MW00782177

© 2021 Michelle Kaye's Holistic Detective Agency

Michelle Kaye, LCSW
Better Than Good Enough: A Parenting Book for the Rest of Us
All rights reserved. No part of this publication may be reproduced,
stored in a retrieval system or transmited in any form or by any means,
electronic, mechanical, photocopying, recording or otherwise without
the prior permision of the publisher or in accordance with the provi-
sions of the Copyright, Designs and Patents Act 1988 or under the
terms of any licence permitting limited copying issued by the Copyright
Licensing Agency.

Published by: Michelle Kaye's Holistic Detective Agency
Cover & Text Design by: Erica Murach

BETTER THAN GOOD ENOUGH

A PARENTING BOOK FOR THE REST OF US

BY MICHELLE KAYE, LCSW

Table of Contents

Dedication

This book is dedicated to the memory of Valerie Feichtenschlager.

Valerie's husband Valentin moved to San Francisco from Austria in 2017. My husband Jeff met Valentin out drinking one night. The next day, Jeff brought him over to our house for a BBQ, and he immediately became a part of our family. A short time later, Valerie moved to San Francisco to join her husband. For the next six months, Valerie took care of our baby Fritz and his friend Tanner once a week. When Valerie told us she was pregnant, we were overjoyed because we knew she was going to be the most amazing mom. We unloaded half of our old baby stuff onto the unsuspecting couple.

Valerie gave birth to Lisbeth Hazel on November 4, 2018. Valerie and Valentin gave Lisbeth the name "Hazel" after my daughter, whom they had come to love. Valerie passed away on November 6, 2018 from complications following Lisbeth's birth.

Valerie: thank you. For taking such wonderful care of Fritz, for being in our lives for such a short and beautiful time, and for creating the sweetest baby girl in the world. Lisbeth turned two just as I was finishing this book, in November of 2020. She is a sweet and observant little girl, just like you. I can't wait to see her roll her eyes at her dad's corny jokes the way you used to. Valerie, you would be so happy and proud to see how wonderful Lisbeth is, and what a great dad Valentin is.

That Time a Worldwide Pandemic Destroyed Society, and I Spent Four Months in Quarantine with My Two Small Children

It is July of 2020. I am writing this paragraph, wearing a mask, sitting far in the back of the outdoor patio at a cafe. A few weeks ago, the COVID-19 cases were decreasing and we were on a good trajectory. Now, the numbers are spiking again, bars and beaches are reclosing in California, and I am feeling hopeless and desperate and sad.

When I started this book six years ago, I never in a million years could have imagined this would be the way I would finish it. Like everyone I know, I have days where I feel completely depressed and hopeless, and other days where I feel okay. We have been incredibly lucky. My husband and I both still have jobs. I have spent the past four months working from home (while taking care of my children full time.) In the weird reality that is the present moment, the freedom and flexibility to do three jobs (teacher, mother, employee) at the same time puts me head and shoulders above most other people. That said, it fucking sucks. Next week, my daughter will go to camp and my son will go back to daycare. I will still be juggling work and childcare for a long, long time (forever?), but it does feel like the end of an incredibly frustrating and difficult, yet also beautiful and precious, time in my life.

Question: How has the pandemic changed the thesis of this book?

Answer: I was totally right about everything.

The thesis of my book is about the importance of everyday interactions with children. The importance of these moment to moment interactions, and of examining how you are reacting to your children and learning from your reactions.

In a world where so many of us are stuck at home…and will be in some form or another for a long, long time…these interactions are even more important. Unfortunately for my work and my personal life, the only people in any position to teach children right now are those in quarantine with them. But how can we ask parents to do this? Especially parents who are worrying about things like food. How can we also ask them to be experts on early learning and emulate the activities of the preschool classroom? Even as an early childhood expert, I'm struggling.

The pandemic has also made it clear that I must finish this project. Finish it. Publish it. Put it out into the world, so all the parents out there who are trying to do it all on their own can read it.

Dear reader, my wish is that when you are reading this, you aren't wearing a mask because masks aren't a thing anymore.[1] I desperately hope while you are reading this, you are living in a world that has backyard BBQs and drag brunches and outdoor summer music festivals and science

---

1 Except in a kinky way.

museums and all of the things that make life worthwhile. I cannot wait to live in that world with you. I hope you and I can one day look back at this mess and learn from it and maybe even feel nostalgic for some part of it. Dear reader, *It was so much harder than you are remembering.* I cannot wait to be in the future with you, looking back and thinking about everything we have learned. And how we maybe, maybe, maybe got out of this together.

CHAPTER 1:

Parenting Books Are Seriously the Worst

Why Should You Waste Your Time Reading This Book?

Parenting books are the worst. They are long and boring, tell you everything you are doing wrong, and make you feel like you are doing a terrible job. Anyway, who has time to read? Even if you do have time to read, why would you read a book? Why not just get online and scroll through clickbait headlines? Or look at pictures of puppies snuggling with babies? Or even better, look at pictures of toddlers having tantrums for no apparent reason? Like this picture of my daughter Hazel collapsing in the middle of a bridge out of sheer toddler bloody-minded-ness.

Or, if you are going to read a book, how about a book about something *other* than being a parent. *Anything* else. Like the Hunger Games trilogy or, if you want to seem smart, the newest David Mitchell novel. Something to take your mind off the everyday, boring, amazing, wonderful, stressful reality of taking care of tiny human beings.

Here's the thing, though. You really do need help. You have a million questions and concerns. A million reasons for pulling out your smartphone at 4 a.m. and typing something into it. Something like:

What does it mean if my baby's poop smells awful?
Why won't my baby sleep without a nipple in his mouth?
Why won't my twenty-six-month-old stop crying?

You might have noticed that when you do type all those questions into Google, the answers you get are less than ideal. Usually, they're just from other parents who are also up at 4 a.m. asking the exact same questions. Or you get answers that make you feel even worse than you already did. For example:

Baby poop smells awful…because he is going to die.
Baby won't sleep without a nipple in his mouth…keep nipple in his mouth until he is twenty-one.
Your twenty-six-month-old won't stop crying…because he has a serious mental illness/disability/personality disorder.

The internet is a never-ending stew of bullshit. False beliefs spread even faster than true beliefs.[2] Anything you type into Google will be confirmed or denied if you scroll long enough. Which is why lots of people still believe that vaccines cause autism…or that a man bun with a goatee is a cool hairstyle.

---

2 Cailin O'Connor and James Owen Weatherall, *The Misinformation Age: How False Beliefs Spread*, (Yale University Press, 2018).

So, here is my advice. Take this book as a potentially more reliable and less stress-inducing alternative to posts by random moms on the internet from five year ago. But don't take it as more reliable than your own best instincts, the advice of your pediatrician, and whatever your amazing grandmother told you. Because let's face it, your grandmother is probably right.

Who the Hell Am I to Give You Parenting Advice?

I'm a Mom

The best parenting advice I ever got was from my husband.[3] When my daughter was an infant, I had been stressing about her sleep for days, maybe weeks, possibly thousands of years. I kept having the same conversation with my husband. And when I say "conversation," I actually mean I kept saying the same thing over and over again and he kept nodding his head or appropriately sighing. I asked, "Should I just let her cry? Should I go get her? Should she co-sleep? Should we take her bottle away? Should I give her a pacifier? Are pacifiers bad for her?" And on and on and on and on.

One day, he had listened to enough of this and said, "I think we need to stop talking about this. This problem isn't going to last forever. Let's talk about something else."

And that was it. That was all it took. The spinning in my brain stopped. I didn't have the answers. She still struggled with her sleep. She still struggles with her sleep sometimes. Six years later I'm still trying to de-complicate and understand the infuriating mystery that is baby sleep (more on that later.) But what Jeff did for me that day was make it okay for me to live in the ambiguity. To exist in the knowledge that I didn't know what I was doing. He reminded me of what I had forgotten about development. That it develops. As soon as you have solved one of

---

3 I realize how surprising and controversial that sounds. Don't worry. I'm not some lunatic who only has positive things to say about my co-parent and posts #blessed every time I put a photo of him on Instagram.

your baby problems, another one presents itself. And again and again. As soon as baby Hazel mastered crawling, she began to stand up. As soon as she was standing, she was working on walking. Now, she's six years old and my biggest problem is that she can read my text messages.[4]

Children don't ever rest in their development. They don't stop at one stage for long enough for you to master being the parent of that child at that age. And if you are crazy enough to have more than one child, you might think to yourself that you know what you are doing since you have done it before. That is a mistake. Chances are, your two or more children are going to be as different from one another as they are from houseplants. So, the best thing you can do is just admit that you are a complete novice, an amateur at parenting this child at this exact age. Do your best to solve the problem in front of you without driving yourself batshit crazy in the process.

I'm a Social Worker

When people at parties ask me what I do for work,[5] I tell them I'm a social worker. I will probably always answer that way, no matter how far away I get from doing actual case management and "social work." I say this because I think like a social worker. I never think about a human being as a separate entity; I think about "person in environment." My first instinct is always to figure out where the person I am speaking to is coming from. I start from a place of "what does this person already know?" I often joke with my friend Sara that as long as a parent isn't actively harming their children, I don't judge them. The job of raising small human beings is hard. The last thing people need is to be judged while they are trying their goddamn best. You know that person who scowls at you in the airport while your three-year-old is screaming their

---

4 That's a lie. That's so not my biggest problem. But she can read my text messages and it is definitely going to blow up in my face.

5 As I am editing this in July of 2020, I am finding the word "parties" extremely triggering.

head off? I am the exact opposite of that person. And not just because I'm not an asshole. My training and expertise have taught me to see two-year-olds lying on the floor of airports and think, *Oh look, a normal child*, not, *Should I report that parent to the authorities?*

I'm a Baby Person

Long before I was a mom, I was a person who loved babies. My sister and I started babysitting for neighborhood infants when we were thirteen years old, getting paid $4.50 an hour! Seems alarming that people trusted us to do this. It was the 90's. Standards were low. One of the kids we babysat is now an undergraduate at Cornell now though, so maybe paying pre-teens below minimum wage to babysit your two-month-old is a good idea.

My whole life I have loved everything about babies: how they smell, how they feel, how they talk, how they look at you. I never imagined I could make babies my career, and I feel so lucky that I have. After getting my master's degree in social work and spending several years working with infants and toddlers with disabilities, I went through the Post-graduate Fellowship Program in Infant-Parent Mental Health through UMass Boston and became certified as a Mental Health expert for ages 0-3. The program helped me to integrate theories of infant mental health with what I already knew about babies. I developed a "blended model" informed by the best practices in the field of infant mental health. My current job is as a Clinical Director of Child, Youth, and Family Services at a non-profit, overseeing our family therapy and early intervention programs. In my private practice, I work with young children and their families using a blend of what I know from my own life experience, expertise from my training and education, and what I have learned from talking to parents of kids under three about their little ones. There are many fantastic theories, modalities, and therapy models out there, and I have drawn from many of them. However, I'm extremely suspicious of anyone who is too fixated on a particular style or technique. It's not just that every child is different. Every situation and every age is different. The best thing you can do for yourself and your child is to have many tools in your tool belt, so you'll have a lot of things to try when you really need to fix a problem.

If you are reading this as a parent who doesn't give a shit about someone's resume and is just here for some practical tips from a mother who's been there, you can skip the next few sentences. But if you are the kind of person who needs to see someone's resume before you will trust that they know what the fuck they are talking about,[6] here are a few of the therapeutic modalities I am trained and certified in: Reflective Practice, Nursing Child Assessment Satellite Tool, Newborn Behavioral Observation, Marte Meo, Early Start Denver Model, Kimochis, Social Thinking Curriculum, Zones of Regulation, Applied Behavioral Analysis, and Cognitive Behavioral Therapy. Enough of this. Just look me up on LinkedIn.

I love learning new therapeutic modalities to use with parents and children. But I get very worried when people are too tied to only one thing. The most confident person I have ever spoken to was a 22 year old who just finished her training in Montessori. She told me "it will be very easy, very easy indeed, for me to create and teach a small Montessori class for your daughter. This will be very simple indeed." Okay sweetheart. That's cute.

Years ago, I worked with a parent of a child with cerebral palsy. Before the baby was born, the mom had researched RIE parenting (Resources for Infant Educarers.) That isn't a typo. The parenting philosophy is for Educares...not educators.[7] RIE is a parenting philosophy that is founded on the principle that "Baby knows best." RIE encourages parents to follow their child's lead, and not to force a child into completing a

---

6 I am totally one of those people.

7 Cute, right?

developmental task he isn't ready for. It's a beautiful notion that I think probably works well for lots of parents. As a pregnant mom, this mom had fallen in love with this technique. Sadly, her baby was born with a disability. Children with cerebral palsy do well when they get lots of physical intervention early on. Physical and occupational therapies are very effective at helping these children to walk, manipulate objects, and do other tasks they might not be able to do otherwise. Because the mom was dedicated to RIE parenting, she declined occupational and physical therapy services in favor of a more child-led approach. After months of working with the family, I was able to show this parent how she could still be very child-focused in her approach, while also allowing her child to receive these much-needed services. The problem with being too fixated on one model is that it doesn't allow you to adapt when things don't go as planned.

Here's a tip for parents when looking for help for their children. When someone (especially a young person who doesn't know shit yet) is too tied to their one model of treatment, be very suspicious. It feels good to be sure of yourself. But the more you learn as a professional, the more you know what you don't know.

I Specialize in Helping Children with Disabilities

My career has been focused on early childhood development. I spent my first few years as a therapist working in community mental health with children, teenagers, and their parents. A few years after graduate school, I started working for Early Start, California's program for infants and toddlers with developmental delays. After that, I worked for an autism services company providing Applied Behavioral Analysis to children on the autism spectrum. I now work at a non-profit providing inclusion services in preschools. My knowledge and expertise about disabilities has informed my work with typically developing children as well. The best practices for children in special education are the best practices for all children. My own children don't have autism or developmental disabilities, but most of the techniques that help my clients work for them as well.

For over a decade, most of the professional conversations I have had with parents have been with parents of children with disabilities. If you are a parent of a typically developing child and you think your job is hard, your job is a fucking cake walk compared to what these families go through on a daily basis. Parents of children with disabilities are some of the most caring, compassionate, hard-working people I know. They do everything they can to help their kids, and they do it while the world judges and scoffs at them. During the four months I was quarantined with my own small children, I would often think about how easy I had it compared to a parent quarantined with a child with a disability. I have learned more from these families than they have learned from me. They have taught me how to advocate and how to stare judgment in the face without blinking. Perhaps most importantly, they have taught me what it means to provide support to a child who is struggling. That it isn't about swooping in and saving the child from the jaws of a cruel world; it's about bolstering the child's support system.

Did I Invent Some New Parenting Philosophy or What? What Is My Model?

I'm a mother of two young children. So, I've been there and I'm still there. Infant sleep completely bewilders me. Every day that I don't scream at my kids, I regard it as a minor miracle. I'm about as far from being the perfect mom as you or anyone else is. But like you, I love my kids more than anything in the world and I try very hard to do a good job.

75% of brain development happens in the first five years of life. The early years of our children's lives are crucial to the people they later become. So, if you make even one tiny, tiny mistake, you have basically ruined them and you may as well just give them up for adoption.

Kidding! But isn't that what it feels like? In my work with families, I have seen that 100% of parents feel guilty 80-90% of the time.[8] If your kids are in daycare, you feel guilty for not keeping them home with you. If they are home with you, you worry that they aren't getting enough peer engagement. If they don't take swimming classes, you fear they will never learn to swim. If you take them to too many activities, then they are overscheduled. If you take your child to daycare during a worldwide pandemic, you worry about them contracting a deadly virus. If you keep them home with you, you worry about losing your mind and about them turning into weirdos who don't know how to socialize. As a parent, you are going to feel terrible about something that you did or didn't do, no matter what you did or didn't do. The only solution is just to accept this and be okay with it. Embrace the ambiguity.

I'm convinced there are no easy answers for any of your burning 5 a.m. questions. There is no magic sleep solution and no amazing, perfect way to wean a twelve-month-old from breastfeeding. Your two-year-old is going to have a tantrum about a sandwich being cut incorrectly. Your five-year-old is going to act like a complete asshole on a playdate. The best thing you can do for yourself is accept that these things are going to happen and as soon as you solve one baby problem, another problem will pop up.

What you can do is make good, informed decisions about what you will try. Then just try things and see what works. Look at yourself and the decisions you make and reflect on why you are making them. When this doesn't work for you and the particular child you have that week, you can just try another tool in your toolbelt.

This book is not about children and it is not about parents. It is about the relationship. It is not going to offer you solutions that you can stick on your child like a Paw Patrol Band-Aid. The ideas in this

---

8 That statistic is based on rigorous and peer-reviewed, evidence-based research. Or, I guess you could say, me just talking to people.

book are based on my own personal experiences, the experiences of my clients and friends, and the best evidence-based practices in the world of infant mental health. But rather than just giving you the suggestions (which you could find in one Google search), I have examined them through the lens of relationships. If you do a quick Google search of "how should I respond to a tantrum," you will find this:

You really don't need a book to tell you that. But is that really how you are responding to your child? Reeeeeeeeeeally? Come on, Mama... tell me the truth! This book examines why it is so challenging to follow the advice we find on Google. Why it is so hard for me to follow it, for my clients to follow it, and for you to follow it. I can't promise that reading this book will make it any easier. But maybe it will help you feel like less of an asshole. Or still an asshole...but in good company.

The psychoanalyst Donald Winnicott is responsible for the phrase "good enough mothering."[9] Good enough mothering refers to the natural process that occurs in infancy when the baby realizes that its mother cannot be everything for him 100% of the time. This is a necessary process for the baby to realize that the mother isn't omniscient and that the baby has to also be able to attend to his own needs and to on occasion, god forbid, wait for something. A good-enough mother is a

9 D.W. Winnicott, *The Child, the Family, and the Outside World* (Harmondsworth: Penguin, 1975).

normal mother. One who isn't attuned to her child 100% of the time. Every once in a while, she wants to close the door when she uses the bathroom. Or eat something. Sometimes, she just wants to mindlessly scroll through Chrissy Teigen's Instagram.

We don't need to be perfect. We are good enough. We want to be better. And that is what this book is about. My journey to being better. And I'm taking you with me.

What Should You Do If I Offend You?

I'm really sorry about any language in this book that you find offensive. I tried really hard not to swear but I just couldn't fucking do it. I've limited my swear words to times when it is absolutely 100% necessary and no other word will do.[10]

Also, I'm Jewish, so if you find the errant Yiddish word in here that you don't understand…blame my mom.

Lastly, a word about gender.

A few months before I finished this book, J.K. Rowling took to Twitter to complain about the use of the phrase "people who menstruate" instead of "women." She later clarified her statements…by publishing a transphobic op-ed.

I was super bummed about this whole thing. I love Harry Potter. Like so many others, I found it profoundly disappointing that Rowling could be so ignorant. One good thing that came out of this, though, was that this exchange also caused me to reflect on my own bias. In the first draft of this book, I used the term "pregnant women" instead of "pregnant people." I used the term "mother" instead of "parent." Not all people who give birth to babies identify as female. Not all primary

---

10 I'm really fucking sorry.

caregivers are mothers.[11] I have attempted to check my own gender biases during the editing process. But for any bias that you find, I apologize.

A parenting book I read, which will remain nameless,[12] included one tiny little sidebar about same-sex couples in the introductory chapter. The whole book was "your husband this" and "your husband that." There are a lot of assumptions embedded in this: that only moms were reading the book, that all moms have partners, that all moms have male partners, and that all moms have male partners they are legally married to. So, the authors thought they could make up for this by including one paragraph that said something like, "We know there are same-sex couples in the world too. When we say 'husband,' we really mean partners. All the advice we give is 100% applicable for same-sex couples as well."

Ummmmmmmmmmmmmmmm.

Okay, so that is clearly super problematic. Everything is not 100% the same for same-sex couples. Queer couples are of course going to have different parenting experiences than I do, and to assume otherwise is ignorant. Where you are from and what you have experienced determines everything about how you parent. Parenting is one of the most culturally specific practices human beings have. I am completely aware that my own thoughts about parenting are 100% biased and based on my own cultural background. I am a straight, white, non-religious Jew living in one of the most liberal places on the planet (the Bay Area.) I am blessed to be healthy, have two healthy kids, and to be a member of the middle class (not by San Francisco standards, obviously, but by normal standards.) As a social worker in the Bay Area, I have been lucky enough to work with every kind of family imaginable. I have worked with wealthy gay dads in Palo Alto and single moms in the projects in San Francisco. I have been

---

11 If you are raising a child with another human being and you are unsure if you or the other person is the "primary" caregiver, ask yourself this simple question: "How many diapers have I changed in my life?" If the answer is anything less than 65,000…you aren't the primary caregiver.

12 I know you are *expecting* me to name the book, but I just won't do it.

lucky enough to have clients from across the world. Practicing cultural humility is extremely important to me. I know what I don't know, but I'm also open to being reminded of it. I try to not just represent my experience but also acknowledge that I am representing my experience.

Here I am, trapped in my own experiences. Painfully aware that how I see the world is not the way the world is, but just how the inside of my head looks. So, if you are reading this book and you think I got something dead wrong, please write to tell me.

Send an email with the subject line "Here's something you didn't get" to michelle@kaye.com.

My Biases

In the interest of full disclosure, I should probably let you know a few of the biases I carry around with me like the half-eaten snacks my kids hand me when they can't find a garbage can.[13] It doesn't matter if somewhere in my brain I know these are biases I should get over. I can't. Because that is how bias works.

1. Before 2020, I was very laid back about hand washing. Then COVID-19 happened and my children acted like I had asked them to remodel the bathroom every time I told them to wash their hands.

2. Even though I give them to my kids because my husband thinks we should, I don't really believe in children's vitamins.

3. I also don't really believe that sugar makes children hyperactive. My husband would disagree, citing the evidence that Fritz acts like a complete nutcase whenever we give it to him. However, he is also a nutcase without sugar, so despite evidence to the contrary, I can never fully get behind the whole sugar-makes-children-hyper theory.

---

13 When you're a mom, you *are* the trashcan.

4. I don't believe in Zodiac signs, essential oils, amber necklaces, placenta pills, spiritual healing, spiritual readings, "sending good vibes," good energy and bad energy, or basically anything else that doesn't have a body of research to back it up.[14] I will occasionally *pretend* to believe in Zodiac signs. When someone says, "I'm an Aries, so I have a hard time interacting with Scorpios," I *want* to respond, "Are you seriously saying that because you were born in April and I was born in November the stars have somehow determined that we can't possibly get along? Really? You genuinely believe that? Do you also believe in witch burnings?" But I actually say, "Oh okay, interesting!" Because we live in a society, so we have to put up with other peoples' socially acceptable bullcrap.[15]

5. I'm bad at faking that I believe in any of that stuff. Even though I fake it all the time because I live in the Bay Area and I want to have friends and a job.

6. I categorically refuse to buy anything from a multi-level marketing scheme because I listened to a podcast about them and they are dumb.[16]

7. I don't believe kids need to go to the dentist every six months, or that they need to floss, or brush their teeth if they passed out in the car and were carried inside. Basically, I'm a pediatric dentist's worst nightmare.

8. I think "life coaching" is a scam. Some of us spend two years getting a master's degree, collect thousands of supervised therapy

---

14 I do believe in the interconnectedness of all things. But more on that later.

15 I'm sure a good portion of you are probably thinking, *This lady is a Scorpio? I'm not sure I can read a book by a Scorpio.* That's just a gamble I'm going to have to take.

16 Here's a fun drinking game you can play while reading this book. Every time you read the sentence "I listened to a podcast…" take a shot.

hours, then pay more money to take a super hard exam. Other people hang a placard outside their door that says "life coach" and then advise people to follow their hearts.

Who Are My Children and Am I Seriously Going to Talk About Them for the Next 200 Pages?

Yes. So, I should probably introduce you.

This is Hazel. She is spunky, spirited, talkative, emotional, intelligent, hilarious, and when she grows up, she wants to be "a scientist who studies magic in the ocean." Here is what she looked like when I started writing this book:

And when I finished it:

This is Fritz. He is sweet, affectionate, a total jock, in a good mood 99% of the time, and emotionally uncomplicated. He's the most Zen person I have ever met. Doesn't think too much about the future, doesn't worry about the past. He likes to throw balls as hard as he can into my face when I'm not looking.

Here he is when I started writing about him in this book:

And when I finished:

This is me with my kids after two months of quarantine. I love this picture because you can't tell I'm barely holding my shit together:

If you find yourself uninterested in these children, you should probably stop reading right now and go back to the Hunger Games trilogy.

When Did I Write this Book?

I took a year sabbatical from my job, left my two kids with a full-time au pair from France, went to a writers' retreat in New Mexico, and wrote this book while drinking matcha lattes and eating avocado toast.

No. None of that happened. Except the avocado toast. If it had, nothing I have to say about parenting would be at all relevant, because I would basically be Gwyneth Paltrow[17] complaining about having to raise kids on a movie set.

I wrote this book on the notepad app on my phone when I arrived five minutes early for a therapy session. I wrote this book with a breastfeeding baby on my lap. On the treadmill at the gym. Standing up in the kitchen waiting for the water to boil for mac and cheese. At the playground while other parents gave me dirty looks for being on my phone. While rubbing Hazel's back at night. In the bathroom, hiding from my kids. In the closet, hiding from my kids. I wrote this book in the tiny, tiny spaces left between my full-time job and my children. I started writing

17 I have spent years making fun of Gwyneth Paltrow. Then my husband and I saw her on The Politician and she looks the same as she did in Shakespeare in Love. Jeff goes, "Maybe all that crazy shit she sells actually works!"

in the days following Hazel's birth, when we had a president we were slightly disappointed with but liked on a personal level. I finished this book with a complete lunatic refusing to leave the White House after losing an election, during the worst pandemic in a century.

I recently listened to a podcast[18] about Deep Work that depressed the hell out of me. If you want to be equally depressed, it is the episode called "You 2.0: Deep Work" from the podcast Hidden Brain. The episode was about how important it is to give ourselves time to do deep work, like writing a book. Professor Sophie Leroy from the University of Minnesota conducted research on something called "attention residue." She found that when lab subjects were given difficult puzzles to solve, it took them a while to get back on track once they were distracted. Let's say for example that you are writing a sentence of an autobiographical parenting book and one of your children pours milk over their sibling's head. When you finally do turn back to work on your book, you may have absolutely no idea what you were going to write about. You may also wonder if it is appropriate for you to give parenting advice to anyone, since you are clearly raising a sociopath.

On the one hand, this book would probably be two billion times better if I *had* written it when cut off from children and technology on a New Mexico writers' retreat. On the other hand, it's probably meaningful that I wrote it in the same manner I have done everything for the past six years: while balancing ten other things.

As I kept writing over the course of these six years, I kept changing my mind about things that I felt so strongly about in the beginning. I became less and less sure that the approaches I discussed were the right ones. That's what happens when you get older: you get less sure of yourself. I have tried to keep as much as I could of what I've written over the years. If reading this book feels a bit like watching someone criticize themselves…that's because that's what it is.

18 Drink.

This book was written in the same manner you will probably read it. Slowly, bit by bit, over the course of six incredibly long, incredibly short years.

CHAPTER 2:

Fish is Fish

"Every particle in the universe…affects every other particle, however faintly and obliquely. Everything interconnects with everything. The beating of a butterfly's wings in China can affect the course of an Atlantic hurricane. If I could interrogate this table leg in a way that made sense to me, or to the table leg, then it could provide me with the answer to any question about the Universe" (Adams, 92).[19]

Let me start by telling you the philosophy that is at the center of everything I do. Not just the parenting stuff, or the work stuff, but everything. It is the lens through which I see every part of my existence. And like all good philosophies, it can be explained by referencing a children's book.

One of my favorite children's books of all times is an old book from 1970 called Fish is Fish, written and illustrated by Leo Lionni. You

---

19 Douglas Adams, in *The Long Dark Tea-Time of the Soul: Dirk Gently Series #2* (New York: Simon and Schuster, 1988), 92.

should just buy the book right now if you don't already have it. But I'll go ahead and tell you the whole plot, so if you don't want a spoiler...to a children's book...skip to Chapter Three.

Fish is Fish is a story about two friends, a fish and a tadpole, who live together in a pond. The fish doesn't know the tadpole is a tadpole. He thinks they are just two fish best friends living their best fish lives. One day, the tadpole turns into a frog and mysteriously disappears from the fish's life. Tragic, I know. Later, the frog reappears and tells the fish all about life on land. Here's a short excerpt of their exchange:

"Where have you been?" asked the fish excitedly.

"I have been about the world—hopping here and there," said the frog, "and I have seen extraordinary things."

"Like what?" asked the fish.

"Birds," said the frog mysteriously. "Birds!" And he told the fish about the bird, who had wings, and two legs and many, many colors. As the frog talked, his friend saw the birds fly through his mind like large feathered fish.

"And people!" said the frog. "Men, women, children!" And he talked and talked until it was dark in the pond.

But the picture in the fish's mind was full of lights and colors and marvelous things and he couldn't sleep. Ah, if he could only jump about like his friend and see that marvelous world.[20]

The frog and the fish are discussing birds and humans, but the mental representation each of them has of these images is completely different. Because the fish has never seen a cow or a person, he starts with what he knows, which in this case is a fish, and adds cow and human-like details as described by the frog. In the book, the fish never learns how incorrect his mental representations were. Later in the story, he becomes so obsessed with seeing cows, people, and birds that he jumps out of the water and almost dies. The frog saves him. At the end of the story, he realizes that "fish is fish" and he should be content with who he is.

But that moral is not what I find inspiring about the book. What I love about the story is the way Leo Lionni illustrates what a bird, cow, and human would look like as imagined by a fish. A fish who has no context to know what they actually look like.

The point is: raising a child is not the same as purchasing a bunch of parts from Ikea and following instructions to put together a dresser.[21] Your

20 Leo Leonni, *Fish Is Fish*, 1st ed. (Knopf Books for Young Readers, 1970).

21 Parenting is hard. But putting together a dresser from Ikea is even harder.

child is not just a smaller version of you, responding to the instructions you give him. Everything we encounter in our lives is only a mental representation of the thing itself. It is colored by our emotions, our experiences, and the way we see the world.

Yesterday, a parent of a child diagnosed with autism asked me, "What can we do to help him?"

I could have answered, "You should make transitions as easy as possible by using warnings and timers; you should encourage social thinking by asking him lots of questions about what others are thinking and feeling; you should give him lots of body breaks when he is overstimulated." Instead of answering this way, I asked, "What do you think of the diagnosis? What are you concerned about? When do you think your child is at his best? What is hardest for him?"

What would I have accomplished by only responding to the child I saw in front of me? I was not seeing the actual child. I was seeing my own mental representation of that child based on ten years of experience working with children with autism. So, whatever I said, it would've been colored by all of my assumptions and beliefs. Yes, my assumptions and beliefs are better informed than how the fish imagines cows, because I have seen a child with autism before. For that matter, I've also seen a cow. However, I am still only able to see the child in front of me through my own limited prism, colored by my previous experiences with children with autism.

Advice from professionals with experience and knowledge is helpful. But this in and of itself is not enough.

What I need to know is: What is the parent's mental representation of their child? What does the child look like in the eyes of the parent? The more I can answer these questions, the better I will be able to relieve their anxiety and strengthen the parent/child relationship. In one year, the parents will be able to master all the strategies I mentioned above. But what should they do today? This week? Where should they begin? What will make the biggest change in the life of that child is for his parents to begin to see him in a different light. For them to see his potential and feel hopeful and excited about his development. And that work can only start once I know how these parents see him today. Only then can I begin to be helpful to them.

My friend Yasmine once wrote of her childhood: "I didn't grow up speaking French to my mom; I grew up *in French* with my mom." Our perception of our world is shaped by the experiences we had in our childhoods. The languages we spoke, the way we felt—these experiences color absolutely everything. Our perception of our childhood creates the people we become.

Research on childhood trauma backs this up. Remember that movie that made us all cry back in the 1990s? No, I'm not talking about *Now and Then*. I'm talking about *Life is Beautiful*. The father and son in that movie are put in a concentration camp. The father pretends they are in a super fun overnight camp and his son is spared the trauma of the Holocaust for as long as possible. How a child responds to traumatic events in their lives is not just about how horrific the event itself was. It is also about how the child made meaning of the event, and this is largely influenced by how the adults in their lives made sense of it. For survivors of childhood abuse, the fact that the adults in their lives couldn't or wouldn't protect them can be as damaging as the abuse.

To simplify: the meaning you make out of an experience is as important as the experience itself.

Your child is their relationship with you, their caretakers. And how you feel about your child, about their day, about their behavior, is everything.

It is for this reason that you won't find very much straight advice in this book. Annoying, right? People ask me for advice all the time. Professionals, children, parents, family members, friends. If you want me to give you advice, you really have to pin me down and force me. I see the world as endlessly complex. So, I *do* generally answer questions with more questions. I'm totally that stereotypical TV therapist who answers a direct question with, "I wonder why you are asking me...." If that frog had asked that fish, "What are you imagining a human looks like?" he would have very quickly found out the fish had a totally wack mental representation. But he never asked that question. So, the fish never did acquire a more accurate mental representation.

I know what you are thinking and yes, my way of responding to the world does mean that I get interrupted by men a lot.

The good news is, if you are looking for a book that will give you super straightforward clear answers about everything you should do to be a parent, there are five billion of those on the market. But it's not this book.

Here's the thing, though. Knowing how to potty train your kid, or how to get your kid to brush his own teeth, is only going to help you for a very specific moment in time. The "brush your teeth" parenting and the "pee in the goddamn potty" parenting moments are fleeting. Before you and I know it, our kids are going to be schnorring the car keys. And then you are going to have to purchase the "how to get your kid through high school without killing themselves or anyone else" book. Your book budget is going to have to be enormous to get through this thing.

But what *Fish is Fish* teaches us applies to everything. If we as parents can learn how to see our children not only as the people they are but as the people they are in our mind's eye, we are doing both them and ourselves a great service.

We do our best parenting when we do more than just look at our child's behavior and respond. You will see your child's behavior and have an emotional response to it. But remember that you are looking out your own individualized window, colored by your own experiences, cultural beliefs, and probably how much caffeine you had that day.[22] Try to understand what your own window looks like. Try to see if there is

---

22 I try to keep my caffeine intake to under seventeen cups of coffee per day.

another window around, and consider if you can look out of it, if the behavior will look different from that window. Look at the behavior from smart windows, evidence-based research windows, and the windows of your friends and family and super-wise grandmother.

Okay, enough with the windows. Let me share a more concrete example.

When my daughter started transitional kindergarten, I had to fill out a questionnaire about her. One question asked: "What worries you about Hazel?" I wrote that I worry about her being mean to other kids. Hazel is well liked by her peers. I often describe her as "catnip" to kids. She's super creative and she's a natural leader. But sometimes she tells kids what to do. And she is honest about things that I wish she kept to herself. I wanted her teacher to know all this about her, so I jotted it down.

After I wrote it, I sat there staring at the page and reflecting on who I was as a child. Most of my memories from kindergarten revolve around being extremely shy. I had a few close friends, but I was quiet around kids I didn't know. I remember being scared of the loud, bossy, big and beautiful confident girls on the playground. Hazel would have terrified me. I looked down at the way I answered this question and realized that my answer had as much to do with me as it did with Hazel. I worry about her being too bossy because bossiness is a trait that frightens me. I can't stand bossy people, and I'm one of the least bossy people I know.[23] Even when some bossiness would come in handy, like when I'm interacting with those who I am literally the boss of, I have a difficult time conjuring it.

My aversion to bossiness in girls is about more than just my own early memories. We live in a society in which bossiness in women and girls is frowned upon. Remember that time America elected a completely incompetent man over the woman with all the experience? My reaction to Hazel's natural personality is also about my own internalized sexism.

23 Again, this is why I get interrupted by men a lot.

This is the soup in which Hazel is growing up. She is a naturally bossy person with a mom who is bossy-averse. Her natural bossiness will no doubt be affected by my natural dislike for it. However, my awareness of this fact makes all the difference. It allows me to take a minute to reflect before I have a knee-jerk reaction to Hazel telling a group of kids, "Okay, I'm the veterinarian and you are all the pets." Rather than jumping in, I can pause and notice my inclination to jump in and then decide if I need to or not.

I see these sorts of patterns in my clients every day. A few years ago, I worked with a very social little boy whose parents were terrified he would be bullied. When I started working with the family, my first step was to go to the school to talk to his teacher about the bullying behavior. The teacher swore up and down that it wasn't happening. At school he was well liked and had lots of friends. During my next meeting with his parents, they disclosed that they had both immigrated to the States as small children and struggled to fit in. I helped his parents reflect on how their own experiences of being ostracized put them on high alert for this behavior. When their child received a diagnosis of autism, this confirmed their deepest fears. After reflecting, these parents realized that their mental projection of their child was different from how the child really was.

As the psychoanalyst Donald Winnicott said, "There is no such thing as a baby." A baby only exists as part of her relationship with her caregiver. And that baby is shaped completely by how that caregiver sees her, and how she sees her caregiver, and how she perceives her caregiver sees her, and how she perceives her caregiver perceives that she sees her…

It is all very complicated.

CHAPTER 3:

Are You Ready to Have a Baby Yet? Take This Quiz and Find Out

1. How long can you wait for another human to eat a piece of toast before you completely lose your mind?

   a) Two seconds

   b) Ten minutes

   c) I have infinite and infallible patience and will give this small child as long as she needs to eat

2. How interested are you in talking to other adults about their children's nap schedules?

   a) I will immediately fall asleep out of boredom if anyone mentions a nap schedule in my presence.

   b) That sounds awful. Is that seriously something that people do?

   c) Totally fascinating. Can't wait.

3. Rank the following in order of most to least gross: poop, vomit, pee, slime, and Cheerios that have been ingested and then spit back into the bowl due to professed sogginess.

   a) Poop, vomit, slime, pee, Cheerios

   b) Cheerios, pee, slime, vomit, poop

   c) If they all came from my own child,
      none of them are gross.

4. How many things can you do simultaneously?

   a) One

   b) Three

   c) 500,000

5. Which of the following can you afford with your current salary?

   a) $1000 a month for childcare, $100 a month for
      swim class, $500 a month for dance classes

   b) $100 a month for diapers, $50 a month for wipes, $5000 a
      month for organic yogurt squeezy snacks

   c) All of the above

6. What happens to you when you don't get enough sleep?

   a) I despise everyone who looks at me.

   b) I start hallucinating.

   c) Nothing at all; I am the picture of calm and
      composure and can take care of multiple
      other human beings as well as myself.

7. Your ideal restaurant is:

   a) One that serves beautifully plated vegan food

   b) A small Italian bistro with dark
      lighting and cloth napkins

   c) Family night at Round Table Pizza

8. What do you like to listen to in the car?

   a) NPR

   b) Heavy Metal

   c) "Who Took the Cookies from the Cookie Jar?"

9. Scenario: You see a two-year-old standing on top of a table holding a bread knife. You:

   a) Leap into action immediately, removing him physically from the table.

   b) Attempt to coax him down gently using rational, gentle language.

   c) Do nothing. You're in the middle of writing an email and it is the only five minutes he has been entertained all evening. You will get to him once he has leapt off the table and the butter knife has impaled him. Hopefully the damage won't be permanent.

10. What do you fantasize about?

   a) Waterskiing in the Caribbean

   b) Skydiving off the Grand Canyon

   c) Sleeping in a hotel room by yourself. Silky sheets. Cold, air-conditioned air. Terrible TV on in the background. And no one else is there. No one. Literally…no one.

Unless you answered C to every question above, I have bad news for you: You aren't ready to have a kid. Sorry! You can give this book back to whomever gifted it to you. Also, feel free to re-gift. This book is a great re-gift. You have my blessing.

The truth is, very few of us are ever 100% ready to have kids. If you are going into parenting with no hesitation, no regrets or trepidation, you probably lead a boring life. There will never be the perfect time to have a baby. Friends and clients of mine who have been trying to get pregnant for years still have some doubt, right up until that baby comes screaming out. When I was in the process of pushing Hazel out of my vagina, I screamed at my husband, "This was a MISTAKE!" And then I met her and everything changed.

The social scientist Daniel Gilbert wrote a book called *Stumbling on Happiness* that discusses how bad most human beings are at predicting how they will feel about future events in their lives.[24] Turns out most of us do a poor job of it. Daniel Gilbert recommends using other people as surrogates for our own experiences, and predicting how we will feel about events based on how people felt about similar events in their lives. This technique apparently works well for movies and television. A few days ago, I decided to watch the Jennifer Aniston movie *Rumor Has It* despite the fact that it has a score of 20% on the website Rotten Tomato. I saw that it was rated 20% and thought to myself, well…I like Jennifer Aniston and I like romantic comedies…I will probably like it. Spoiler Alert: the movie was terrible! The tomato people were right!

If people based their decision to have children only on how they thought they might feel, most people would never have them. You *like* sleeping in! You *like* having conversations with other adults without someone yelling "Mom!" every ten seconds. Why would any of us ever want to give up our kid-free lives?

Because our decision to have children isn't rational. For many of us, the biological necessity of parenthood is an itch we have to scratch. I have always envied the Oprahs of the world who never feel that desire to be parents. Imagine how much I could have accomplished if I didn't want to be a mom. I would have my own network! Or at the very least, this book would have taken me less than five years to write.[25] Unfortunately, that was never me. I have been obsessed with babies ever since I was a baby myself. I always knew I was going to be a mom, and I was super

24 Daniel Gilbert, *Stumbling on Happiness* (Vintage Books, 2006).

25 Also, this book would be about fantasy and science fiction novels or the show Buffy the Vampire Slayer, since other than babies those are my main interests.

excited both times I was pregnant with my kids…but still terrified and not 100% sure it was the right choice.

Based on the above quiz, you might think I am giving the whole "having kids" thing a Tomatometer of 20%. Here's the good news. There is still one more question left on this quiz:

    11. How will you feel lying next to your sleeping baby staring at his chest rise and fall?
        a) Content: like lying on your back in the grass watching the clouds go by.
        b) Happy: like walking across the stage at your college graduation.
        c) Indescribable joy. It feels like there is an invisible cord connecting you to him. You imagine your entire life with him. Him as a fetus growing inside of you. Him crying in those seconds following his easy birth. Those early months when his personality began to shine through. Then you imagine him as a teenager, dirty and grumpy, rushing in and out of the house. And him as a young man giving you a quick hug on a return trip from college. You imagine him being taller than you, taking care of you. You imagine it all in those moments when you stare into his tiny perfect face, and you realize that nothing in your life has ever given you the feeling you get from him and his sister. There isn't another feeling that has ever come close. It isn't just that being a parent is the biggest feeling you have ever had; it is a feeling that doesn't even compare to any other feeling. It is a feeling that changes what it means to feel things.

It's C. The correct answer is C.

BETTER THAN GOOD ENOUGH

CHAPTER 4:

The Ten Most Annoying Things People Say to Pregnant People and…One Thing It Is Totally Cool to Say

1. **You won't (sleep, drink, go out to dinner, have sex) again for eighteen years. You will see!**

   First of all: this is bullshit. Both times I was pregnant countless people told me that I wouldn't sleep for eighteen years. Eighteen years! Really, your eighteen-year-old is waking you up in the middle of the night to breastfeed? Sounds like you have bigger problems than I do. The reality is, kids are only little for a few years. While you are in it, it feels like an eternity. But they get bigger and bigger and more and more independent (or so I'm told.)

   People also like to make the suggestion that you should "sleep now" because once the baby comes you won't get any sleep. Is there some "sleep bank" I'm not familiar with where you can store excess sleep so you can use it later? Additionally, sleeping while pregnant suuuuuuuuuuuucks. There's this big belly that makes it totally uncomfortable to try to sleep and there's a tiny little alien wiggling inside of you. Oh, and you can't sleep because you are tossing and turning and worrying about how the hell you are going to take care of this little person, and what you should call the little person, and if birth will be as bad as people say, and if you will be able to do a natural birth, *and* also worrying that you are worrying too much and it's stressing out the baby.

And I love how people think they are the ones breaking the news to you that babies don't sleep. Really? Oh, wow. Thanks.

The "advice" that you won't be able to drink or go out to eat after the baby is born is also complete bullshit. When grown-up people tell me their lives stopped being fun after they had children, I immediately assume they weren't that fun to begin with. You know who I am talking about. These were the people who went to bed at 10 p.m. in college because they wanted to get up early the next day and go for a hike.[26] As soon as they have children, they like to tell people who don't have kids yet that they should party now because kids change everything. It's a ruse! You people weren't even fun *in college*! Now you are using your kid as an excuse for societally-approved non-funness.

Also, as I am writing this six months into a global pandemic, can I just say how much having a baby is not a good excuse for not having fun. You know what's a good excuse not to go out to a bar or restaurant? All of them being closed. Also, a deadly virus. As someone who is usually on the giving end of the "Come out! You only live once! Have one more drink!" equation, I feel like I got the last laugh with this one. Over the past six months, I have been tempted to call up all my friends who turned down my invitations to go out because they were "tired' or "had a Zumba class in the morning" and tell them, "I was right! Don't you wish you

---

26 I went for hikes in college too. "Hikes" to the bonfire pit to get wasted.

had come out with me?! Never say no to me again!" Because you just never know when a global pandemic will destroy a year's worth of fun.

In conclusion: do not let them tell you that your life is over and you will never have fun again because you are having a baby. A global pandemic will destroy your fun. Not a baby.

2. You can have a few beers while you are pregnant. It is fiiiiiine... our parents drank and we all turned out fiiiiiiine.

People love talking about how many drugs our moms did back in the seventies and eighties when they were pregnant with us. First of all, this isn't true. Even though there wasn't as much known about prenatal health a generation ago, pregnant people were aware that what they put in their bodies had some effect on the fetuses they were carrying. I find it hard to believe that pregnant people in the seventies and eighties were sitting around doing shots during prenatal exams.

Let's give our mothers and grandmothers some credit. Just because white middle-aged male doctors hadn't published a bunch of research about it yet doesn't mean that women didn't know how to take care of themselves and their babies. We need to remember to look at the history of maternal health through a critical feminist lens. The medical establishment may have thought it was okay to smoke and drink during pregnancy. This does not inherently mean that aunties and grandmothers and sisters were giving the same advice.

There has been ample research since then showing the negative effects that drugs, alcohol, and tobacco exposure have on a growing fetus. Pregnant people should be very thoughtful about what they put in their bodies. The growing fetus is a very small, fragile, and sensitive thing, and even a small amount of a toxic substance can affect it. If a pregnant person feels uncomfortable drinking while pregnant, that makes sense.

Here's a good piece of advice to carry with you: DON'T TELL PREGNANT PEOPLE WHAT TO DO WITH THEIR BODIES!

3. There's a lot of evidence showing that it's totally fine to smoke weed during pregnancy.

Somebody literally told me this when I was pregnant. They got their evidence from www.stonermoms.com. #fakenews

DON'T TELL PREGNANT PEOPLE WHAT TO DO WITH THEIR BODIES!

4. Oh no, you're pregnant! Don't drink that beer!

Most doctors will tell you that one glass of wine a day during pregnancy is fine. So, everyone needs to stop harassing the pregnant lady in the corner of the party sheepishly sipping her tiny glass of chardonnay.

A few years ago, I met a visibly pregnant woman at a wedding. Everyone was having a wonderful time and she was standing around drinking water like a loser. I was going to the bar and asked her if I could get her anything. "Like a small sip of champagne?" I suggested.

"I want one," she whispered, "but I don't want anyone to judge me!"

So, I went to the bar and asked for half a mason jar full of champagne,[27] and put a beer koozie around the jar before handing it to her. "Now no one will know!" I whispered conspiratorially.

Not five seconds later, the woman's friend came rushing up to her. "What are you drinking??" she asked, scandalized.

"Oh, it's just juice," the pregnant woman answered.

"Oh," her friend said with a laugh. "For a second I thought it was champagne but I know that you would never do that!"

No wonder she was nervous, I thought.

DON'T TELL PREGNANT PEOPLE WHAT TO DO WITH THEIR BODIES!

---

27 "Mason jar" is Northern Californian for champagne glass.

5. You are pregnant. Don't move or carry anything. Just relax.

I was a home visiting therapist during both of my pregnancies. I traveled up and down the hills of San Francisco, wheeling a rolling suitcase and sitting on people's floors playing with their babies. In culturally diverse San Francisco, a lot of the families whose homes I went into were not okay letting a pregnant woman work so hard. I tried to do my job, but as soon as they saw my pregnant belly, the families would prop me up with pillows and feed me cookies and tea. At the other extreme, at eight months pregnant I had a white tech dad stand in his doorway texting while I lugged a rolling suitcase up a flight of stairs.

The latest research indicates that it is okay for pregnant people to move around and carry objects just as they normally would. You shouldn't strain yourself or carry anything so heavy that it would put your back out. However, the latest research shows it is good for pregnant folks to be active. It keeps your baby regulated and used to moving around in the world. Babies who are exposed to lots of moving around prenatally are being prepared for all the bouncing and moving around they will experience once they are out there in the world.

However, just because that is what the research says doesn't mean it is always culturally appropriate for pregnant folks to behave this way. I'm a super active person. It was difficult for me to give in to the families who wanted me to slow down, sit on their couches, and not work. Eventually, I realized that it came from a good place. People who want to take care of fully functioning, healthy, energetic pregnant folks can be annoying. It is less annoying, however, than the asshole who pushed me out of the way on Market Street in downtown San Francisco when I was nine months pregnant.

6. How are you feeling?

I must admit that I am guilty of asking pregnant folks this innocuous, well-meaning question. However, I remember being *so over it* during my pregnancies. For the most part, I felt okay. Tired, sick of being pregnant, sometimes literally sick, but okay. So, there wasn't much to report. The question "how are you feeling?" is distinctly different from "how are you doing?" in a few crucial ways. "How are you feeling?" implies that you might be sick. It specifically asks you about your body, which maybe you just don't feel like talking about right at that moment. If you are looking for a good alternative to the "how are you feeling" question, try, "How are you doing?" Same sentiment. Less invasive.

7. You are *definitely* having a boy!

When I was pregnant with Hazel, we didn't find out if we were having a boy or girl. As my husband put it, there are very few fun surprises available to us in this life. Throughout my whole pregnancy, *everybody* told me I was having a boy. They gave lots of reasons for this: my belly was sticking straight out, my skin was clear, the baby was super active. At my work baby shower, my coworkers even hung up a "Congratulations, It's a Boy!" banner. I finally asked my OBGYN if there was any evidence that you could predict the sex of the baby from the shape of the belly. She explained that there was zero science behind any of it. It was 100% old wives' tales.

I love a good old wives' tale as much as anyone. And I don't like to question people's cultural beliefs without cause. The problem with some of these old wives' tales is that they are sexist. All of the "negative" traits of pregnancy are attributed to having a girl. I didn't gain a lot of weight during that pregnancy and didn't have skin issues caused by hormones. People told me, "It's a boy because girls steal your beauty." How sad is that? Before we are even born, we are accused of making our mothers old and ugly by stealing their beauty! During the last few months of my pregnancy with Hazel, she moved around constantly. Everyone assumed an energetic fetus was going to create a bouncing baby boy. Not the case! For nine months, Hazel squirmed, kicked, and prodded me. She was kicking like crazy the moment she came out. Hazel is fully female, in her sex assigned at birth and in how she identifies. But she's also exactly like how she was as a fetus: vivacious, energetic, and kicking the shit out of everyone around her.

When I was pregnant with Hazel, a neonatal surgeon explained to me that how a fetus acts during pregnancy has more to do with your placenta than the baby. Even though we read all kinds of things into what our little ones are doing when they are inside us, most of this is determined by the behavior of our placenta and how our bodies react to the hormones pulsing through us.

Also, gender is a social construct, so it doesn't really matter if you are having a "boy" or a "girl" anyway.

8. You are *huge*. You look like you're ready to pop!

I *hate* this expression. I think it is the use of the word "pop" that turns me off the most. Babies don't pop. Have you seen a birth? It's not a "popping." If only!

Also, it doesn't matter if a person is pregnant. No one wants to be referred to as "huge."

9. You look too big/too small for thirty weeks.

People absolutely don't mean to do this, but they freak pregnant people out when they say this. No one wants to be too big and have an abnormally large baby that requires a c-section or a difficult birth. But being too small is scary too. That could mean that the baby isn't growing. The truth is that very few of us really know what size is normal for a given gestational age. Even doctors need to measure you and look at a chart. Ever notice that your OBGYN or midwife never says, "You look so big!" when you walk in to see them? They don't say anything until after they have taken out their tape measure and measured you. No professional ever "eyeballs" this.

The person who tells you that you are too big or small is almost always male, and because his wife had three kids thirty years ago, he is convinced he's an expert on maternal size for gestational age. You know what actually is too small? The amount of prenatal experience a man needs to have before he feels comfortable telling a random woman in the grocery store that her belly is the wrong size.

Ugh...that guy. Don't even get me started.

If you ever find yourself tempted to comment on how big or small a pregnant person is, just stop for a minute and think. Does she really need your input on her size right now? Does she really want you to stare at her belly for a few minutes before commenting on the shape of her stomach? How would you feel if she did that to you? Being pregnant doesn't make it any less weird to have your body stared at by strangers.

10. Can I touch your belly?

No.

Unless you are a baby or small child yourself, in which case, yes.

11. Did you have that baby yet?

Luckily, some brilliant person created a website for this:[28]

---

28 "Have You Had That Baby Yet?," Have You Had That Baby Yet?, accessed August 12, 2020, http://haveyouhadthatbabyyet.com/.

The One and Only Thing You Should Say to a Pregnant Person

You look great!

That's it. I don't tell them they are glowing (because sometimes they are glowing because they are gleaming with sweat); I don't tell them they are big or small or round or pointy. I just say, "You look great."

Because pregnancy *is* beautiful. But they probably feel like a hot, sweaty, giant mess right now, so the nicest thing to do is to remind them

CHAPTER 5:

Fetus is Fetus

**WARNING: This chapter is going to be kind of a bummer.
Deal with it.**

This book was completely different when I started writing it. My
original instinct was to speak from a place of authority based on my
professional experience. I thought I would talk about my own experiences
and my own children only when it helped to illustrate a broader point.
This is not an autobiography, and therefore I am under no obligation
to disclose more about myself than I feel comfortable disclosing. I can
hide all kinds of things from my audience, like the fact that I gave my
children cotton candy last night right before bed and then forgot to
brush their teeth.[29]

But just because a book isn't an autobiography doesn't mean it
shouldn't contain stories that are hard to tell. In fact, the opposite is
true. Our experiences are almost always more universal than we expect.
The more we remain silent about the things that make us and others

---

29 If Hazel and Fritz's dentist is reading this…I'm truly sorry.

uncomfortable, the more our experiences stay hidden and unexplored. Pregnancy is only acknowledged and discussed when it results in its preferred outcome (a healthy baby). The truth is that most pregnancies *don't* result in a baby. As many as 50% of pregnancies end in miscarriage, many of those before people even know they are pregnant. And yet, *no one ever discusses this*. As a result, let's say you are a perfectly healthy twenty-seven-year-old woman who gets pregnant after a few months of trying. You are excited and scared, but mostly excited. Then you find out you are going to have a miscarriage and you *feel like there is something fundamentally wrong with you*. Why? Because in your entire life, a life filled with social justice and activism, reproductive rights conferences and deep friendships with other women, you have never had a deep conversation with another woman about miscarriages. So, when you hear that you will miscarry, the very first thought in your head is that this must be retribution for ending a pregnancy a few years prior.

I met my husband Jeff during our first week of graduate school. We had a whirlwind courtship that consisted of passing notes in class, going on dates to all-you-can-eat-sushi places and half-off-appetizers happy hours,[30] staying up late writing papers about attachment theory, and swimming in places we weren't supposed to. By the end of our first summer together, we knew we would never be apart. We also knew we weren't ready to be parents.

I found out I was pregnant while visiting Jeff in San Francisco two months into our relationship. I was twenty-four years old. Jeff and I had just fallen in love. We had just started graduate school and embarked on these new careers together. I knew I wanted to have kids someday and I already knew I wanted to have them with him. But I also knew that it wasn't the right time. We were fully immersed in the cocoon of early love. We knew that this baby, who would have been born within the

---

30 If our relationship was a book, the first chapter would be called Broke and Happy and the latest chapter would be titled Mo Money Mo Problems.

first year of our relationship, would make it really hard to maintain the honeymoon of early love. Also, we were broke. Remember the sentence about all-you-can-eat-sushi restaurants? That was the kind of people we were back then: all-you-can-eat-sushi people. Not we-have-money-for-diapers people. Also…I had spent the weeks before I found out I was pregnant having multiple beers every night. It was grad school!

For the first year of our relationship, we were long distance. Jeff was in San Francisco doing his practicum hours and I was still in Massachusetts. I found out I was pregnant in San Francisco the day before I was due to fly back to Massachusetts. I remember sitting on the airplane on the way home feeling like an alien had invaded my body. I felt like I wouldn't be normal again until the alien was gone.

I went to my OBGYN a few days later and explained the situation. I asked, "So…if theoretically a person drinks casually during early pregnancy…what effect exactly…?"

The doctor I saw was nice, gentle, and non-judgmental when I told her I didn't want to keep the baby.

"So, when can you perform the abortion?" I asked.

She was totally thrown by my question. "Oh! Um, no…you have to call Planned Parenthood."

"Right, um, of course," I answered, feeling like a moron. I guess it should have been obvious to me that I couldn't get an abortion at my doctor's office or a nearby clinic. Of course, I had to go to a special abortion-performing place fifty miles away.

Oh, right…I suddenly remembered. This was one of the top three things lunatics shouted about on the internet. There was an entire group of people out there who thought I should have this baby. Despite the fact that I was in a social work graduate program and had been thinking about the issue of reproductive choice my entire life, the whole abortion debate hadn't been on my mind until the moment the doctor brought up Planned Parenthood. I was just thinking about my body, my life, and my boyfriend's life. Why would anyone other than me and Jeff have any interest in this mundane medical procedure? And why did I have to travel to a totally different clinic, an hour away from where I lived, to have it done?

You know what people don't spend a lot of time thinking about as part of the abortion debate in this country? Women who don't want to be pregnant anymore. They are just trying to get the medical care they need. They are not trying to be in the center of some big controversy.

I called Planned Parenthood and made the appointment. Then I called Jeff and he bought a plane ticket to Massachusetts. The day of the procedure, we drove the hour to the Planned Parenthood clinic and passed protesters holding signs with weird pictures of aliens on them outside of the clinic. *Why are they holding pictures of aliens?* I wondered. *Oh right, those are fetuses.* I paid someone at the front desk $400 in cash[31] and sat down to wait my turn. The waiting room was full of women and girls who appeared to be in a similar predicament. Some of them were teenagers with their moms; others were in their twenties and accompanied by men sitting a few chairs away from them, like they barely knew each other.[32] I looked around and wondered if I was making the wrong decision. I wasn't sixteen years old. I was in love with the guy who got me pregnant. We were graduate students. My parents had money (kind of) to help me. Why didn't I just have the baby? Was this selfish? Was it the wrong move?

And then I ran out of the clinic crying and went to the nearest alien-sign holding anti-choice protester I could find and begged them to send me to a "crisis pregnancy center" instead.

No. That is not what happened. Even in my moment of doubt in the waiting room, I knew this was what I was going to do. It wasn't a

---

31 I will once again remind you of the all-you-can-eat-sushi anecdote. $400 in cash! Imagine how much sushi that could buy?!

32 Judging by the body language. I have no idea what the deal actually was.

baby growing inside of me. It was a bunch of cells that were going in a direction I didn't want them to go, and I needed to get them fixed so I could finish my degree and start my career.[33] I wondered if I was making the right decision. The same way I always wonder if I am making the right decision when I buy a pair of jeans without trying them on. It was doubt like that. Little "d" doubt. Not big "D" Doubt.

When the nurse called my name, I followed her into the scary Planned Parenthood back room.[34] They asked me a million questions to determine if I was being coerced into this by some creepy guy, made me fill out a DMV-sized amount of paperwork, and then brought me into the far back of Planned Parenthood. It was probably more complicated, but my memory of it is that I lay down on a table and a really nice lady held my hand, while two surprisingly cheerful and friendly abortion doctors suctioned a fetus out of my vagina. The whole thing took about two minutes. I knew right away that the alien was gone and that I was back to being an un-pregnant person. For the first, but not the last, time in my life, I appreciated that lifting of weight. That feeling of non-pregnancy. A feeling you don't notice until you are not-not-pregnant.

I was put in another room where I was given juice and incredibly delicious crackers. Within a surprisingly short amount of time, I was sent on my way. While I was going through this medical procedure, Jeff had gone to a diner to eat a nice brunch.[35] He brought me back an omelet I scarfed down, because abortions make you hungry.

I didn't end up regretting that decision. The abortion, I mean. The omelet I did come to regret because I was still a little woozy after the whole alien-removing thing. Every once in a while, I will remember that if that group of cells had turned into a child, that child would have been Fritz and Hazel's older sibling. But then everything would have

33 And keep drinking PBRs.

34 Where they harvest baby parts.

35 This is totally how my husband works. He's like, "How long is this abortion going to take? I'm going to get a bite to eat."

been different. Would I still have finished graduate school? Would Jeff and I have stayed together? Would there have been a Fritz and Hazel? Having kids has been so much harder than I could have ever predicted, and *I was ready for them.*

I felt ready to have children four years after that day at Planned Parenthood. Jeff was forty, I was almost thirty, and it finally felt like the kind of thing we could sort of kind of manage. As soon as the I'm-ready-to-have-a-baby light switched on for me, I couldn't switch it off. I went from not feeling ready to feeling reaaaaaaally ready. So, we started trying and within a few months I was pregnant.

Totally ignoring convention, I immediately told all my friends. I remember how my friend Carolynn looked shocked when I explained that I was only a few weeks along and hadn't been to the doctor. Carolynn is a very careful, always-look-both-ways type of person. "Shouldn't you wait until you go to the doctor before telling people?" she cautioned.

"Why?" I remember asking, genuinely not getting it. I was just so confident that everything would go perfectly for me. Why wouldn't it? I was twenty-eight years old and in perfect health. Of course, there would be no issues.

Well…you can guess how this story ends. At that first appointment, my OBGYN looked at the ultrasound and made cautious "we will see…I'm not sure" sounds that doctors make when they don't want to scare the shit out of you but also don't have anything good to say. Immediately, my heart sank and tears sprung to my eyes. I had spent the past six weeks getting to know the fetus growing inside of me. I had thought about the baby nearly constantly. It already felt like a child to me. I was already starting to feel like a mother. But the pregnancy likely wasn't going to be viable, my doctor patiently explained. It was possible that we had miscalculated ovulation and we should do bloodwork to determine if it was a viable pregnancy or not, and then go from there.

I can't remember how many days passed between that appointment and the final news from my doctor that the pregnancy wasn't going to be viable. Looking back, I only remember the overwhelming sadness. I had just started to fall in love with the idea of this fetus, with the idea that I was going to be a mother. And already I had failed, before I had even begun.

For the first time in years, I started thinking about my abortion again. Was this somehow happening because of the abortion? It made absolutely no sense to connect the two events, but in my mind, they were inherently related. It felt like I had rejected someone and then years later, decided I was into them, only to have them turn around and reject me. Somehow, I had brought this on myself by not just having a baby when I had the chance.

When my doctor finally called to tell me that the pregnancy wasn't viable, it felt like a relief after so much anxious waiting and wondering. Okay. Now I could move on. Also, I decided that meant I could drink, so I went ahead and did that. Which helped. My doctor recommended a D & C, a surgical procedure to allow a safe first trimester miscarriage. Wanting this non-baby out of me as soon as possible, I took the first appointment they had: November 1, 2013…my twenty-ninth birthday.

A few days before the procedure, I met with the anesthesiologist who would be operating on me. He met with me in his office to explain what would happen and get my consent. I acted the way I always do when I'm trying to get through boring or unpleasant things; I asked as few questions as possible so it would be over faster. I handed the doctor back the consent forms, and he placed them on the desk beside him, capped his pen, and turned to me.

"You know…" he began. "My wife and I have six kids. When we were pregnant with our fifth child, we found out that the pregnancy wasn't viable and she had to have a medically-induced miscarriage. Now, I can tell that you are being very stoic about this, but I just wanted to say…even though we knew intellectually how many pregnancies end in miscarriage, it didn't change anything for us. We were both very sad for a long time, her even more than me. And we still think about it, and about that baby. So, I just wanted to tell you that it's hard. And that I know it's hard. Just because miscarriages are common, that doesn't mean they are easy."

I burst into tears in his office. He handed me a tissue and we hugged. That little bit of kindness and understanding, that humanity in the midst of a sterile medical environment, meant so much to me.

The doctor was right. The sadness stayed with me for months, right up until that six-week ultrasound appointment with my third pregnancy, when I heard baby Hazel's healthy heart beating inside of me. That feeling of losing a pregnancy, even one that had been so short, broke my heart in a way the abortion never did.

Webster's Dictionary defines "pregnant" as "containing a developing embryo, fetus, or unborn offspring within the body."[36] Medically speaking, pregnancy is the same whether or not you want to have a baby. The same process happens in your body if you accidentally got pregnant due to some birth control malfunction, or after months or years of trying. But the experience of pregnancy is completely different from one pregnancy to another. As a pregnant belly grows bigger, the parent creates a mental representation of the cells growing inside. During my first pregnancy, there was no baby. The mental representation I had was of an alien. That was what those cells inside of me meant to me. During my second pregnancy, the mental representation was of a baby whom I would someday know. When that pregnancy ended abruptly, I lost that imagined baby. I don't believe I lost a baby, but I lost a mental representation of a baby, and that was something I had to grieve.

36 "Pregnant," Merriam-Webster (Merriam-Webster), accessed August 12, 2019, https://www.merriam-webster.com/dictionary/pregnant.

I have friends who have been trying to get pregnant for years. I have friends and clients who lost babies in the first trimester, or in the second and third, and I have a friend who experienced the birth of a stillborn baby. And of course, I have watched friends and clients get pregnant and give birth to healthy, beautiful babies time and time again. Every one of these pregnancies is emotional in its own way. The emotions start with the mental representation of the pregnancy. As a society, we only like to discuss pregnancy as the beginning of the journey toward a baby. But it is so much more than that. Pregnancy is its own journey, sometimes nine months and sometimes way, way shorter. That's why I thought it deserved its own chapter.

I'll try to be less of a bummer from now on.

CHAPTER 6:

The Five Most Annoying Things People Say to Parents of Newborns and…Five Helpful Things

Eventually, you will have that baby. When you do, it is almost guaranteed that people will have a whole new cadre of annoying things to say to you. People love giving advice to new parents. It generally comes from a good place, but that doesn't stop it from being incredibly irritating to hear the same thing over and over again. Especially when you are feeling exhausted and overwhelmed. The problem with having a baby is that it is an experience every person on the planet can relate to. Most people have kids. And everybody used to be a baby. So, we all think we know a little something about both sides of the equation.

Another completely exasperating fact of having a baby is that the people who know the most about creating and taking care of babies are women. Plenty of men know lots about both of these activities. However, let's just be completely honest for a second. What percentage of overall baby creation, rocking, diaper changing, feeding, etc. has been conducted by people with female organs? I can't even begin to answer this question, but let's just say…to be fair…well over 50%.

And yet. One group of people seems more comfortable bragging about their expertise and giving advice than the other group. And guess what? It isn't the women.

To the men who are reading this book: you are all amazing and I love you. Especially since you are reading a parenting book. Good for you! I hope you are doing it in public, so people can give you the standing ovation you deserve!

I have coined a phrase for the kind of explaining that men like to do to women about how to take care of babies: it's called manbabysplaining. Get it? Like mansplaining but about babies! And the great part about this term is that it can also be interpreted as calling the men babies. After pushing two babies out of my vagina and listening to men complain about vasectomies, that seems appropriate as well.

Let me give you an example of manbabysplaining at its best—or worst, depending on how you look at it. Last year, I was sitting next to my friend Ron a few weeks before his wife gave birth to her first child. "How are you feeling about things?" I asked him.

He answered, "Well, I'm definitely nervous…but I think that's normal. How did you feel before you had Hazel?"

I opened my mouth to answer, but before I could, the man sitting on the other side of him interrupted. "Oh man, bro, it's going to be a ride! It's going to be crazy! When those contractions start coming, make sure you are counting them for her. And make sure to massage her feet. I've had three kids and with my first one, oh man, I was totally freaking out before the baby was born…"

The manbabysplainer continued for several more minutes before Ron finally interrupted him pointedly to ask me, "So, Michelle...you have given birth to two children... How was that for you?"

Manbabysplainers are a professional hazard for me. They are almost all well-meaning dads. It's not their fault they have been raised to answer questions, even those directed to the woman sitting next to them. I will turn to the mom and ask, "So, how was the pregnancy?"

The dad will immediately answer, "Totally normal! Everything was great!"

To which the moms will respond, "Are you fucking nuts?? I threw up for seven months straight!"

I once went to a home visit where the dad had helpfully filled in the application ahead of time. As I started to go through it with the mom who was at the visit (the dad was at work), she turned to me and earnestly asked, "Wait...is this supposed to be about me?? This has nothing to do with my pregnancy."

And then there are the less well-meaning dads who like to manbabysplain to me about child development. They will very earnestly tell me, "Most babies talk between eighteen and twenty-four months," and, "Most brain development happens in the first five years." I always nod and smile politely, but I want to respond with, "Wait...I didn't realize that the first five years of brain development was important! Holy shit!"

Poor men. It must be so hard to have to know everything all the time.

I actually understand the instinct that fathers have to answer questions about pregnancy and breastfeeding, even when they weren't the ones experiencing it firsthand. It feels so incredible and salient to them that they feel as if they can speak about it with immense authority. Having a baby is both the most incredible and the most ordinary thing that will ever happen to you. It is completely mind-blowing. I still look at my kids and think, *How did I make you???* Somehow my body, completely separated from my conscious self, created this incredible little person who walks around, talks, rolls her eyes at me, and one day will probably criticize my politics for being too conservative. How amazing is that? And somehow, *my body* did this! Without me being able to explain how?! Mind blowing.

On the other hand, there are seven billion human beings on the planet and, with a few exceptions, all of them were created within the bodies of other human beings. This Onion Headline summarizes this perfectly:[37]

Giving birth is the most boring and redundant thing that can happen to you. And yet, it is simultaneously the most amazing and incredible thing. Your world is turned upside down in an instant. How will you get through these first few weeks with this new crying, pooping, tiny little bundle of joy? How will you make sure that your autonomous self isn't completely swallowed up by this creature? What is happening in your baby's brain during these first few weeks, and how can you help him learn and grow?

While you are asking yourself these questions, walking around in a state of shock and semi-consciousness, people are going to say the same dumb shit to you. Just so you feel prepared, here are the Five Most Annoying Things People Will Say to You. Followed by Five Non-Annoying Things You Can Say to Parents of Newborns when they have a baby (take note, all ye manbabysplainers.)

---

37 The Onion, "Miracle of Birth Occurs For 83 Billionth Time" (The Onion, October 18, 2017), https://www.theonion.com/miracle-of-birth-occurs-for-83-billionth-time-1819565067.

The Five Most Annoying Things People Will Say to You

1. I remember when my kids were young. It goes so fast! Enjoy it while you can!

Years ago, I promised myself that no matter how tempted I might be, I will *never* say this to a parent of a newborn baby. I have since broken this promise many, many times (see below example.) I understand that when people see parents of newborns, they can't help but think of their own children. Fine. KEEP IT TO YOURSELF! This is such a condescending, obnoxious thing to say. First of all, it's depressing to new parents to remind them right away that their babies will one day be obnoxious, temper-tantrum-throwing toddlers, or, even worse, rebellious teens. Also, why do people think new parents need to be reminded to enjoy their babies? What do they think we are doing? I once commented to my friend Sara, mother of two, that she should enjoy these years while she could. "Yeah, I'm enjoying them. I'm enjoying them," she grumbled, grabbing her son milliseconds before he hit his younger sister with a bat.

Even worse than the people who look at newborns and say, "I remember when my sixteen-year-old was that old," are people who look at newborns and say, "I remember when my nephew was that old... Enjoy it while you can!" Congratulations on your experience of being an uncle. Unless you were an uncle who adopted his niece and nephew after their parents died in a car crash, keep that shit to yourself.

Human beings love being the voices of authority on every subject. As I mentioned earlier, this is an attribute more commonly associated with human males. Therefore, people love to portray themselves as the voices of authority because they had a baby before you. As voices of authority, they feel compelled to make you aware of two very basic facts: 1) Children grow up, and 2) You should enjoy them.

How are parents of newborns supposed to respond to this comment? I mean seriously, how can they respond to it graciously. "Oh, wow! You mean my baby is going to grow up? Shit!"

2. Get some sleep!

This is another piece of advice that comes from a good place but is completely ridiculous. You aren't going to sleep for at least a few weeks, most likely months, possibly years. It is just not going to happen. That baby is going to have to eat every two milliseconds throughout the night. I don't know why people tell you this unless they are planning on coming over and sleeping at your house with your baby.

If they are planning to come to your house and breastfeed your baby while you sleep...then this is an *amazing* comment.

3. Can I hold him?

I am 100% guilty of asking new parents this. Even though I know this can be an obnoxious thing to ask, I will keep on doing it until the day I die. Newborns are unbelievably adorable, squishy little balls of love. If you are a baby person like me, you probably find it impossible to resist touching these little creatures. I am the weirdo at the cocktail party staring at a newborn across the room and drunkenly whispering to my husband, "Do you think that lady will let me hold her baby??"

"No," my husband usually whispers back, "I don't think she is going to let a drunk stranger hold her week-old infant." This is how I act while my children are still relatively young and cuddly! Can you imagine how crazy I am going to be when they are all grown up and I don't have any babies of my own to cuddle?

Offering to hold a newborn can often be a gracious and welcome act. I once gave in to my desires and asked to hold a newborn at a party. The baby's mother was extremely grateful. "Thank GOD," she said, "I can finally go to the bathroom." The poor lady had been standing there for who knows how long needing to pee. But there is a time and a place for holding newborns. Before you ask to hold a newborn, make sure you are doing it not just for your own purposes but in a way that is helpful for both parent and baby.

When a tiny, tiny baby has finally fallen asleep, swaddled in his mother's arms, do not ask to hold him with your grubby, snotty little hands! Sometimes new parents will want to be nice and will un-swaddle and hand him over to you. Next thing you know, the baby is screaming his head off. Nice going.

It truly is important to keep newborns as far away from germs as you can for the first few months. Visitors should wash their hands. Sick people should stay at home. I'm generally very laid back about these things. However, these tiny people don't have developed immune systems. You should feel 100% justified in being stern and just saying no to a well-intentioned person who asks to hold your newborn with their grubby, snotty little hands. Tell them to get their own newborn.

This is particularly true now, during a global pandemic. One of the many, many, many terrible situations that COVID-19 is responsible for is creating a world in which grandparents cannot hold newborn babies without fear of catching or giving a deadly virus. Fuck you, COVID-19.

4. Here, I will rock him.

Taking a crying newborn away from his parents may seem like a nice thing to do. This is not always the case. Again, read the room. Often what you accomplish in doing this is making the new parent feel incompetent and inexperienced. I understand that baby people and experienced parents are just trying to help, but sometimes they are also trying to prove that they are baby whisperers. Some people really do have a magic touch when it comes to babies. My sister, for example, can basically put a baby to sleep by looking at it. Dwight from the television show *The Office* apparently has the same effect.

However. Most babies, most of the time, prefer their parents. Dr. T. Berry Brazelton (a pediatrician who was a pioneer in the field of infant-mental health) had an incredible experiment he did with new babies to illustrate this. Brazelton would have a mom talk to her newborn baby in one ear and he (the stranger) would talk to the baby in the other ear. Almost all of the time, the baby would turn to his mother. He did the same experiment with fathers. The results were similar; most of the time the baby would turn to the father. The newborn babies showed immediate preference for the voices they had been hearing for nine months in the womb.

Here is my favorite part of the experiment. When the newborn babies did not naturally turn their heads to their parents, Dr. Brazelton would gently and subtly turn the babies' heads toward the parent. Why did he do this? It was more important to Dr. Brazelton to build up the confidence of the parents than to show them what an amazing baby whisperer he is. Dr. Brazelton knew the babies would be better served by having parents who felt confident about their own abilities than by him showing that he was great with babies.

New parents will learn how to calm their own babies. They *will* become experts on their own little ones. You can help by offering solutions or just by sitting back and observing what a great job they are doing. All babies cry. It doesn't mean they are failing as parents. Sometimes sitting there in sympathy and compassion while the parents figure out how to soothe their baby is more helpful than soothing the baby yourself.

There is a strong parallel between the way we as providers, or as friends of new parents, treat parents and how we want parents to treat their young children. If you step in and do everything for a child, his face will get washed, his pancake will get cut, and his clothes will match perfectly. But he will not learn how to wash his face, cut his pancake, or put on his clothes. However, if you offer gentle coaching and wait while he tries things and makes his own mistakes, he will learn how to do these things on his own. I practice the same strategy with new parents. I sit quietly and supportively nearby while they figure out how to soothe their baby. I ask questions rather than give answers. "Is that a hunger cry? Or is he just tired?" Even asking a question like this can help parents think about how different cries sound, if this isn't something they have thought of before. I offer help when they need it. I try not to offer suggestions they don't ask for. Babies cry. And the process of crying and being soothed is an integral part of the relationship building between parent and baby.

5. Bring the baby!

People love inviting parents of newborns to stuff and saying, "Bring the baby!" When I had Hazel, I was the first of most of my friends to have a baby, so my community was still very new to the whole "people have kids" phenomenon. Well-intentioned friends were constantly suggesting I bring the baby to movie theaters, bars, boats, etc. People said it to me so many times that eventually even I thought I could bring her to these things. Hazel was never convinced, though. I remember a few times I got somewhere and Hazel just looked at me like, "Why am I here? You know I'm a baby, right?" Although, my sister and I did bring Hazel to the third *Hunger Games* movie when she was about a week old and it went surprisingly well.[38]

We live in such a fast-paced world that it is hard for most of us to just slow down and enjoy our downtime. I know this is an irritating suggestion, but if at all possible, enjoy that newborn period! They sleep most of the time. Except, of course, if you have a colicky baby and then bless your heart, you are a saint and a martyr and we should all worship you.

---

38 We went to a matinee on a weekday and there was only one other person in the theater. We put little baby earphones on her. Hope had already seen it and left the theater with her when she started crying.

When your baby is tiny, you should spend all day on the couch watching Netflix and cuddling. Pretty soon they will be three years old and keeping them at home will be like keeping a rabid puppy in a shoebox.

So, seriously, enjoy it while you can!!! They grow up so *fast*!

Haha. :)

Five Non-Annoying (and Actually Helpful) Things You Can Say to Parents of Newborns

1. You are probably doing everything right.

Before I had kids, I remember worrying so much about how to hold my baby, how to rock my baby, how to play with my baby and talk to my baby. I had already been in the field of infant mental health for years, and when I had Hazel, I was halfway through an infant mental health postgraduate program. Still, I felt like a novice and was certain I would mess it up.

There is so much information! Overall, it is great having so much information at our fingertips. But it is also overwhelming. When I was pregnant for the first time, I thought I had to take every prenatal class or workshop or I would fail as a parent.

Confession: my husband and I are birthing class dropouts. We attended one class and then never went back. The first thing the teacher did was split us into groups. All the men sat together and all the women sat together. One of the men in Jeff's group announced that he was going to insist his wife stay home once she had the baby. Jeff responded, "Really? I'm trying to be the one to stay home when the baby gets here!" We immediately knew this was not our scene. So, we decided to just wing it.

One of the many workshops I meant to sign up for but didn't was on breastfeeding. Then little Hazel came along and an hour after she was born the nurse gave her to me and said, "Okay, try to feed her."

"Um, okay," I replied, wishing I had taken the breastfeeding class. I took my newborn baby and placed her on my nipple. She immediately started sucking away.

The nurse came back and said, "Oh, wow! You must have taken a breastfeeding class!"

"No," I replied. "But Hazel took one!"

Now, obviously this personal anecdote does not represent a universal experience. Many, many women struggle with breastfeeding, those who take breastfeeding classes and those who don't. Breastfeeding was just one of the things that came easily to my baby, but not every baby is like this.

There was a study conducted in 2019 by Brooke Scelza, a professor of evolutionary anthropology at UCLA,[39] that looked at why so many women in the modern world struggle with breastfeeding while women in countries like Namibia don't seem to struggle at all. The hypothesis was that women in more rural countries grew up around women breastfeeding, while in the west we basically require women to hide behind garbage cans and breastfeed babies through overcoats if they want to do it in public. But the hypothesis of the study was incorrect! The reason women in Namibia didn't seem to struggle with breastfeeding was simple: grandmothers. Women in Namibia *did* struggle in the first few days just as often as American women did. Babies had difficulty latching, milk flow was limited—all the same problems we have in the US. However, Namibian women had grandmothers, aunties, and sisters to help them problem-solve these issues. What do we have? Google.

What I got out of this study was this: the struggle is real and it is universal. Everything that we see about childbirth and babies on television is complete bullshit. Remember when Mindy Kaling's character had a baby on the show *The Mindy Project*? And that baby just hung out in the crib all day while Mindy cooked meals and had hours to get dressed in

39 B. Scelza and K. Hinde, "Crucial Contributions: A Biocultural Study of Grandmothering During the Perinatal Period," Human Nature, 30(4), (2019): 371-397, https://doi.org/10.1007/s12110-019-09356-2

decent clothes and do her make-up? Bullshit! Most infants have a hard time. Most parents have a hard time. It isn't you. You're not sucking at this. It's just really, really, really, really hard. Sure, it has happened seven billion times. But it's still really, really, really, really, really hard. Hopefully, you are lucky enough to have sisters and aunties and grandmas (and brothers and uncles and grandpas). But if you don't, hopefully it's a comfort for you to know that there are millions of parents right now who are dead tired, and completely in love with this tiny being in front of them but thinking, *Goddammit, this is so much different from how it was portrayed on The Mindy Project.*[40]

The Marvelous Mrs. Maisel has a similar problem. I adore that show. But has anyone writing for that show ever had a baby? Met a baby? Been a baby? There really is a baby living in Mrs. Maisel's house. They often refer to a baby. Mrs. Maisel and other characters on the show say that a baby exists and occasionally, we even see a baby. But the baby never cries, or wakes up at night, or spits up on any of Mrs. Maisel's beautiful clothes. The baby and her older brother never seem to require anything out of the adults around them other than an occasional pat on the head. Now, I wasn't alive in the 1950s, so maybe that's just how babies were. What is more likely is that the Mrs. Maisel writing staff didn't want baby-duties interfering with the plot. And this seems to be the trouble with most children or babies on shows.

According to Hollywood, babies are boring. Therefore, most television shows deal with the existence of babies by inserting a cute baby into the background of a shot. In 99% of movie and TV scenes involving babies, two adults have a completely uninterrupted conversation with a cute baby cooing in the background. Or, even more unrealistic, a toddler quietly playing in the next room. Dude. If I am having an uninterrupted conversation with an adult and my kids are home, it is

---

40 As I was finishing this book, Mindy Kaling put out a series of essays about parenthood called *Nothing Like I Imagined*. Girl, yeah, we saw your fucking show. We know what you imagined.

guaranteed the children are quiet because they are busy flushing objects down the toilet. If television writers want to create scenes where adults have uninterrupted conversations while small children are home, they should probably have every one of those scenes end with an emergency call to a plumber, because that's the only way it seems realistic.

2. Seriously though, babies are like snowflakes/boxes of chocolate.

It is the biggest cliche in the book, but babies really are like snowflakes. When you are pregnant, people convince you that you *absolutely* need the $300 baby swing, or the baby bathtub, or the bouncy chair. The best gift you can give an expecting couple is cash or a gift card. Because your baby might have loved that bouncy chair, but your friend's baby will probably hate it. You won't know what you need until you meet your little human being.

All babies are born with different sensory profiles. When Hazel was a baby, I had to rock her in a very specific way to get her to calm down. I had to stand with feet apart and bounce twice, very deeply on one side and then the other, dipping slightly and bending forward. I am not kidding. I had to train my husband to bounce the exact same way as me so I could go to the bathroom or sit for a few minutes between rocking. When Fritz was little, he didn't care how he was rocked. As long as you snuggled that little guy, he was happy.

In case you think he was the easiest baby in the whole world, let me tell you, that little man would *scream* every time he was in the car, for the entire time he was in the car. Hazel was two years old and I had to keep her entertained as well, so we spent a lot of time driving to various kid places when Fritz was an infant. It didn't matter if we were in the car for five minutes or two hours; he screamed the whole time. It got so bad that Hazel refused to get in the car with him. I went on a desperate hunt for answers. I emailed my occupational therapist friend. I scoured the available literature. Finally, a suggestion came to me from a random mom on the internet (proving that sometimes random anecdotes on the internet are indeed helpful.) She said that her baby cried in the car until she got a cushion for his car seat. So, I bought Fritz a memory foam baby seat cushion from Babies R Us. The result was immediate. He never cried in the car again. Crazy, right?! What a little Princess and the Pea. He was physically uncomfortable in the car seat. At four years old, Fritz still acts this way. He's a super easy kid overall, but he's sensitive to how things feel.

All babies have sensory needs that are distinctly different from each other. Your baby is going to have a completely different sensory profile than your friend's baby who was obsessed with the swing. So, before you spend money on something, see what that profile looks like.

3. Don't get out of bed until you have to.

If you are the kind of person who goes absolutely insane on no sleep (more about that later), just flat out refuse to get out of bed. When your baby wakes up at 6 a.m. and is cooing and loving and flirting and indicating that this is a great time to get out of bed and start the day, adamantly disagree. Play with the baby in bed and see if after a half hour, an hour, or two hours, the baby will go back to sleep. Chances are, a newborn baby will do this if you give them time. When they do, you will still be in bed and can hopefully go back to sleep. If you get up at 6 a.m. when your baby gets up, then there you are, still dead tired but dressed and caffeinated when it is time for your baby's nap. If you have the luxury (no work or other children to take care of), STAY IN BED.

4. It is okay to be sad.

There is a difference between baby blues and postpartum depression. Baby blues are totally normal and almost universal. Your hormones change. Your entire life has been flipped upside down. If this is your second, third, or fourth kid,[41] you are in shock at how hard this is. You are exhausted and often lonely in this new life where the only person you talk to has a vocabulary of two sounds: "waa" and "coo." New parents feel like they are supposed to be in a state of blissful delight all the time. The truth is very different. Most of us feel sad, at least some of the time, for some of those early days of being home with the baby.

There is so much excitement associated with the birth of a new baby. It is incredibly painful and horrifying, but also exciting. And then there are a few days where everyone is happy for you and you get a million likes on your Instagram pictures and friends come over with gifts. Then everyone is gone and it's just you, on a couch with your pajamas and baby puke, suddenly aware that your life has changed completely. For parents who had a baby during a pandemic, they missed out on all the early bliss of the gift-giving and baby-holding and instead, just skipped to the lonely part.

As I stated in an earlier chapter, if you aren't slightly ambivalent about having children, you are probably boring. Very few people are 100% on board ever, even after they have multiple children. It changes everything about your life. As much as people obnoxiously point this out to you before you have children, you don't 100% understand until that needy little ball of love is lying on your lap and you can't get up to pee because if you move the baby will wake up. Then it suddenly occurs to you that a few days earlier you were a fully functional human being who could pee whenever you wanted, and now you are this. And you will be this forever. "HOLY SHIT THERE IS NO GOING BACK!?" Is a perfectly normal response to having a baby.

It is normal to feel sad, and this is called the baby blues.

Postpartum depression is not baby blues. If you feel very sad for a long time, or even very, very sad for a short time, there are amazing

---

41 Four kids?!

resources out there to treat postpartum depression. You should seek treatment immediately so that you and your little one can get help.

5. Newborn babies are brilliant and interesting.

When I was in the infant parent mental health postgraduate program, I remember one speaker (I wish I could remember their name) talking about how before the field of infant mental health emerged in the 1940s, the common western belief about newborns was that they were incompetent, non-observant little balls of flesh.

This is, of course, complete bullshit.

One of the problems with the amazing field of infant mental health is that most of the scholarly research has historically been done by middle-aged white guys. However, most babies are primarily cared for by WOMEN, and most childcare providers in this country are women of color. I am 100% sure that mothers in the 1930s intuitively knew their newborns were incredible, brilliant things. But they were just at home quietly loving and caring for them while their husbands were off doing research on monkeys and making up dumb theories, like John Watson's belief that loving your children too much is bad for them. John Watson, the father of behaviorism, wrote in 1928:

> *"Never hug and kiss (children), never let them sit on your lap. If you must, kiss them once on the forehead when they say good night. Shake hands with them in the morning…try it out. In a week's time you will find how easy it is to be perfectly objective with your child and at the same time kind. You will be utterly ashamed of the mawkish, sentimental way you have been handling it."* [42]

When I think of how much time we have wasted as a society by only listening to old white dudes…

42 John Watson, *Psychological Care of Infant & Child* (New York, New York: Norton Press, 1928), 82.

Neuroscience now proves what mothers have always known. Newborns are incredibly intelligent, extremely sensitive to their environments, and very reactive to their circumstances.

Dr. Brazelton developed the Newborn Behavioral Observation (NBO) tool as a concise and measured way to show off the skills of the newborn baby. If you haven't already, take a break from reading this and look up T. Berry Brazelton on YouTube conducting the NBO. The Newborn Behavioral Observation tool is used to show off to new parents the amazing skills their tiny little creatures are capable of. From their first moments of life, babies are self-regulating and control the amount of stimulation they let in. They show emotions through cooing and crying. They respond better to the language they heard in utero than to other languages. They show a preference for their mothers and any other caregivers who were around when they were growing.

Knowing that newborns are brilliant and amazing is important information for new parents. Not only does it confirm your suspicion that your little baby is the most amazing and perfect baby ever to be born (she is), but it also helps you to feel less bored and isolated. You aren't just hanging out all day with a cute ball of flesh. You are hanging out all day with an incredibly intelligent creature.

Newborn babies sleep a lot (if you are lucky). When they aren't sleeping, they spend a lot of time crying, fussing, pooping, eating, or getting ready to poop or eat. A newborn only has a few moments every day (usually in the morning) when they are primed and ready for engagement. Those are the amazing moments when your little one opens his eyes and seems to notice you. "Oh, hi!" you say, immediately tearing up. In those moments, few and far between, your baby will start to imitate you. This begins in the first few weeks of life! If you talk to your baby, you will notice that his mouth will start to move to mimic you. Later on, he will mimic a sound and still later, a word.

In the first few weeks, babies will begin to track objects and light with their eyes. Try passing a light over your baby's face and see if he will follow it. He might even get excited if you show him a cool toy and start to kick his feet. During those early days, you don't need to stress yourself out trying to teach your baby rocket science. For god's sake, don't play him Baby Einstein. But you can start to play simple games with him to keep yourself from going crazy from boredom and fatigue.

Babies are so much smarter and more amazing than any of us give them credit for. There is this feeling of ennui that sinks in when you are home with an infant. You feel like you need to be doing something meaningful in those moments between feeding and diaper changing. But remember, you are doing something important. You are helping to create the brain of another person. You are making connections between synapses when you respond with "ba" after they say, "ba." The job of being with a newborn is more vital to the continuation of the human race than any of the other shit we all get paid to do.

Which is why you shouldn't fuck up. And why when you eventually do fuck up, you can totally fix it.

CHAPTER 7:

Everything You Do Matters but It's Okay

Now that we have discussed how amazing and brilliant newborn babies are, let's talk about how the parent fits into this equation. Kristie Brandt, who runs the Napa Infant Parent Post Graduate Fellowship Program at UC Davis and is a brilliant source of information on all things baby, compares the newborn baby to the newborn giraffe. She writes:

"In sub-Saharan Africa, a giraffe gives birth to a calf that falls 10 feet to the ground, lands on his back and quickly sits up. Within minutes he will stand and within hours be able to run alongside his mother. A calf that is unable to accomplish the developmental motor tasks of standing, walking, and running so quickly after birth (something the typical human infant will not accomplish until age 10-14 months) will die by predation or starvation.

The human infant is born, breathes on his own, and is placed in his mother's arms. He, too, must accomplish a crucial developmental task or agenda, or he will not survive: the newborn must attract a caregiver who is competent and willing to invest in his survival. He must attract someone willing to keep him safe, feed him, and fall in love with him." [43]

Babies are primed to make us fall in love with them. The way they smell, the feel of their cuddly little skin, their smiles, their coos. These are their superpowers. Like the ability to move in rhythm to their parents' voices. My sister and I always talk about how we completely distrust people who don't like babies. What kind of person could be immune to this:

(This is Fritz on the day he was born)

Babies may look like they are just lounging around doing nothing, but they are working super hard to be so cute and get you to engage with them. It is through the engagement and relationship with the parent that the baby's brain develops.

Sadly, the brains of neglected children are *smaller* than the brains of typical children:

---

43 Kristie Brandt et al., *Infant and Early Childhood Mental Health: Core Concepts and Clinical Practice* (American Psychiatric Publishing, a Division of American Psychiatric Association, 2013), 8.

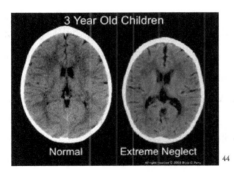

It isn't just that the baby learns new skills from the parent; the baby learns how to learn from his relationship to the parent. This is what the psychoanalyst Donald Winnicott meant by saying, "There is no such thing as a baby." There is no such thing as a baby in a void. The baby can only exist in relationship to a loving adult. Hence, the difference between baby humans and baby giraffes. Baby giraffes are basically just good to go from birth. And baby Komodo dragons must avoid their parents because they might eat them.[45]

Knowing how crucial you are to the development of your baby's brain is empowering. But that's also a lot of pressure. What if you mess up during those early days of parenthood? Is that it for you? You may as well throw in the towel?

Which brings me to Dr. Ed Tronick's Still Face experiment.

If you are in the field of education or psychology, you have probably watched a video of The Still Face experiment. If you haven't, Google "Still Face Experiment." Ed Tronick has been doing this experiment in various ways since the 1960s. The experiment is this: he puts a very young baby in front of her mother. The mother engages with the baby in the way she typically does. The baby coos, talks back, points at interesting things around the room. Then, suddenly, the mother stops engaging.

44 Bruce Perry, "Maltreatment and The Developing Child," *The Margaret McCain Lecture Series* (2005), https://www.childtrauma.org/brain-dev-neuroscience.

45 I told Fritz that fact and he cried.

She drops her head. The baby first tries all her tricks (smiling, pointing etc.) to get her mother back. Eventually, the baby gets angry. When this doesn't work, the baby seems to give up. That's the saddest part of the experiment. The baby seems to decide it isn't worth it. Nothing she can do makes any difference. After this happens, the mother re-engages with the baby. At first, the baby is still mad. She doesn't look at the mother. She's basically saying, "Oh, I see! Noooooooow you want me!" But very quickly, the baby/mother interaction is back on track. The baby has stopped being petty and is back to being in love with his mother.[46]

If you watched this as part of a class on education or development, it is possible that the conclusion the instructor reached about the video was the opposite of what Tronick's research shows. Because the baby has such a strong reaction to the parent in the video, the video is often shown to students to illustrate the importance of maternal/baby attunement. Students are asked to imagine what the baby's existence would be if this were to happen all the time, as in the case of a depressed mother. While this is an important point, it misses Dr. Tronick's conclusion.

This kind of rupture in attunement does happen all the time to babies. By tracking the mother and baby's heart rates, Dr. Tronick found that most baby/mother dyads are only in sync a small percentage of the time. The rest of the time, the baby is looking somewhere else, or the mother is looking somewhere else, or for whatever reason they aren't quite in tune with each other. How often is a baby looking at a mother who is looking at her phone? All the time, right!? Let's not trick ourselves into thinking this is a modern problem. Cave mamas had to look out for lions. They couldn't sit there staring at their baby's face all day.

In healthy attachment relationships, the infant parent pair is *not* always in sync; rather, they are constantly dancing with one another. In sync, out of sync, in sync, out of sync. Students often find it difficult to

---

46 *Still Face Experiment: Dr. Edward Tronick*, YouTube (UMass Boston, 2009), https://youtu.be/apzXGEbZht0.

watch Still Face videos because it feels like the babies are being tortured. But look at how quickly the babies recover! What the Still Face videos show is how the interactions between parent and baby are dynamic; they ebb and flow. The mother is not the perfect mother every second of every day, and that is okay!

I worked with a family a few years ago who had a two-year-old with autism. The hard-working, loving mother was a firm believer in the power of early intervention. As a result, she poured her heart and soul into providing her little guy with every single opportunity for growth and learning. He ended up having sixty hours of intervention per week. Sixty hours! She was doing so much for him that the family didn't have any time just to be a family together. Or for her to go to the gym. Or for them to veg on the couch watching a movie. She was completely exhausted and as a result, she didn't have the emotional energy just to have *fun* with her little guy.

When she had her second baby, that little girl started showing developmental delays as well. At first, we thought it was autism too, because she wasn't making eye contact or responding the way we would expect. What ended up making the biggest difference in the little girl's development was when the mom cut down on the hours of therapy for her older son. She scheduled time for herself just to sit on the couch with the baby and be calm with her. She found time for the two of them to be together. It became clear that the second child didn't have autism; she just needed some more one-on-one time with her mother.

The bad news is that everything you do now really does matter.

But the good news is pretty good. It isn't rocket science! Most babies are born with all the tools they need to win your heart. And you have all the tools too! You don't have to do anything incredible. Just coo at them when they are awake and alert. Make dumb noises. Sing dumb songs. The content of the interaction doesn't matter too much. You can sing "Twinkle, Twinkle Little Star." or you can sing "One Week" by the Barenaked Ladies. If you are doing it with your baby, she will probably find it hysterical and captivating. And you don't have to do it for twenty-four hours a day. If someone texts you, you can look at your phone. And if your baby coos at you while you are doing this and you miss the cue, it's okay. There are more coos coming.

CHAPTER 8:

Why Knowing about Attachment Theory Will Mess with Your Head

There are some pieces of information that can only affect the learner in positive ways. For example, learning how to change a tire.[47] Or learning the difference between "affect" and "effect." These are not dangerous pieces of information that could change your entire life and make you question everything you have ever known.[48]

---

47 When we were little, my dad told me and my sister that we would never need to know how to do this because we could just flag down a man to do it for us. My sister reacted by getting offended and later learning how to change a tire, a skill that has served her well for years. My reaction: "Okay, sounds good, thanks!" I can't change a tire. I can barely change a lightbulb. Since I'm married to an electrician, I haven't changed one in eleven years.

48 When my sister was proofreading this, she wrote, "Unless you're me, and the difference between 'affect' and 'effect' and everyone else's inability to grasp the concept haunts you like a physical poltergeist throughout every hour of your waking life."

There are other pieces of information, however, that, while valuable, can also completely derail your world view in a way that isn't always welcome. Like listening to Neil deGrasse Tyson talk about basically anything. Or accidentally overhearing coworkers talk about your leadership style. Learning about attachment theory falls into this second category of knowledge. It can be helpful, but it can also completely change the way you think about yourself, your childhood, your parenting style, and the future success of your children.

I learned about attachment theory in graduate school over ten years ago. Since then, I have watched friends, family members, and clients go through the illuminating and often terrifying process of learning about attachment theory and then immediately reevaluating their existence. Just in case you haven't spent a semester, or even an afternoon, learning the basic principles of attachment theory, let me give you a brief overview. Then you can go off and examine your own childhood through the lens of attachment and process what it means for your children's happiness. When you are done doing that, you can return and read the rest of this chapter.

Attachment Theory derives from the work of the psychoanalysts John Bowbly and Mary Ainsworth. Bowbly and Ainsworth's central thesis was that all human babies must form a strong attachment to at least one primary caregiver to survive. Seems pretty obvious, right? Their work focused on the hypothesis that human babies formed a strong attachment to a primary caregiver *even if* that caregiver was abusive, neglectful, or unreliable. Humans (as well as human-like animals) would rather become attached to a mean parent than be unattached.[49]

This theory was tested by the psychologist Harry Harlow in a particularly brutal experiment that PETA activists still have nightmares about. Harlow took a group of baby rhesus monkeys and separated

---

49 Inge Bretherton, "The Origins of Attachment Theory: John Bowlby and Mary Ainsworth," *Developmental Psychology* 28, no. 5 (1992): 759-775, https://doi.org/10.1037/0012-1649.28.5.759.

them from their mothers. He then had the baby monkeys bond with "surrogate" mothers, who were made of either cloth or wire. The wire monkeys had food and the cloth monkeys had no food but were soft and cuddly. The baby monkeys all showed strong preference for the cloth mother monkeys. The baby monkeys would go to the wire monkeys for food, and then return to the cloth monkeys. Harlow added an additional element, where the baby monkeys periodically heard a loud noise. They would immediately run to their cloth mothers for comfort. Lastly, he engineered an experiment where the cloth mothers hurt the babies with spikes. The baby monkeys still preferred their cloth mothers, even though they hurt them.[50]

Harry Harlow also isolated baby monkeys in dark cages by themselves for a year to see what would happen to them. In conclusion: everything we know about human behavior is derived from a bunch of psychopathic white men in the 1950s. Let's see what happens to baby monkeys when we isolate them for a year! The history of social science is a dark, dark place.

The most famous experiment related to attachment is Mary Ainsworth's Strange Situation Experiment.[51] Although these human babies weren't isolated from their mothers for a year, the experiments can still be difficult to watch. Again, I direct you to type "Ainsworth Strange Situation" into YouTube. But if you are the kind of person who learns better by having a video described to you than by watching it, I will break it down for you.[52]

In the Strange Situation experiment, a mother plays with a toddler in a room with a one-way mirror, and a bunch of creepy scientists on the other side of the mirror take notes. The room has fun age-appropriate toys, and the mother and toddler play for several minutes until the child

50 "Harry F. Harlow, Monkey Love Experiments," Adoption History: Harry Harlow, Monkey Love Experiments, accessed August 13, 2020, https://pages.uoregon.edu/adoption/studies/HarlowMLE.htm.

51 The Strange Situation | *Mary Ainsworth, 1969* | *Developmental Psychology*, YouTube (Psychology Unlocked, 2017), https://youtu.be/m_6rQk7jlrc.

52 NPR listeners are those kinds of people. I don't want to watch the documentary on exotic birds…please just describe it for me in detail.

feels fairly comfortable being in the room. It isn't Chuck E Cheese, but it is fine. Then a stranger enters the room. The baby looks at the stranger like "Who the fuck is this?" but accepts it. A few minutes later, one of the scientists taps lightly on the glass. The mother says to the child, "Okay, I'll be right back, sweetheart," and leaves the room. The baby tries to follow the mother, but the mother leaves without her. The stranger tries to comfort the baby, who very sensibly loses her shit. The mother returns a minute later and picks up the crying baby. The crying baby immediately settles down.

This is what "secure attachment" looks like. When the toddler is in a strange situation, he wants his mother to comfort him. When the mother is unavailable, he is distraught. As soon as the mother returns, the toddler settles down. According to Ainsworth's research, 70% of children are securely attached.[53]

So, what about the other 30%? These children were found to be "insecurely attached." This category of insecure attachment breaks down into two subgroups. There are the "insecure avoidant" and "insecure ambivalent/resistant."

The key moment in the Strange Situation experiment is what the baby does when the mother returns to the room. In the insecure/avoidant videos, when the mother returns and picks up the toddler, the baby turns his face away. He looks sad and sullen. He doesn't look at his mother. Basically, he's still pissed. He doesn't want to get burned again, so he's not expressing too much happiness at seeing her. The secure child forgives his mother for leaving. Right away, he's like, "Oh good, you are back, let's play!" But the insecure/avoidant baby doesn't want to engage with his mother.

53 Mary D. Salter Ainsworth and Silvia M. Bell, "Attachment, Exploration, and Separation: Illustrated by the Behavior of One-Year-Olds in a Strange Situation," *Child Development* 41, no. 1 (1970): 49. https://doi.org/10.2307/1127388.

The insecure resistant/ambivalent baby is also not comforted by his mother's return. He keeps crying even when she comes back. When she offers him a toy, he slaps it out of her hand. He's still mad at her, even though she came right back. It's as if this baby is harboring a deep-seated grudge against her that he just can't get over.

Research on these attachment styles has shown that they continue throughout the lifespan of a child. When the insecurely attached babies from the Strange Situation experiment were interviewed twenty years later, they continued to show patterns of insecure attachment toward romantic partners or other loved ones. What does this look like in an adult? At its most severe, it can look like a personality disorder. At its least severe, it can look like someone who has difficulty maintaining healthy romantic relationships because they don't trust that someone is going to stick around.

Based on my own extensive research (a.k.a. conversations about this with friends, colleagues, and clients), it is impossible to watch these Strange Situation videos and not analyze your own attachment style. Most people will immediately think about that time they were twenty-five and didn't trust that their boyfriend was being faithful, so they threw a potted plant at him in a fit of rage. Or we will think about that time our eighteen-month-old was throwing a tantrum and we didn't offer comfort when we should have. Did we set him up for a lifetime of insecure attachments? Will he act ambivalent toward his future partners because his parents didn't respond to his feelings?

On the one hand, I love Attachment Theory and I love the Strange Situation. I love that it validates the importance of the parent/child relationship as the most critical determinant of later relationship success. Prior to Bowlby and Ainsworth, pediatricians in the United States were routinely counseling mothers not to hug their children as it might spoil them. So yeah, unless you are a baby rhesus monkey, Attachment Theory has had an overall positive effect on your life. It is a good reminder for all of us to be responsive to our babies' emotional needs, even when they are driving us crazy. They are born primed to be attached to us. And the more consistent we are with giving warm, gentle, attuned attention to them, the more likely they are to seek that out in the world. And the more likely they are to give it to their children. Because they will know what attuned attachment looks like.

Every time I watch those Strange Situation videos, I wonder about the mothers of the insecurely attached infants. Were they told they would be put on blast for their bad parenting? Forever? On something that didn't exist yet called YouTube??? Would they ever have consented to this? How much did they pay these poor mothers? I'm glad we no longer tell mothers they shouldn't hug their babies. The pendulum has swung all the way to the other direction. Now, instead of telling them they will spoil their kids by hugging them too much, we tell parents they will destroy them by hugging them too little.

So, what do you do when you suspect you might have an insecurely attached baby? Or if your insecure attachment style is affecting your child? Should you give your baby up for adoption right away? Or wait a few years and see how everything pans out?

Parenting in the internet age means knowing too much. Parents living on the prairie in the nineteenth century didn't know that they were creating insecure attachments in their children…and they probably wouldn't have cared if they did. They had nine kids! Who cared if one was fucked up?! Nowadays, most people only have two children and the internet has convinced us that we suck at raising them.

What good comes from this worrying? If you interpret the Strange Situation videos as evidence that you are a bad parent, you are not doing yourself any favors. But it is helpful to think about our behavior toward our children through a compassionate, forgiving lens.

Rather than thinking this: *Oh my god, I am terrible. My mother was a stressed single parent when I was a baby and as a result did not always respond to my bids for attention. I developed an ambivalent attachment style because I didn't want to rely too strongly on any one caregiver. I always struggled in romantic relationships and now I am a stressed single mother myself and I am repeating this same pattern with my own child. I hate myself.*

You can think this: *I can see that my baby sometimes responds with ambivalence when I walk into a room. I wonder if I have a hard time consistently responding to him when he needs my attention. I haven't been paying enough attention to him since I started working. I need to find a few little moments when I get home from work for us to be together and work on our attachment.*

I believe in Attachment Theory. I believe that the way we respond to our babies affects how they will respond in future relationships. But I also believe that people are malleable, and nothing is finite. We can grow and change. The more knowledge we have, the more we can make changes in our lives. But knowledge itself is not enough. We need to be loving and forgiving with ourselves and each other. We need to have the ability to look at our behavior and ourselves critically but not judgmentally. For hundreds of years, we have blamed our mothers for everything that is wrong with us. Mothers have been told to hug less, or to hug more, or to hug the same amount but differently, depending on which psychoanalyst is popular. My suggestion is that we give parents full credit for how important we are in the lives of their babies, and also give ourselves a goddamn break.

Both are possible.

CHAPTER 9:

Everybody Hates Babies

What? That's crazy! That can't be true! Everyone loves babies! They are welcome everywhere and anywhere!

Nope. False.

As I have already lamented, I live in the Bay Area. It is insanely expensive, it is slightly cold 80% of the time, and it is full of rich, judgmental pricks. Unfortunately, all of my friends and family are here, so I'm essentially stuck.[54] Because I live in the Bay Area, my perspective on society is distorted. However, I do think there are probably some echoes of my experience everywhere in our country/world.

One of the hardest adjustments to make when you become a parent is getting dirty looks everywhere you go. Most places parents go with children, we will get dirty looks if our children do basically anything: cry, touch things, move, whine, talk, breathe…you know, any of the things human children do.

I have gotten dirty looks/words from strangers when my children:

---

54 Also, I love it.

1. lay on the floor of a yoga/dance studio
2. attempted to touch toys in a toy store
3. whined/cried at a grocery store/mall/parking lot/community center/playground/Planet Earth

This is probably worse in the Bay Area (where we have more dogs than children) than in most other places, but it is not a phenomenon unique to here. We don't live in a society that accepts children. This is weird given that a) everyone was a child, and b) most people have a child. Nonetheless, if you have children you are expected to leave them at home, but also to stay at home with them and not leave your children to be raised by someone else; basically, you are expected to be a shut-in, which luckily is possible now with Amazon Prime.

Older adults and parents of kids and adults with disabilities experience the same feeling of being shunned by society. God forbid an older adult drives a little slow, or an adult with a disability takes a bit longer ordering at Philz Coffee. Everyone around the person acts like they are an ER doctor getting called to a surgery. We live in a society. Some people are old, some people are young, and some people have disabilities. Can we *please* allow all of these people to order at Philz?[55]

I never say anything to anyone because I prefer to shoot passive aggressive looks over my shoulder, but here is the dialogue I have in my head every time I take my children anywhere with me:

Guy at Jiffy Lube after giving us dirty looks for ten minutes: "They really shouldn't touch those tires. They are really dirty.

Me: "Dirty, huh? Oh, man! That's a huge fucking deal because my children have never encountered dirt before! Whatever should they do? I don't allow them to use their hands to touch things at all. Other than,

---

55 I know people outside of the Bay Area don't know what Philz Coffee is, but I'm not changing that reference in the hopes that someone, somewhere, someday will read that, Google Philz Coffee, and end up ordering a Jakobs Wonderbar and thus changing their life.

of course, carefully-inspected toys not manufactured in China. Thank you so much for speaking up and questioning my parenting! I will ensure that they sit on these uncomfortable chairs for the remainder of the time we are in here and not touch anything. In the meantime, please take as long as you possibly can with my oil change."

It is true. No one likes babies.

You love babies, obviously, or else you probably wouldn't be reading this. As a society, we have decided that children do not belong in public spaces. There is room for well-behaved, quiet, not-crying-and-not-moving children, but not actual real-life children.

So, what are parents to do? Do we stay at home all day but also not let our children watch too much television (or else their brains will crumble and die)? Or do we go through the world constantly correcting their behavior? There's no good answer. It's hard for parents, and it's even harder for children.

I went out for dinner with my extremely well-behaved niece when she was three years old. She sat at the table waiting for her food while the adults around her engaged in boring adult conversation (blah blah Big Five blah blah tiles replaced). She picked up her fork and started stabbing the table with it. "Please stop that," she was told. She took her spoon and started spooning ice into her mouth, causing it to splash onto the table. "Stop it," another adult whispered. She picked up her straw and started blowing bubbles into the water. "You need to stop doing that," she was once again reminded. My niece threw up her hands, exasperated and asked, "So, what can I do?"

Seriously, though. What do we expect children to do during these extremely boring everyday situations? They are children; being wiggly and curious is part of who they are. These characteristics are viewed by society as bad behavior. They are just childhood. We don't live in a society that accepts these behaviors as part of everyday life. What if we did?

What if there were restaurants where the tables surrounded a giant play structure? I don't mean an indoor play place that also sells food. I mean an actual good restaurant that happens to have a play structure in the middle. What if every bathroom had a child-sized toilet? Or a changing table? We feel grateful when these things exist, but we should require them! We should walk out of public restrooms and ask, "Excuse me…where is your child-sized toilet!?"

Five years into this whole parenting journey, I decided to change the way I approached public spaces with my children. Rather than constantly apologizing and telling my children, "No, no, stop, stop, don't do that," I decided to accept whatever consequences were coming my way. I decided that children should be as welcome in public spaces as anyone else.

A year ago, I had to go into a local urgent care clinic for a TB test. My husband was working, so I took the kids with me. As soon as we entered the waiting room, Fritz noticed a very interesting round table with a hole in it. Naturally, he did this:

And then this:

In case it isn't clear from the picture, that is a miniature pumpkin that Fritz is throwing into the middle of the table. I'm not sure exactly what the donut-shaped table was designed to accomplish...but it likely was not intended to be used as a basketball hoop for a pumpkin.

A few years ago, I would have immediately told Fritz to cut it out. Then I would have taken the pumpkin away from him if he didn't listen (which he wouldn't). But now? Five years into this thing, I'm done with bending over backwards to make my kids behave in public settings. If the clinic didn't want Fritz to throw pumpkins around their waiting room, they shouldn't have built a table with a hole in it. If they have a problem with it, *they* can tell him.[56] I'm over it.

During my final editing of this book in late 2020, this whole society-doesn't-value-children theory was proven like never before. In California, bars and restaurants were reopened and COVID-19 cases immediately spiked. Schools didn't reopen in the fall as a result of the spike in cases. What if we had made the collective decision to value reopening schools over bars and restaurants? What if we had decided to put the developmental needs of our children above all other concerns? What would a society like that look like?

I would love to find out the answer to that one day.

---

56 If they *do* tell him they have a problem with it, I will judge them, look at them passive-aggressively, have an inner dialogue about it, and then process it in book format.

CHAPTER 10:

If You Don't Breastfeed Your Baby You Are a Literal Monster

There is a radio program in San Francisco called Forum, which is exactly what it sounds like. A older white liberal man interviews important people about relevant (mostly local) issues. As long as you overlook his not-so-occasional name-dropping, as well as him referencing classes he has taught at Berkeley and books of poetry he has read/published...it is pretty good. In fact, Forum was the site of my one and only fifteen minutes of fame. Many years ago, Michael Krasny asked the (now deceased) mayor of San Francisco about a radio piece I had written criticizing Twitter for not paying pay roll. Michael Krasny asked Mayor Lee, "What do you think about Michelle Kaye's argument that tech companies are getting too big of a break?"

Mayor Lee responded, "Well, it sounds like Michelle Kaye is anti-progress."

I was in my car looking for parking when I heard this and my first thought was, *Wait… is this coming out of everyone's radio or just mine?* The mayor of San Francisco insulted me by name. So, that was the biggest thing that happened to me in my twenties.[57]

Years later, I was once again listening to Forum while looking for parking in downtown San Francisco. On this particular morning, the Forum topic was breastfeeding. Most likely, Michael Krasny had a few guests on to discuss this topic, and I assume at least one of them was female. However, the guest I remember was a middle-aged male doctor promoting the health benefits of breastfeeding. In my memory of the program that day, the discussion consisted of two old men talking about boobs. At the time, I was an exhausted breastfeeding mother of two on my way to work. I was already rolling my eyes before I had even absorbed what they were saying.

When I tuned into the program, the doctor was explaining to Michael Krasny and the listeners how important breastfeeding is to the development of children. He was explaining how breastfeeding has been linked in evidence-based studies to all kinds of positive effects for infants and young children. He continued to expound on how these positive effects last throughout our lifetimes. I just did a two-second Google search on the effects of breastfeeding and here is what I found:

The Benefits of Breastfeeding | Parents
https://www.parents.com/baby/breastfeeding/basics/the-benefits-of-breastfeeding/

11 Benefits of Breastfeeding for Both Mom and Baby

- Breast Milk Provides Ideal Nutrition for Babies
- Breast Milk Contains Important Antibodies
- Breastfeeding May Reduce Disease Risk
- Breast Milk Promotes a Healthy Weight
- Breastfeeding May Make Children Smarter
- Breastfeeding May Help You Lose Weight
- Breastfeeding Helps the Uterus Contract

More items • Jun 1, 2017

11 Benefits of Breastfeeding for Both Mom and Baby - Healthline
https://www.healthline.com/nutrition/11-benefits-of-breastfeeding

---

57 And I include giving birth to Hazel when I was twenty-nine. Babies are born every day. It isn't every day that you get personally insulted by a politician.

The positive effects of breastfeeding are incredibly well documented now that it isn't the 1970s and formula companies aren't allowed to peddle their bullshit anymore. But this doctor was arguing that breastfeeding has even *more* long-term, positive effects for children than was previously thought. His argument was that if you breastfeed your child, he will go to Harvard, and if you don't…well, then whatever happens is your fault.

After the doctor had gone on and on about the miracles of letting babies suck on your boobs, a mom called into the show about her experience breastfeeding her four-month-old. She explained, "My baby has an incredibly difficult time breastfeeding. He has a hard time latching and so he gets frustrated trying to get enough milk and ends up crying. My nipples are sore from him biting them and I'm totally exhausted from trying all of the time. It is a miserable experience for him and for me and I end up breaking down in tears every time I feed him. I know breastfeeding has all kinds of benefits, but I'm exhausted. Is it okay for me to give him formula?"

The doctor answered, "Given the incredible benefits to both baby and parent of breastfeeding, I would strongly encourage you to keep going. I understand that the journey is hard but in the end it is worth it."

Sounding completely deflated, the caller responded, "Oh, okay… thanks." It clearly wasn't the answer she was hoping for.

"WHAT THE FUCK???" I screamed into my radio. Seriously? The last thing a burnt-out, exhausted mother who already feels like a failure needs to hear from a doctor is that yes, she should continue exhausting herself because it is worth it for her child's future. Mothers who can't breastfeed already feel like they are failing their children, and this guy was making it even worse!

It was also just such a one-dimensional answer. Sure, if you think the only thing that contributes to the long-term health of babies is the nutrients that they absorb and the hormones that are released from breastfeeding, then I guess this answer makes sense. But we are so much more than the nutrients that make up our body! Brain research continues to show the importance of early attachment during those first few years, particularly the first year. I would argue that this attachment, this relationship between an infant and its primary caregiver, has a bigger contribution to future child health than the amount of nutrients a baby absorbs through breast milk.

Of course, breastfeeding often contributes to and strengthens that attachment, and when successful breastfeeding takes place it helps with attachment as well. The moment that Hazel first attached to my nipple to feed, I received a rush of oxytocin that felt like nothing I had ever experienced.[58] It turned out Hazel had taken a breastfeeding course in my uterus and had absolutely no problem knowing what to do. In my case, breastfeeding kicked off the strongest feeling of attachment I have ever felt.

But a stressed-out mother, with an increased heart rate, crying and begging her baby to latch…think about how that stress is impacting the infant. I doubt there is much oxytocin being released to the mother's brain in those moments. As she continues to feel that stress and anxiety every time she goes to feed her baby, think about how many of the early moments between mom and baby are being spent with the mother and baby stressed and anxious. One half of the dyad is begging the other one to eat. The other half of the dyad is not understanding why he can't get milk more easily. This is time that could be spent babbling, cooing, laughing, and napping on the couch watching Netflix shows. Even if you *only* focus on future health outcomes for the baby (and don't consider the mother at all), the baby will be healthier if his mother is free to make the choice that is right for her, not the choice that her doctor thinks she should make.

---

58 I went to raves in the early 2000s, and seriously, the Hazel/breastfeeding drug was the strongest.

Also, can people whose boobs don't produce milk stop telling other people what to do with their milk-producing boobs? Oh. Also, can people whose boobs do produce milk please stop telling other people whose boobs produce milk what to do? That would be great, thanks.

I have spent most of my career talking to parents about their concerns with their children. Time and time again, I have found the concern that brings parents the most pain and anguish is feeding. Whether it is a two-month-old who won't breastfeed, or a five-month-old who won't take the bottle, or a five-year-old who won't eat, feeding problems *kill* parents. Parents feel so defeated by them, so utterly helpless. I had a mom once explain to me what it felt like to have a three-year-old who wouldn't eat. "It is like my *one* job, to make him eat," she said. "And he just won't do it."

This line summarizes why parents find eating problems so unbearable. If your kid won't stop throwing tantrums, if he isn't walking yet, if you can't toilet train him, these are problems—but they aren't life and death problems. Feeding feels so urgent to us because it is related to our children *living*. Even if the feeding issue itself isn't life or death, like the kid is eating but the only food he will eat is garbanzo beans,[59] it still *feels* like life or death. And so generally, parents approach eating with life or death urgency. Unfortunately, that is exactly the wrong thing to do.

If you follow me on Instagram, you are aware that I am currently embroiled in a years-long struggle to get my son to eat a vegetable. Any vegetable. At the time of this writing, he is four years old and I can count the amount of non-potato vegetables he has digested on one hand. He doesn't believe that vegetables are truly food. Or maybe they are food for other people but certainly not for him.

---

59 I didn't make that up. I really know a kid who will only eat garbanzo beans.

He is not a fan.

Fritzi's relationship with vegetables has helped me understand what my clients find so challenging about feeding issues with their kids. I sometimes fantasize about placing food directly into his stomach, bypassing his mouth and taste buds completely. In my weaker moments, I have attempted to shove food into his mouth (an approach that I do not recommend you try, not only because it doesn't work but because it is tantamount to child abuse.) I routinely avoid reading articles about kids' nutrition. At this point, it is better for me not to know. Fritzi's favorite restaurant order is "ketchup with a hotdog please." I am pretending that subsisting primarily on ketchup is a perfectly healthy lifestyle for a four-year-old boy, and I don't want to be told anything different.

Feeding therapists will recommend the exact opposite of the "shoving food into the mouth" method of feeding. You want to keep putting vegetables on your child's plate *without* making a big deal out of it. If you attempt to force them to eat the vegetables, they will realize quickly that you think vegetables are gross and are something they need to be forced into eating. But if you start off gradually by just encouraging them to keep the vegetable on their plate, they may eventually just get curious and take a bite. And if not, oh well. My aunt has a theory that children just magically absorb whatever nutrients they need to survive through whatever food they are given. I love this theory because it basically comes down to "Don't worry, they will survive and eventually eat like a normal human being and even if they don't, oh well."

Kids eventually get old enough to respond to logic. Sometimes. Hazel understands that vegetables help her grow, and she wants to grow bigger so she can become a scientist and take over the world. Therefore, she started eating vegetables—and then, incredibly, liked them! On her own. Once I stopped stressing out about it all the time. Who knows, maybe Fritzi will eventually come around as well.

Breastfeeding is the same way. Some babies come out of the womb knowing exactly what to do and how to do it. Other babies need a little coaxing. Some babies need a *lot* of coaxing. But the best approach is to meet your baby where your baby is and try to get that baby to suck your nipples; if she doesn't, you are not a failure as a mother. Your baby is not a failure as a baby. Did you know that they sell this stuff called "formula" in stores? In your neighborhood!

This is a screenshot of a text message with my friends Yasmine and Ariana. Yasmine's baby Roxie spent a week in the NICU, so she had a hard time latching afterwards. On top of everything else, Yaz felt guilty about Roxie missing out on key attachment/breastfeeding moments early on.

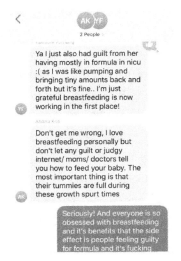

We live in a society that is so quick to judge mothers for what they are doing or not doing. Every day, another *Slate* article comes out about what parents should do differently. But we don't pay enough attention to what this guilt is doing to us and to our children. We are all doing the best we can. We are muddling our way through. And the very *last* thing we need is to be told what we are doing or not doing is going to cause lifelong damage to our children.

I have a hunch. My hunch is you will read that, agree with me in principle, and continue to stress about what your child is eating or not eating. Despite knowing that forcing food into your child's mouth is not a good plan for instilling a lifetime of healthy eating habits, you will still try to do it. I have a hunch you will do what I do, what our parents did: you will bribe them. You will tell them they can't leave the table until they have finished all their Brussels sprouts. Or, "Three more bites of carrot or no television!"

Even as those words leave your mouth, you will think to yourself, *This is dumb. This is not going to instill a lifetime of healthy eating. This is only going to encourage this child to think of carrots as something to be swallowed and tolerated, instead of savored.* Even so, you will say it... again and again. Because eating is so emotional for parents. Seeing my children eat healthy foods (on the rare occasions they do) fills me with joy. I'm prouder of Hazel when she eats a carrot in front of other people than when she uses the word "parched" correctly in a sentence.

It's okay that you will do this. It's okay that you will do this knowing it is not the best approach to healthy eating. Because you are doing it for yourself. This is how you show love to your child, and how you show yourself that you are showing love to your child. There probably aren't many children out there who hear their parents yell at them to eat more vegetables and think to themselves, *They must really love me, because they care what I put in my body.* However, forcing our children to eat healthy foods is about the relationship, and on some level, children know this.

My mother-in-law is from Germany. When we visited her family in the Bavarian countryside a few years ago, every day we were treated to a gigantic feast. I'm not used to eating a hamburger, followed by a steak and potatoes, followed by a cheese platter, followed by dessert. But in the German countryside when family is visiting, that's how they roll. So, every meal consisted of Jeff's relatives asking him in German why I wasn't eating more. It wasn't about the food. It was about love. In Germany, and in so many cultures throughout the world, sharing food is about sharing love.

It's like that with our children too. When we say, "Eat your carrots," we are really saying, "I love you." It's very important to remind your children of that when they get upset because you scream EAT YOUR CARROTS at the top of your lungs. It's just our way of saying we love you, really.

CHAPTER 11:

Get Some Sleep

Is your eight-week-old baby sleeping through the night? Yes? WELL, GOOD FOR FRICKIN YOU!!!!!!!!!!!

Please skip this chapter and go give yourself a huge pat on the back.

Okay, now that those people are gone…let's get real. When I started writing this chapter, I was in a pretty good place in terms of my relationship with infant sleep. Fritz had slept in his crib for two nights in a row and I was feeling like, this isn't too bad, I think I've cracked this tough baby-sleep nut. I wrote a very cheery passage about how to transition your baby from snuggling your boob all night to sleeping in his crib without bouts of unrelenting crying and screaming.

And then…

The next night happened. I picked up my baby and rocked him. I held his hand through the crib. I rubbed his back. I climbed in his crib with him.[60] I climbed out. I touched his face. I put a blanket on him.

---

60 This is something I don't know: am I the only person who has routinely crawled into my children's cribs with them to get them to sleep?

He. Would. Not. Stop. Crying. Finally, after hours of waking up every time I wasn't touching him, Fritz passed out at 4 a.m. I passed out at 4:10. At 5 a.m., Hazel woke me up.

#toddlerlife #babylife #thisissofuckedup

I have found infant sleep to be one of the most confounding problems I have encountered in my personal and professional life. After eleven years of thinking about baby sleep and five years of living with it, I still feel like I don't have a simple, satisfying answer to this problem. Which is one of the reasons I wanted to talk about it in this book. Because if there is anything that will require you to be okay with the ambiguity, it is dealing with baby sleep.

First of all, babies don't actually sleep through the night. None of them. Like all human beings, they wake up throughout the night. Some babies magically know how to put themselves back to sleep without intervention. Which is just awful for their parents, because those parents never get to experience the blissful feeling of being awoken every forty-five minutes for eight hours straight.

In Jennifer Senior's book *All Joy and No Fun*, she talks about how parents of young children can be divided into three camps. People in the first camp adjust to a lack of sleep without any major hiccups. People in the second camp find it slightly challenging but do okay. Then there is the third camp: parents who go completely insane.[61] I am a proud member of this group. You know you belong to this camp if:

1. You have broken down sobbing uncontrollably at 4 a.m. and begged your baby to go to sleep.
2. You have been so tired that you tried to hand the cup of coffee to the baby and didn't notice until you took a sip from the bottle.

---

61 Jennifer Senior, *All Joy and No Fun: The Paradox of Modern Parenthood* (Little, Brown Book Group, 2015).

3. You fantasize about sleeping in a bed, all by yourself
with nobody to interrupt you, like some people have
fantasies about winning the lottery.

Before I had kids, I took sleep for granted. I remember being a
teenager and saying, "I will sleep when I'm old." When I was in high
school I would get home at 3 p.m., do my homework, take a quick power
nap, then stay up until midnight listening to Pink Floyd and braiding
my hair. After college I used to stay up late binge-watching shows just
for the hell of it, knowing I could always sleep in. Oh, how far in the
rearview mirror those days seem now.

When you don't have children, if you go to work after a night of
drinking you know somewhere in the back of your mind that the magical
sleep reservoir is in your future. You are midway through your shift at
work thinking, *After this I'll go home, order Chinese food, and pass out in
front of the TV.* When you have young children, there is no magical sleep
reservoir in your future. You are exhausted at work thinking, *After work
I will go get the kids, make dinner, play with them, clean up after them,
put them to bed, yell at them to go to bed, scream at them to go to bed, beg
them to go to bed, and then eventually I will go to bed. And then they will
wake me up five times before morning.*

Fucking exhausting.

Because I fall into the camp of people who lose their minds with no
sleep, I have spent a lot of time in the past years researching baby sleep.
I have read books, gone to classes, and spent an embarrassing amount
of time on mommy blogs looking for answers. My thoughts about sleep
are informed by my understanding of how babies' brains work, as well
as by my own experience.

Here's what I have found:

1. Cry it Out is bullshit.

"Crying it out" is the idea that you should just let babies cry until they pass out. It is a philosophy that new parents are often presented with in this way: Your great aunt is visiting you during the baby's naptime. You are attempting to talk to her about her upcoming African safari, but you keep getting interrupted by the baby crying from the other room. "So sorry," you keep saying as you run to the baby's room. Eventually, your great aunt helpfully tells you, "You know, in my day we just let the babies cry until they wore themselves out. Have you tried that?" Thanks, Aunt Suzie.[62] Great advice.

Let's look at the best possible outcome of Cry it Out. Your baby cries so much and so often with no response that she eventually gives up, determines that no one loves her anymore so there is no point, and falls asleep. That is just about the saddest thing I have ever heard in my life.[63]

There have been a few interesting studies showing the negative effects this has on the brain. When you think about it, we shouldn't require research to tell us to stop letting our babies cry at night. Babies are tiny, fragile creatures that could be gobbled up by coyotes if they aren't cuddled and protected. And they know it! When your baby is crying at night, she is saying, "Heeeeeeello! I literally weigh eleven pounds and can't even roll over yet! Come get me!!!"

I know there is a whole industry that has popped up around letting babies cry it out. I also know that people have been letting babies cry it out, at least in the United States, for a long time. My own parents have stories about letting me cry it out in a hotel room and guests calling the front desk and saying I was being tortured. And yet somehow, I turned out fine-ish. Although, who knows how well I could have turned out if I had been cuddled at night like I should have been. Maybe I could

---

62 In case you are wondering if Aunt Suzie is real, she isn't. Or maybe she is, but in any case, she isn't my aunt.

63 With the exception of baby monkeys left in isolation for a year.

have been one of those Wall Street types who makes a million a year moving money around instead of having a meaningful job helping people for pittance.

I realize that many, many people have done this to babies and these babies (including me) have turned into fully functioning adults. However, I am just not convinced this is a practice we should continue. Not only is it stress inducing for infants; it's also extremely stressful for parents. No one *wants* to do this to their baby. I once sat next to a woman at a sleep-training class who burst into tears when she talked about leaving her baby to cry it out. "I don't know if I can do it!" she said between tears.

Her husband put his arm around her, and the instructor encouraged her, "I know you can do it." But they were both missing something here. Maybe the reason she was so emotional about not leaving her tiny infant to cry himself to sleep at night was because it isn't right.

Sometimes the things that don't feel right *aren't* right.

So, if there is another solution to getting babies to sleep that doesn't involve stressing everyone the fuck out, I think we should try it.

2. Co-Sleeping = bad but kind of amazing.

I once had a pediatric resident at my doctor's office (who looked like she had just graduated high school) tell me that if I was going to co-sleep, I should have my baby on the outside of the bed, rather than between me and my partner. Her reasoning was that it was better for my baby to fall off the bed then for my husband to roll on top of the baby. Clearly, this is a completely insane thing to say and just proves how clueless (some) doctors can be (sometimes).

In her defense, I'm sure she was just repeating something from her medical training. The American Academy of Pediatrics recommends:

Infants should sleep in the same bedroom as their parents—but on a separate surface, such as a crib or bassinet, and never on a couch, armchair or soft surface—to decrease the risks of sleep-related deaths.[64]

Fine. I get it. They have to go with the most medically safe and evidence-based recommendations. That's their calling. When I was in the hospital when Fritz was born, I kept falling asleep with him breastfeeding. The nurses kept coming into my room and waking me up to tell me to put him in the bassinet. Every time I did, he woke up and started crying. Thus, neither of us got any sleep.

What could be more natural and normal than a breastfeeding mother asleep cuddling her newborn baby? Remember the coyote? It's a dangerous world out there and these little newborns are teeny-tiny and delicious. Cuddle them!

Also, have you ever cuddled with a baby? There is literally nothing better.

Here's a picture of my sister, the world's best baby whisperer, cuddling my little man Fritz.

For thousands of years, in every culture on Planet Earth, mothers have slept with their babies. Why are we telling people not to do this? The American Academy of Pediatrics recommends babies sleep in the same room as their parents for the first year, but not in the same bed.

---

64 "Safe Sleep Recommendations," AAP.org, accessed August 13, 2020, https:// www.aap.org/en-us/advocacy-and-policy/aap-health-initiatives/safe-sleep/ Pages/Safe-Sleep-Recommendations.aspx.

They recommend babies not sleep on couches, in car seats, in rockers, or any of the places that babies typically fall asleep. They recommend that babies not be left to sleep in the arms of a sleeping caregiver, even if the sleeping caregiver is the best baby whisperer in human history (a.k.a. "Auntie Hope").

From the standpoint of most-safe and less-likely-to-cause-death-or-injury, these recommendations make sense. I cannot imagine being an ER doctor and having to perform CPR on an unresponsive infant. That would happen to me exactly one time and I would become a complete tyrant who went around waking every baby I saw sleeping anywhere other than a firm surface away from blankets and other people. If I were a pediatrician or a nurse, I would probably give all these recommendations to my patients, even this one:

If your baby falls asleep in a car seat, stroller, swing, infant carrier, or sling, you should move him or her to a firm sleep surface on his or her back as soon as possible.[65]

Seriously…can you imagine waking up a three-month-old who has finally passed out in a swing just so you can put them in a crib?

When I had Hazel, I got spooked by all the recommendations of the medical establishment, and so I started her off in the crib. For the first few weeks, I got up every forty-five minutes to feed her. Eventually, I put her in bed with me, so I didn't have to get up to nurse. Finally, I got some sleep. Little Fritz was in my bed from the day I got him home. That way, I could nurse him at night while still half asleep. My insomnia-induced insanity with him was lessened considerably. I was crazy for other reasons (like having a newborn and a toddler), but I couldn't blame it solely on no sleep deprivation.

---

65 "Safe Sleep Recommendations," AAP.org, accessed August 13, 2020, https://www.aap.org/en-us/advocacy-and-policy/aap-health-initiatives/safe-sleep/Pages/Safe-Sleep-Recommendations.aspx.

In conclusion: co-sleeping worked for me. And my children lived through it. Especially for those first few months when they were feeding all the time, it worked miracles. However, it's not for everyone. Some women have told me they can't sleep when their baby is in bed with them. Safety is a huge concern if you have a partner in bed with you who is a deep sleeper or is just not down with the whole idea. Luckily, we live in a world of endless consumer goods and they sell all sorts of nets and co-sleepers, which let you have the baby right by you in bed without the safety risk. If you co-sleep or even have a baby nearby in a co-sleeper, you will at some point need to transition the baby to another room and that will absolutely suck. However, I would argue it is 100% worth it for the sleep you will get by having the baby in there for the first few months.

3. Babies need a lot of help to go to sleep.

There are few things that infuriate me more than the way Hollywood depicts putting babies to bed. I just watched the show *Atlanta* in which a mother places a baby in a crib, turns off the light, closes the door, and goes to sleep herself. The whole thing takes about thirty seconds.

Are. You. Kidding. Me.

Babies need rocking, cuddling, feeding, sucking, singing, and swaddling to go to sleep. They cannot do it themselves! It's a skill they haven't learned yet. So, we have to help them. The problem is that once we help them go to sleep, they have a hard time going to sleep on their own. And therein lies the fundamental conundrum of baby sleep.

The trick is to slowly and steadily help them to help themselves. This is not dissimilar to how we teach children and teenagers basically everything. We have to ease babies from not being able to put themselves to sleep to soothing themselves.

Slowly.

Steadily.

One.

Step.

At.

A.

Time.

4. Slow and steady will work eventually.

You will reach a point when you are ready for your baby to sleep by himself with minimal wake-ups. This point is different for everybody. After the first twelve weeks, most pediatricians say it is okay for a baby to go through the night without eating. Their stomachs are big enough to store food, so they don't need to eat during the night. Some parents are ready to get babies to sleep on their own as soon as they hit that twelve-week mark. Some parents are okay waiting until their baby is twenty-four months.

Sleep is the first test of your parenting style. Parents face a decision at twelve weeks of how much or how little they are going to intervene to fix their baby's sleep. For some parents, they jump fully into the problem, research it as much as they can, and tackle it head on. For others, they just hope that the problem will work itself out and that the baby will eventually sleep through the night on their own. For my little ones, I basically just waited until I literally couldn't deal with it anymore and then I tackled the problem head on.

Whether it is at twelve weeks or twelve months, most parents are going to come to a point where they are ready to intervene. And then what do you do?

First, you need to believe it will work. Just imagine a very distant time in the future when your baby will sleep through the night and you can go back to being a normal human who can get up to pee at night without having to tiptoe like a burglar to the bathroom for fear of waking the beast and kicking off an hour-long rocking session. For every baby, there will come a time when they will sleep through the night. Even if it isn't until the child is three years old, it's going to happen. You have to believe it. This too will pass.

Secondly, don't focus too hard on the end goal. If you want to get the baby sleeping through the night without using Cry it Out, you need to take it night by night. The goal is not to get your baby sleeping through the night in a week. If that is the goal, then there are going to be tears. Slow and steady will win the race, but it will take a loooooong time. You are trying to help them, day by day, just move a bit further along on the trajectory of sleep. If tonight she sleeps for four hours in a row, tomorrow night can she sleep for four and a half? Give yourself an end goal that is a few months out.

The book I found most helpful for me when it comes to sleep was *The No Cry Sleep Solution* by Elizabeth Pantley. This woman raised four kids and she knows what she is talking about. She encourages families to take a log of each day in the life of your baby and track what you did, what worked, and what didn't work in terms of sleep. She also has some awesome little tips in there, like how to remove a nipple from a baby's mouth without waking him up.[66]

When I was twenty-five, I never would have imagined that "how to remove a nipple from baby's mouth without waking him up" would be like, the most important information I could possibly learn. But it legit changed my life.

So, if you are the kind of person who likes to have a very detailed method to follow, I recommend buying her book and following it like the Torah. I am not that kind of person. I prefer for someone to just give me the gist and then I can improvise.

---

66 Elizabeth Pantley, *The No-Cry Sleep Solution for Toddlers and Preschoolers: Gentle Ways to Stop Bedtime Battles and Improve Your Child's Sleep* (New York: McGraw-Hill, 2005).

The Gist of Slow and Steady:

Every night, focus on getting a little closer to your goal than you were the night before. To make slow and steady work, you need to have big goals and then smaller goals to help you reach those big goals. Then you need to have nightly goals to help you reach the smaller goals that will ultimately help you reach the big goals. I know, this is sounding like some stupid "How to Become a Millionaire from Home Without Trying" motivational thing. But seriously, it is the best way to think about sleep training.

When Fritz was ten months old, he could only sleep if he was cuddling me, breastfeeding every two hours. This was fine when he was a newborn, but by the time he was ten months old I had had enough. Also, Jeff was like, "Can you please get this giant baby out of the bed?" Rather than focusing on getting Fritz to sleep in the crib, I first focused on getting him to stop breastfeeding at night. Around this time, he basically weaned himself during the day, so I felt like he was ready to wean at night too. Breastfeeding to go back to sleep is the most invasive form of soothing for all involved. There is only one person who can do that for any given baby. So, anything you can do to transition a baby to literally anything else will make your life easier.

For Fritz, my long-term goal was to get him to sleep in his crib, with a few nightly wakings. I started out trying to help him go back to sleep on his own. To do this, I needed to very slowly and gradually decrease the amount of soothing he required to go back to sleep.

I broke down the problem like this:

Step 1: Transition from soothing him by breastfeeding to soothing him by bottle feeding.

Step 2: Transition from soothing him by bottle feeding to soothing him by rocking him every time he wakes up and then cuddling him.

Step 3: Transition from soothing him by cuddling in bed to soothing him by rocking him and then putting him back in the crib.

Step 4: Transition from soothing him by rocking him to soothing him by touching him in the crib.

Step 5: Letting him soothe himself with no intervention.

I gave myself one month to do this. I don't think I could have done it in less time, and I probably should have given him even more time. Don't start sleep training when you are on vacation, during a crazy work week, or when you are just feeling stressed and anxious already. I started the steps with Fritz after we came back from vacation, while I had a bit of time before starting a new project.

Step 1: Getting from Step 1 to Step 2 took me about a week. I started by seeing if I could get him to go an extra hour at night without breastfeeding. When I started, Fritz usually woke up to feed around 9 p.m. That first night, instead of breastfeeding him at 9 p.m., I gave him the bottle at 9 p.m. It wasn't until he woke up at 11 p.m. that I breastfed him. The next night, I gave him the bottle at 9 p.m., again at 11 p.m., and was able to prolong breastfeeding until 2 a.m. And on and on. Within a week, I had him weaned from breastfeeding at night to just bottle feeding at night.

Step 2: The next step was to wean him from the bottle. That first night of weaning from the bottle, I rocked him when he woke up at 9 p.m. and didn't give him the bottle until 11 p.m. The night after that, I prolonged the bottle until 2 a.m. A few nights later, Fritz didn't need the bottle at night. However, I still had to cuddle him in bed or else he would wail.

Step 3: I finally had Fritz weaned from needing milk at night. But he was still sleeping in the bed with us, and every time he woke up, he would need to be rocked back to sleep and then cuddled. The first night of Step 3, I rocked him to sleep and then got into the crib with him and snuggled him until he fell asleep, then snuck out of the crib. That whole process took me about two hours, but at the end of it, I had a baby asleep in a crib. For only one hour before he woke up. When he woke up, I rocked him until he was asleep again and put him back in the crib. Of course, he woke up again and again and again. Nevertheless, I persisted! That first night I got no sleep, but I demanded that Fritz not get into bed with us until 11 p.m. The next night, I rocked and placed him, rocked and placed him, until finally relenting and putting him in our bed at midnight. I made sure that each night he spent just one hour longer in his crib, until eventually we made it until 6 a.m. Yay! Step 3 took me a completely exhausting week and a half.

Step 4: Finally, I had Fritz sleeping in his crib. However, he was still waking up two to three times throughout the night, which was fairly normal for a ten-month-old. Every time he woke up, he needed to be rocked until he fell back asleep. The first night of Step 4, I made sure to only rock him three times throughout the night. The other times he woke up, I would stroke his back, rub him, and hum in his ear but not pick him up. The next night, I only picked him up twice throughout the night. The next night, only once. Finally, I had a few nights in a row where I only touched him and rubbed him and he would go back to sleep in the crib.

Step 5: The last step was to get Fritz to go back to sleep without any intervention from me. He did this step on his own. Rubbing his back wasn't making that much of a difference. When he woke up in the night crying, I would wait, without rubbing his back, and eventually he went back to sleep on his own.

BETTER THAN GOOD ENOUGH

Using this approach, I went from Fritz sleeping in my bed and breastfeeding every one to two hours to Fritz sleeping in his crib and waking up one to two times throughout the night but staying in the crib. It took me about a month to get from Step 1 to Step 5. And then, of course, three months later he had a major sleep regression, and I had to spend another four weeks slowly and steadily getting him back on track. It sucked, but luckily, I had gained confidence from the first slow and steady training that I was able to do it again.

Here are some key points to keep in mind to make slow and steady work:

1. You Need to Be Ready: Before launching into any kind of sleep training plan, ask yourself this question: Are you ready for this? If you have so much else going on in your life that you aren't ready to rock the boat, hold off. Because if you are going to try to change a sleep behavior at 2 a.m. when you are already completely exhausted and delirious, you have to want it. Otherwise, just let the baby do whatever that baby wants to do so you can live your life. Seriously, don't drive yourself crazy. There will be a time and place for you to train this little demon later.

2. Baby Has to Be Ready: If you are absolutely killing yourself trying to sleep train a baby, maybe your baby isn't ready. Remember, babies are learning how to sleep. You know that expression, "sleep like a baby"? Well, unless that expression means "sleeping like a person who doesn't actually know how to sleep and is waking up all the time and needs tons of assistance to go back to sleep," then that expression makes no sense. Some babies need more help than others to talk, some babies need help to walk, and some babies need help going back to sleep. So, if you are in an absolute all-out war with your baby over this,

maybe it isn't the right time. A right time is bound to come. Or if not a right time, a better time. At least, the time can't get worse than right now, right? Because right now isn't working.

3. Make Nightly Goals: To make this work, all you need to do each night is do slightly better than the night before. Make super achievable goals so that you feel you are making progress. All you are trying to do is chip away at the sleep habit, not change it overnight. If your baby needs to breastfeed to go back to sleep, can you get her to go one more hour each night without breastfeeding?

4. The 100 Rule: Something as simple as counting can be a helpful way to keep yourself from going crazy while trying to get babies to sleep. If you have ever tried to put a baby to sleep, I'm sure you know what I am talking about. You have been at this for an hour; every time you put the baby down, he opens his eyes and wails. All you want is to drink a glass of wine on the couch and watch PEN15. You can literally *smell* the chocolate bar your partner is eating in the other room. Finally, the baby falls asleep in your arms. You are 100% convinced he is asleep. In disbelief that the moment has arrived, you put him down in his crib. He immediately starts wailing. Your hopes and dreams are dashed in a matter of seconds. Try this: Count. Wait until the baby is not moving. And by not moving, I mean dead weight in your arms, breathing heavily, not kicking her little feet or stretching her little hands. As soon as this happens, start counting. Count to 100. If she moves at *all*, start over at zero. As soon as you reach 100, put her down in the crib but keep your hand on her. Count to 100 again. Don't cheat! I know you

want that chocolate, but I'm telling you, this technique will pay off. As soon as you reach 100, remove your hand from her back but stay in the room. Lurk over her. Even if your door doesn't creak and she can't hear your footsteps, babies have a weird sixth sense that alerts them when you are leaving a room. Lurk over her and count to 100 again. Now you can leave the room. Did it work? Are you eating chocolate? You're welcome.

5. I will not stress about naps.

One of the best pieces of advice I ever got about baby sleep came from a sleep course I took when I was struggling with Hazel. The instructor said, "Do not worry about naps." And then she looked each of us parents in the eye one by one and repeated it: "Do. Not. Worry. About. Naps." Those five words probably added five years to my life. Trying to keep a baby on a nap schedule *will* make you lose your mind. It is not a matter of *if*, it is a matter of *when*. You can have a nap schedule. You can try to stick to a nap schedule. What you are not allowed to do is kill yourself over that nap schedule. Believe me, it isn't worth the pain.

Remember, this whole thing is temporary. Years from now, someone at a party will ask you, "How did your baby sleep?" You will think for a few minutes before responding, "Pretty good I think!" You won't remember the delirium, the sweat, the tears, the desperation. You will just remember their quiet, beautiful little face, sleeping "like a baby."

Another thing about naps. Don't let them ruin your day. Don't leave the party or the zoo or the socially-distanced beach hike because of a nap. The nap schedule isn't as important as everyone makes you think. The nap propaganda has to end. Life is too short for that shit.

6. All of this is harder than anyone tells you.

Sleep training your baby is going to be a lot harder than what I just described. This is because I am looking at sleep training in the rearview mirror, and so is literally anyone who ever writes or talks about sleep training. The human memory is inherently flawed. We tend to remember things as easier than they actually were. What makes this especially true for sleep training is that we are doing it in the middle of the night, while we are only semi-conscious. So, we tend to remember these stressful moments with our babies as we would remember a bad dream. In retrospect, it doesn't seem as terrible as it actually was.

Just yesterday, I was having a conversation with my friend Erica, who has a five-week-old baby. She told me a few times she has woken up in the middle of the night and yelled at her husband, "I CAN'T DO THIS ANYMORE!!" We laughed about this together. This behavior seems funny when you are sitting in the light of day, with a beautiful sleeping baby on your lap. Or years later when your children are sleeping through the night. It is funny how crazy sleep deprivation makes us. But in those 3 a.m. moments, when your brain is screaming at you to just keep sleeping but you know you can't, and you know that not only do you have to wake up, but you have to wake up and be responsible...it doesn't seem funny at all. It seems like a life and death moment. And even though when we look back at these moments we can laugh, we shouldn't in any way diminish how stressful they actually are.

I just want you to know that I see you, Mama. And I know this shit is way harder than I just made it sound.

Sleep training your baby will make the already stressful 3 a.m. wake-up moment even harder and more stressful. I am a firm believer that no matter what you do, eventually that baby will sleep train. He isn't going to be a forty-year-old who wakes up every forty-five minutes to breastfeed...I hope. So please, be kind to your 3 a.m. self. It's okay to do nothing. It's okay to keep the status quo and just try to get some fucking sleep.

CHAPTER 12:

The Imperfect Baby and the Imperfect Parent

"We live in strange times. We also live in strange places: each in a universe of our own. The people with whom we populate our universes are the shadows of whole other universes intersecting with our own. Being able to glance out into this bewildering complexity of infinite recursion and say things like, "Oh, hi, Ed! Nice tan. How's Carol?" involves a great deal of filtering skill for which all conscious entities have eventually to develop a capacity in order to protect themselves from the contemplation of the chaos through which they seethe and tumble. So give your kid a break, okay?

Extract from Practical Parenting in a Fractally Demented Universe."
-Excerpt **actually** from *Mostly Harmless* by Douglas Adams[67]

---

67 Douglas Adams, *Mostly Harmless* (Hitchhiker's Trilogy, V.5.), 160. New York, NY: Ballantine Books, 2000.

When you were pregnant or preparing to adopt, who did you imagine your child would be? Did you imagine your child would emerge fully formed as a tiny replica of yourself? Did you imagine yourself curled around a snuggling, cuddly, chubby, gooey baby like a mama kangaroo?

Don't lie. You tooooooooooootally imagined this.

If you are like me, you have been imagining being a parent for as long as you can remember. And snuggling, sleepy, loving, sweet caregiving has always played a prominent role in your imagination.

I recently found these two images on my mom's fridge. Me with a guinea pig at age nine. Me with my baby Hazel twenty years later.

The guinea pig was less work.

Donald Winnicott talked about how the mother (or caregiver) holds space for the baby during pregnancy. She dreams about the baby, imagining what the baby will be like when he enters her life.[68] This baby is the imagined baby, the perfect baby, the cuddly, adorable, non-crying baby who appears in almost all television shows and movies about babies and literally nowhere else on Planet Earth. The imagined baby is essentially a guinea pig. Or, less squeaky than the guinea pig. Then the real baby arrives and this baby is *never* the imagined baby.

68 D. W. Winnicott, *The Child, the Family, and the Outside World* (Harmondsworth, Middlesex: Penguin, 1975)

It could be something small, like you thought your baby was going to have a vagina and he has a penis. Or you thought the baby would be blonde and she is a brunette. Or bald. Or giant or tiny. Or it could be something life altering, like your baby was born premature or born with a disability. Whatever the case, you now have to restructure your brain around this real baby, and kiss the imagined baby goodbye.

This is doubly true for children born with disabilities. Maybe someday I will write a book exclusively for parents with children with disabilities, as that is my specialty and my passion. I have come to understand and sympathize with what these families experience during the early years of their children's lives. The experience of having a baby born very premature or with a disability *is different* from having a typical baby. However, all parents go through a miniature version of making a mental adjustment when their real baby replaces the imagined baby of pre-birth.

Even when babies are born perfectly healthy, they are often born in unanticipated ways. Here in the Bay Area, there is a huge emphasis on natural childbirth. According to the CDC website, 32% of all births in the US in 2015 were through C-section. That is higher than in most countries in Europe, and seems to be on the rise in the US. There are documented adverse effects for babies who have a C-section versus a vaginal delivery. Babies born via C-section have lower immunity because they didn't have a chance to pass through the birth canal. There was even a recent study showing a link between C-sections and higher rates of autism and ADHD.[69] When my friend sent me an article showing that latest study, my immediate reaction was this:

---

69 Gene Emery, "Possible Link between C-Section and Autism, ADHD," Reuters (Thomson Reuters, August 28, 2019), https://www.reuters.com/article/us-health-csection-brain/possible-link-between-c-section-and-autism-adhd-idUSKCN1VI1VS.

This knowledge about what creates the healthiest outcomes for parents and babies is a positive thing. I'm glad we are living in an era where hospitals feel pressure to perform fewer C-sections, and pregnant folks are more empowered about all of their birthing choices. It's fantastic. But unfortunately, this emphasis on natural childbirth can leave women who don't have that option, or don't make that choice, feeling like failures. In response to a doula extolling the long history of women giving birth naturally, a friend of mine said, "True. Women have been giving birth at home for thousands of years. And you know what those women giving birth on the floor of cabins on the prairie would have loved? A frickin' hospital!" I mean really, can you imagine telling a woman giving birth in a hut in the middle ages that you had the choice of using painkillers during birth but you refused it? That mama in that hut would slap you across the face.

Women have given birth at home unmedicated for thousands of years. They continue to do so across the globe. It is also true that lots of babies and mothers have died in the process. The best-case scenario is that everything will go perfectly and she will deliver at home, unmedicated, surrounded by a loving doula and lots of candles and incense. I have had lots of friends and clients who dreamed about delivering this way. And for those who were able to pull it off, it sounds wonderful and amazing.

However, not all mothers are so lucky. My friend Ariana found out a few days before her expected due date that her little one was breech. Instead of a home birth, she ended up having a planned C-section in a hospital. Of course, as soon as Ariana and her husband found out a home birth wasn't possible, they switched gears and started planning for a hospital delivery. Luckily, their little girl Amaya is five years old and perfect. But it doesn't mean that Ariana isn't still grieving the loss of the home birth she had imagined during pregnancy.

A well-meaning friend once asked her if she was nervous about exposing Amaya to germs, since Amaya was the product of a C-section and didn't pass through the birth canal. Rude! Why are we making parents feel endlessly guilty for choices they made to protect the health and safety of their babies? Many parents who have C-sections often feel as if their births don't "count" because they don't experience labor in the way most women do.

The same is often true of women who have epidurals. I had an epidural with Hazel. However, my labor was four days long followed by four and a half hours of excruciating pushing before I delivered her vaginally. Also, the epidural ended up falling out and didn't do me much good. When people (particularly men) discover I had an epidural, they act as if the experience must have been easy and simple. This is wrong on so many levels. You can still have intense pain even with an epidural. Also, even if you have reduced pain, minimal pain, or no pain, why does this matter? Does it somehow not count as a birth? Male partners of women who give birth "naturally" are often extremely proud of their partners and treat them like conquering heroes. "She gave birth totally naturally. No drugs." It's amazing how even the most feminine of acts, childbirth, can be turned into a pissing contest.

Some women are lucky enough to have their ideal birth. I have a few friends who have given birth at home, surrounded by doulas and incense. My good friend is a doula who has assisted at dozens of successful home births. But let's be real. The majority of us don't get to have the birth we imagined. When that baby is ready to come out, most of us throw away that imagined childbirth and accept the childbirth that is happening. Whether or not we like it.

Sometimes, it isn't the baby who is different from how you imagined they would be; it is you. I once commented to an acquaintance at a party that I was "nothing like the mom I thought I would be." The acquaintance looked at me with sympathy, as if I had just told her my hopes and dreams for my life had been crushed. I was equally surprised by her reaction, because I hadn't actually meant it as a bad thing. It is just true.

Before I was a parent, I dreamed of creating elaborate projects for my kids to do every night, of taking them on amazing adventures every weekend, of feeding them vegetables and naturally sourced meat, of raising them without television or sugar. It's not that I don't do *some* of those things. I am a pretty fun and creative mom, maybe slightly more than half of the time. But before I had kids, I had no idea how incredibly annoying three-year-olds can be, and what lack of sleep does to your energy and propensity for adventure. So yeah, I'm not the parent I thought I would be. But that's okay. I'm still pretty good.

When I was pregnant, I told a friend of mine that our baby would just have to figure out how to fit into our lifestyle; we weren't going to adjust our lifestyle to the baby. Jeff and I were living in a one-bedroom, rent-controlled apartment at the beach. We spent our weekends at the beach, drinking, and going to concerts. We liked to sleep in on Saturdays, then drink mimosas and eat crepes on Sundays. We were both working as social workers at a nonprofit, making basically no money.

"The baby will just have to learn to fit into our lifestyle."

Cute, right?

When I became a mom, I was surprised to discover that I found parenting kind of, well, boring. I love babies and I love parents. I love being with babies, talking about them, holding them, and talking to their parents about them…in my professional life. However, during the first few months when I was home with Hazel, I felt bored much of the time. And then I felt guilty about feeling bored.

Because parenting *is* boring, in addition to being exhausting and frustrating and oh yeah, incredible and amazing. Babies cuddle, but they also cry. A lot. And for a long time.

The first three months of a baby's life are often referred to by professionals as the "fourth trimester." I love that term. It acknowledges how not fully formed these tiny people are. They need us for everything, and their brains are growing at an incredible rate in relation and in reaction to the stimulation we provide them with. However, there is a big difference between the fourth trimester and the previous three. Now, the baby is out in the world! The baby still feels so much a part of us and yet, it is separate. Able to communicate its own needs and wants. Able to be a different person from what we projected the baby to be. And we ourselves are completely different from the parents we thought we would be. The fourth trimester is the hardest one. It isn't just about dreams of perfect childbirth and a sleepy, cuddly breastfeeding baby. It's the real thing. You are different from who you thought you would be. Your baby is different from who you thought she would be. And this whole thing is so much goddamn harder than you thought it would be.

A few months ago, I sat on my friend Erica's couch, holding her five-week-old baby girl while she told me how things have been for her. Erica had her own baby years after watching her sister and most of her close friends have theirs. She told me, "I had no idea how hard this would be."

"Really?" I responded, "I'm surprised to hear you say that, because you've seen all of us have babies already and you saw how hard it was for us."

"Yeah," she explained, "but I wasn't really in it. It wasn't happening to me. You guys would tell me 'breastfeeding makes you really hungry,' and I would think, whatever, I've been hungry before. But yesterday I literally tore a hole in a plastic Tupperware because I was starving and trying to get to the food."

So, as a culture, let's give the mamas (and all caretakers) a break, shall we? We know more now than we ever did about how young brains develop and about the importance of natural births. About feeding kids healthy foods and keeping them away from screens. But there is another important component to the infant-parent relationship that we often lose sight of: the parent. How important is it for parents to feel confident? It is an immeasurable thing. How do you measure something like that? But I see it all the time in my work with parents of children with delays or disabilities, or who were born through C-section or in-vitro fertilization. There are a lot of people telling you everything that didn't go well with your baby, either because of something you did or maybe just due to luck of the draw. There are a lot of voices in your ear doubting you and making you crazy.

There is such a wealth of information out there for parents that even those of us who have children without any complications can feel overwhelmed and confused. These early weeks/months/years are so important...what if we make a mistake and it has lifelong consequences for our little ones? Then, what happens when everything doesn't go perfectly? When beyond your control you aren't able to breast feed, or you can't have a "natural birth," or when doctors and nurse and lactation consultants and social workers are telling you that you *should* worry because maybe there is something wrong. How do you turn off the constant chatter in your head telling you to worry? How can you just stop, and chill and relax with your baby?

Last night, I sat on the couch with my best friend Yasmine, her partner, and their five-week-old baby. It was a quiet, sweet domestic moment. The three of us were watching *PEN15* on television, and she was breastfeeding her baby. Suddenly, Yasmine started crying. A few days before, her pediatrician had recommended "no screen time" for her baby. The three of us had laughed about this recommendation. Her baby was too little to notice the TV, let alone be negatively influenced by its presence. I had never heard someone make this kind of recommendation for a child this young. We had laughed it off just a few hours before, making fun of the overly cautious doctor.

But what Yasmine's partner and I had failed to notice was that it wasn't possible for Yasmine to laugh off any recommendation, no matter how silly. Her baby had had a challenging birth, followed by a week-long stay in the NICU. During the same pediatrician visit where screen time was discouraged, her doctor had also expressed concern about the baby's weight gain. The birth and NICU experience had left Yasmine, a new mom, feeling shaken and unsure of herself. It was tough for her to feel confidence in her own instincts as a parent. Was screen time irreversibly damaging for her tiny baby? She didn't know. And she couldn't just relax into the moment without feeling guilty and unsettled.

This well-meaning pediatrician was just doing his job: giving a new mom the latest evidence-based medical and developmental information to make the best decisions for her child. But he had ignored another need from this new mom—a need to be reassured that she was doing okay. A need to settle on the couch with her baby and her partner and her best friend and watch a silly show about middle school without a little voice telling her she was damaging her baby.

Yasmine tearfully asked us, "When will I stop worrying about every little thing? When will I just relax?"

This is what we need to do. For ourselves and for the other parents in our lives. We need to add another voice to the chorus of voices telling us what we are doing wrong. A voice that comes from within, reminding us that maybe this isn't the perfect baby you dreamed of, and you aren't the perfect parent you thought you would be. But even so, you and your baby are beautiful and unique in your imperfections.

And you are doing your goddamn best.

CHAPTER 13:

There Is Something Wrong with My Kid

Do me a favor. Don't Google "when should babies say their first words." I know you really, really want to. But don't!

I spent five years working at the Early Start program, California's Early Intervention Program. Early Start provides services for children under three with developmental delays. A big part of my job was taking calls from parents who were worried that their child was delayed. Most of these parents had reasons to be concerned. However, many, many, *many* parents called me because of something in a Google search that freaked them out.

A surprising number of these calls were about wheel spinning. The day before I started this chapter, baby Fritz (twelve months old at the time) turned a car upside down and started spinning its wheels. He did this once, glanced up at me with a smile, and then looked back down at the car he was holding and spun the wheels again. This was very exciting for Fritz. When he spun the wheels, they both looked cool and made a super fun rushing sound. How amazing! Fritz spun these wheels for about three minutes before becoming bored and moving on to something else.

So, what? Well, if I were relying on Google searches for most of my information on development, this simple play activity might have completely freaked me out. Wheel spinning is on most of the online lists for "early signs of autism."

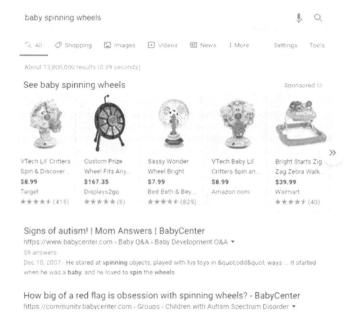

See above screenshot. The first thing Google does is direct you to five plastic baby things you can buy (which are all terrible.) Then Google announces that your infant has autism. No wonder parents freak out.

Let's examine Fritz's interaction with the car more closely.

At one year old, Fritz was endlessly curious. All day, he crawled and walked around from toy to toy to toy, finding new ways to play and explore. He opened every box, turned over every object, and found every opportunity to get into places and spaces he shouldn't.

He played with everything. This endless curiosity is the hallmark of one-year-olds. It is why one-year-olds are so endearing. It's also why they are so frickin' mischievous. Let's say that *all* Fritz did with a car was spin its wheels. Or that he only preferred to play with one yellow square and all he did was lick it or carry it around with him. Or that he didn't play with toys at all but only liked his IPad. Or that he was hyper-sensitive to textures and wouldn't touch anything squishy. All of those would be characterized as "stereotyped or rigid" behaviors and would raise a red flag for autism. It isn't the spinning of a wheel that is concerning; it is how the wheel is being spun and why. If that is the *only* way a baby plays with a car, or if a baby can watch a wheel spin for longer than three minutes without losing interest, call me.

Let's also talk about the way Fritz interacted with me while he was playing with the car. As soon as he realized the wheel made a cool sound when he spun it, he looked up at me and smiled. His smile said, "Look at how cool this is! Please enjoy this with me. Enjoy me enjoying this!" Seriously, my one-year-old said all this! With his eyes! Children with autism or other similar development delays have a difficult time looping adults into their experiences. They are interested in playing with the toy they are playing with. They are less interested in having you participate in the play with them.

Quality and context are everything when it comes to development. The problem with parents Googling lists of milestones is that these lists often leave out the broader context of why the concern exists. Development doesn't happen in a void. It is happening all the time and always within the context of the caregiving environment. You can improve developmental experiences for your child within your daily routines, without having to kill yourself or bend over backwards or pay an extra $4000 a month for the most expensive preschool in the city.

So, do me a favor. DON'T GOOGLE. If you want to honor your child's strengths, look for areas of growth and monitor for developmental delays. There are lots of great tools to use for this online. I would recommend going to the Ages and Stages Questionnaire website and looking at their free resources for parents.[70] There is a developmental checklist you can run through to get an idea of areas where your child might need help. There are also lots of activities on the website that you can do to stimulate your child's development.

Delays in Social-Emotional and Communication Milestones

There are two developmental domains that are most important for healthy development: social-emotional and communication. Early intervention can make a *huge* difference for children who have delays in these areas. Unfortunately, most children with developmental delays in these areas don't receive early intervention. If a child isn't walking, or isn't eating, that is going to be an obvious reason to talk to a pediatrician. But the social-emotional and communication milestones in the first year are less noticeable.

After twelve months, the developmental milestones grow farther apart and are easier to watch for using a developmental checklist. I am going to focus on explaining how they appear in the first twelve months, because those months are the trickiest to understand. We don't have very

70 Visit https://agesandstages.com/ for more information.

high expectations for babies. We sort of expect them to be drooling and banging things on the table. Therefore, when they are still doing this at twelve months and they haven't started walking or talking or pointing at us, we don't get that worried about it. I have worked with many families who missed all the warning signs about a developmental delay because they didn't expect that much from their baby.

This section focuses on two of the five developmental domains typically discussed in early intervention work: social/emotional skills and communication skills. The other three developmental domains not included are motor skills, adaptive skills, and cognitive skills.

Here is what motor skills look like in the first year: child sits, then walks, then runs full speed away from you in Target.

Here is what adaptive skills look like: child drinks milk, then eats some food, then refuses to eat any food that isn't mac and cheese.

Motor and adaptive skills also incredibly subjective and culturally based. Children who don't have developmental delays and disabilities generally develop these skills when and as the adults around them indicate they should. This is particularly true for self-care skills. As a provider working in the culturally rich Bay Area, I have seen this firsthand.

When I worked in Early Start, I conducted home visits where I completed developmental assessments using a tool called the Batelle Developmental Inventory (BDI), which tests children's development to see how they measure up with their peers. I would ask parents, "Does your child dress himself?" and, "Can your child feed himself with a fork?" For many, many families, we found the answers to these questions were "I dress him" and "I feed him." Non-immigrant, white American families place value on independence and self-sufficiency. We are impressed by children who feed themselves, and by people who pull themselves up by their bootstraps![71] This is not the case in many other parts of the world. What is more important than feeding yourself or

71 This is bullshit, by the way. And also, what the hell is a bootstrap?

dressing yourself is being fed and being dressed. More value is based on the collective than on the individual. It is more important that children engage as part of a society—and that they get enough to eat—than it is that they do it themselves.

In the Early Start program, we interpreted scores related to adaptive skills with a grain of salt. I *do not* tell grandmas what to do. And I am certainly not going to tell a Japanese grandmother of a two-year-old not to feed him but to let him feed himself. I only work on adaptive skills with my clients when it is something that they express concern about, or the lack of adaptive skills is creating behavioral issues for the parents. It is an issue when the family thinks it's an issue.

Motor skills develop in a similar way. For most children, they meet the motor milestones that are in line with what their parents want and expect from them. Children go at their own pace. They do things when they damn well feel like it. Unless a child doesn't hit the big ones you can locate from the ASQ website (not from Googling, please), you probably don't have to worry. Is the child two years old and not walking? Three years old and can't scribble? He can do those things? Then he is probably going to be fine.

Cognitive skills are generally tracked separately from social-emotional and communication skills in young children. Cognitive skills are tasks like recognizing that an object is being hidden under a cloth, or knowing what to do with a rattle when handed one. These skills are crucial to the later development of preschool skills like sorting and counting. But they aren't separate from communication and social skills. Generally, children don't learn a cognitive skill because they weren't paying attention when it was presented to them. Small children with autism usually show delays in cognitive skills because when they are given an instruction to "pick up the cup" they don't understand or they weren't paying attention. When social-emotional and communication skills are strengthened in young children, cognitive skills come along as well.

Development is a process, and we should think about how each skill naturally blends into the next. Many parents focus on their child having one word by twelve months old, when what is really important is *how* their child is communicating, and how their child's communication skills are developing, changing, and evolving.

For now, let's talk about two main skills—social-emotional and communication—and how they normally arise during the first year of a child's life, as well as the delays to watch out for.

Why Social-Emotional Skills?

A newborn baby is a beautiful, sleeping, crying, tiny, helpless genius. To an outsider, this baby is completely indistinguishable from the baby doll wrapped in a blanket that everybody uses to represent babies in plays and movies. To an outsider, the newborn looks like an alien and is cute in a creepy, wet, and wrinkled way. To the parent, this creature is the most incredible and amazing piece of flesh ever to appear on earth.

When I meet a new baby, I always remark to the parents, "Oh my god, she's beautiful!" I'm not being insincere, because I do in fact think all babies are beautiful. The parents smile at me with this look that says, "We know! Isn't she the most magnificent thing you've ever seen in your life!?" New parents present their babies to you for admiration, as if they are showing you a rare gem taken from the Crown Jewels. Every new parent genuinely believes their new baby is the most fabulous baby ever. I 1000% believe that's what people thought when they met Fritz and Hazel for the first time. Obviously, they did, because they were the most amazing babies in human existence.

When Hazel was a few months old, I was in Philz Coffee[72] and I recognized the pediatrician who examined her before her hospital discharge. I ran over to the pediatrician immediately, so she could see

---

72 I swear to God Philz Coffee didn't sponsor this book. If they *do* want to thank me for the multiple plugs though, I wouldn't say know to a few bags of beans.

how Hazel was doing a few months after discharge. "Hi!" I exclaimed. "Great to see you again. I wanted to show you Hazel so you can see how she is doing!"

"Great to see you again too," the doctor said, and proceeded to coo over the baby.

It was only after leaving the Starbucks that I realized there was no way in hell she remembered me or my baby. She must examine twenty babies per day in the maternal ward. Here is what the job description for pediatrician on call in a maternal ward must include:

1. Must be able to convincingly pretend to recognize mothers and babies who approach you in Philz Coffee. These women truly believe you will recognize their babies, since they think their babies are the most beautiful creatures on God's green earth. You must play along even though you have no goddamn idea who they are.

Encouraging new parents to believe their newborn babies are incredible and amazing is actually an important medical intervention. As I mentioned previously, Dr. T. Berry Brazelton developed an assessment tool called the Newborn Behavioral Observation (NBO) to demonstrate how incredible and amazing newborns are. The NBO was created "to sensitize parents to their infant's competencies, with a view to helping them understand their infant's behavior and thereby promote positive interactions between parents and their new infant and contribute to the development of a parent-infant relationship."[73]

Most parents present their newborn to you for admiration with the expectation that you will be as shocked as they are by the beauty of their incredible little creation. That is what happens in the best of circumstances. Many parents are too tired, too worn down by their own

73 J. Kevin Nugent et al., *Understanding Newborn Behavior & Early Relationships: The Newborn Behavioral Observations* (NBO) System Handbook (Baltimore, MD: Paul H. Brookes Pub., 2007), 3.

lives or by the trauma of childbirth to admire their newborn as much as they should. Even new parents who do give their newborn the proper admiration don't usually understand all of the incredible things their baby can do. The NBO shows the parents "look at this goddamn genius." Thereby setting the parents up for a lifetime of paying for infant-baby massage classes, swim classes, Mandarin lessons, math tutoring, college, and graduate school. Or, most importantly, it sets the parent up to see their baby as worthy of all the goddamn work they are going to have to put in to take care of this little thing.

Social-Emotional Skills in the first Twelve Months

A baby is born. All of a sudden, the baby is in the world. The baby discovers his hands. He wiggles his fingers and wonders, what do I do with these things? First, you put an object on the baby's hand and he begins to grasp it. You put an object in front of him when he is on his back and he brings his hands together in the middle of his body. Then, he begins to reach out in front of him for an object. When you put your baby on his stomach, he lifts his head up. Then, he begins to put his knees up and eventually rolls over from stomach to back, and from back to stomach. He begins to support himself in sitting by propping up with one arm or another. By about six months, your baby is sitting up by himself.

During the first few minutes of life, neonatal staff issue what is called an Apgar score. The Apgar score measures the baby's breathing, heart rate, muscle tone, reflexes, and skin color on a scale of 1-10. An Apgar score is given for a baby at one minute, five minutes, and then again, if necessary, at ten minutes. You might be thinking, *Jesus, babies are tested as soon as they leave the womb. That seems a bit soon!* But these numbers are useful for indicating what might turn into developmental and health issues later on. If your baby had an Apgar score of 9 and 9, that means the baby had no issues with any of his essential functions during the first few minutes of life. If your baby had Apgars of 1,1, and 9, that tells you he did initially have some issues that were resolved. These first minutes of life are so vital that even though your baby did fine eventually, it is important to know he did have some trouble initially, and to wonder why that was.

Apgar scores help us understand the importance of the first few minutes of life, and also help us to understand how different newborns look from one another, even though they are all portrayed by the same baby doll wrapped in a blanket in every play. And the same six-month-old pretending to be a newborn in every movie.

For a baby who does okay during those first few minutes and days, he has only one job to do for the next few months: sleep. Okay, that's not entirely true. He has three jobs: eat, poop, and sleep. That's 90% of what they do. However, it is important to note that even newborn babies have a few moments each day when they are alert and ready for engagement. Often, babies have a moment like this right when they are born (after they have cried, freaked out about how cold they are and been wrapped in a blanket.) Many babies then have a moment of alertness, where they look deeply into your eyes and tell you, "Wow, I really love you. Thanks so much for everything so far. Don't you want to care for me for the next eighteen or fifty years? Look at how adorable I am." Newborns look at us this way, and most of us feel a surge of oxytocin so powerful we don't recover for decades (except for brief periods when we want to strangle them).

During the first three months, or the "fourth trimester" in a lot of ways, newborns are still *inside*. They are happiest curled up, snuggled, warm, and sleeping. They are totally and completely overwhelmed by the loud, bright world. Even if you don't explicitly know this, you sense it when you are around a brand-new baby. Comfort and warmth are the most necessary and important sensations to them.

Then in the third month, it is as if the baby wakes up! At three months, babies are present in the world. They are looking around, making eye contact with anyone who will look at them. The "social smile" comes on board at around six weeks, but at three months it is robust and heart-melting.

Between three to six months, babies are at their absolute cutest. They recognize you and other family members. They show preferences for the games and toys you share with them. They dazzle everyone around them. Most three to six-month-old babies are okay with being held by grandmas, aunties, and even some strangers.[74] They are the life of the party, the drunk guy with the funny stories who entertains everyone in the room.

There is a reason why six-month-old babies are completely irresistible to everyone. They are still very much babies, tiny and chubby and asking to be snuggled. But they are also so *in the world*. Unlike a two-month-old, a six-month-old wants to interact with everyone around him. When you are sitting in the waiting room of the doctor's office, they make eye contact with everyone. Six-month-olds seem to want to be picked up and cuddled. But don't be deceived, a six-month-old is a trickster. They look at you like they want you to pick them up and snuggle them, but when you do, they scream!

Babies begin to experience themselves as separate from their parents. This freaks them out. They start to whine when they see Mommy moving away from them because suddenly, they realize Mommy *can* move away from them. Holy shit! She is a separate person from me! Not cool, Mom!

Between six and nine months, your baby becomes more particular. He has started to develop stranger danger. He isn't so sure about that particular auntie or grandmother. And that guy with the beard better stay the fuck away from him! Babies at this age start to play back-and-

74 This was not true for my kids. I can only assume it is because I am the greatest mother in human existence, but my kids didn't let anyone else hold them for six months. It was excruciating.

forth social games like peek-a-boo. They begin to point to objects around them and look at your face as if to say, "Isn't that cool?" Babies this age aren't just interested in toys; they are interested in your interest in toys. These babies are extremely social; as a result, they can be more fearful of people they don't know, and more nervous when you leave the room.

Nine to twelve-month-old babies are great at imitation. They are also starting to know the social rules you have enforced on them. This is not to say they will *follow* the social rules, but they are aware of what they are. They have started to show stronger preferences as their independence has started to develop. They will attempt to help with tasks like feeding and dressing—if you are lucky.

Communication Skills

One of the most amazing things about human development is that we are learning how to speak languages *before we are born.* That's right. Newborn babies show a strong preference for the languages they heard when they were in utero. However, when we are born, we are ready to speak any language that is spoken to us, even one that we didn't hear in utero. We can click, roll our r's, pronounce twenty-letter Welsh words… *anything.* And then we transform into incompetent adults who can't even order coffee in Paris. It's tragic. I am horrible at learning languages, so I am blown away by the capability of small children to learn them. Fetuses are the best at this, and then we go slowly downhill from there.

Communication starts at birth. Babies cry to have their needs met (obviously), but a cry isn't just a meaningless, indistinguishable sound. Primary caregivers can identify what their babies need just based on the way the cry sounds. They can recognize the difference between a distress cry, a tired cry, an I-just-pooped cry, and an I'm-bored cry. It may all just be annoying noise to you, but to the parents, it's a sentence. The better we are at interpreting our babies' cries, the better they are at producing cries that make sense to us. The back and forth of communication begins right away, with the baby crying and the parent making educated guesses about what they want.

Very quickly, babies begin to communicate with us in more robust ways. Remember those moments of alertness I told you about? If you can catch a baby in one of those alert moments, when she isn't wet, hungry, tired or just generally annoyed at you, you can begin to have a conversation with her. Almost immediately, human beings start mimicking face shapes. If you make eye contact with an infant and open and close your mouth, you can often get him to do the same back to you. There is a big delay, so you must do it slowly and patiently, but when you see it your mind will be blown. Imitation starts at birth!

Your baby is talking to you! It may not sound like the Queen's English, but he is now saying meaningful things to you all the time. In the beginning, he coos and makes open vowel sounds like "ahhhhh" and "ooooohhh." He exclaims for attention, making a "ba!" or a "ma!" sound. He has different cries: a hungry cry, a tired cry, an angry cry. At six months old, your baby isn't just cooing and beginning to babble; he is cooing and making sounds in your language. Hopefully, you are speaking more than one language to him, and not being lame like I am and raising him as a monolingual English speaker. Not only have bilingual children been shown to be better at languages, but they also have better executive decision-making skills. Sorry, Hazel and Fritz, I totally screwed this one up.

Throughout the first year, the sounds babies make grow more and more robust. Between six and nine months, you should hear your baby babbling. When we say babbling, we mean sounds that are more than just "ah" and "oh." Babbling is "babababababa" and "mamamamama." Babies should go from just making open vowel sounds to making vowel-consonant combination sounds. When they start making these sounds, they are just sounds. The baby is just imitating the sounds they hear from the adults around them.

And then something really cool happens. Your baby is just babbling away going "dadadadadada" and you go, "Oh, dada! Dada is right there!" The baby looks at daddy and thinks, *What is this lady talking about? I was just going, dadadadadada, what does that have to do with that guy over there?* But then this same thing happens again and again. He keeps saying "dadadada" and you keep going, "Yes! Dada!" Eventually, your baby thinks, *Oh, I get it now. Dada has something to do with that guy over there.*

First, they make the connection that "dada" is about that guy. A few years later, they use the word "except" correctly in a sentence. It blows my mind. Have you ever tried to define a word like "except" to a child? It is impossible. Imagine if we had to do this for every word in the English language. Thank god the brains of children are so incredible, because that would be exhausting.

We expect babies at one year old to be able to say "mama" and "dada" or one to two other words of equal significance to them. For example, at one year old my baby Fritz didn't seem to care one bit about who dada or mama was, but if you put a ball in front of him, he would go absolutely crazy: "BALL! BALL!"

Once your baby understands the random sounds he makes with his mouth are somehow associated with real things in the real world, the words should come quickly. We expect one to two words by twelve months old (usually mama or dada), fifteen to twenty words by eighteen months, and at least fifty words by age two. Most speech therapists will tell you it takes about fifty to one hundred words for a child to have enough words to combine two words spontaneously, like "more milk." So, by age two we also expect children to be demanding things in two to three-word phrases. The average three-year-old has two hundred words. Now, if you are still counting your three-year-old's words, then either your three-year-old doesn't have enough words yet or you are kind of being crazy. Basically, a three-year-old should be able to talk.

Before age three, speech therapists don't worry too much about articulation. Most three-year-olds are about 75% comprehensible to a non-familiar listener, and obviously way more comprehensible than that to someone who knows them well. You should expect to be able to understand a three-year-old you talk to every day.

What Do You Do If There Is a Problem?

A pediatric nurse once told me, 70% of the time when the parent thinks there is an issue with a child, they are correct. I have the best pediatrician in the world, and I have been lucky enough to work with many amazing pediatricians over the years. Unfortunately, however, not every pediatrician has a great eye for development. Most pediatricians only have a few minutes to see their patients, so they rely on the parent's report on what the child is doing or not doing. I have spoken to countless parents of children who later received a diagnosis of autism or another condition who told me this:

"I spoke to my doctor about my concerns, but she said let's just wait and see."

Doctor's offices throughout the United States give the Ages and Stages Questionnaire (ASQ) to parents in the waiting room to fill out. The first time I was handed this questionnaire for one of my children, I was overjoyed that my doctor's office was taking this extra step to make sure they didn't miss anything. Then I started filling it out. Hazel was running around the office trying to hide crayons in the furniture. Fritzi was attempting to climb inside the fish tank. I filled out the survey as quickly as I could, so I could get my kids under control. A few minutes later, my doctor looked over my survey and then glanced up at my son, who was attempting to jump off the table and onto my head, and asked me, "So, Fritz doesn't walk yet?" In my haste to fill out the ASQ, I had marked down that he couldn't walk. This was a kid who could already dribble a basketball. I finally understood what pediatricians are up against.

Even when they do their best to collect developmental information from parents, we are too frazzled to provide it.

It is up to you to know when there is something wrong with your child. Trust your instincts. And if you think something is wrong, get help right away. I have spent a decade working in early intervention and I believe in it. It works! When your baby is tiny and malleable, you can change her brain circuitry and get her back on track. By the time she turns six, this will be a lot harder.

The first person to go to is your pediatrician. If you want the services to be covered by insurance, you will have to get a referral from him or her. If they give you the "let's wait and see" answer, tell them you can "wait and see" how much early intervention helps. If you live in the United States, special education services for children under three are covered under Part C of the Individuals with Disabilities Education Act. Just Google "Part C Services" and your state and you can learn who to call.

If you want to do some additional screening before you set these services in motion, you can review your child's development on the Ages and Stages Questionnaire. Or, if you are concerned about autism, you can conduct an MCHAT assessment online. The MCHAT is the best tool to screen for autism, and it's free to do an online assessment.[75]

You can also email me. I seriously love talking to people about their children.

---

75 Visit https://m-chat.org/ for more information.

CHAPTER 14:

If You Are Arguing with a Two-Year-Old, You Are Losing

Here is a quick quiz for you. A toddler and a grown woman with a Master's degree are standing in the kitchen. The toddler is repeatedly pressing a little yellow puzzle piece onto the fridge. The puzzle piece, itself confused about the point of this exercise, keeps dropping to the ground. The toddler is becoming increasingly frustrated and begins to scream. The adult, confused, asks the toddler what she is doing.

The toddler screams, "The magnet won't stay, Mommy!"

"Oh," the adult responds, calmly and patiently. "It's not a magnet, darling. It is a puzzle piece. Why don't you get a magnet and that will stick to the fridge?"

"It is a magnet, Mommy! IT IS!" she screams, as the puzzle piece, predictably, falls to the floor.

"No, sweetheart, it isn't," the adult responds, still patiently but admittedly, with a slight edge this time.

"IT IS!!!!!!" the toddler screams, throwing the—at this point quite alarmed—puzzle piece against the fridge. The toddler falls to the floor, screaming in horror.

"IT'S NOT A MAGNET! IT'S NOT!" the adult screams back at her.

Question: Who is the irrational person in this situation? Is it:

1. The toddler, who has been on this planet for two and a half years, half of which she spent drooling, and has not yet learned how to communicate her strong feelings and desires.

Or

2. The thirty-something-year-old woman with an advanced degree who is screaming at the two-year-old.

Answer: It is you. You are the crazy person. If you are arguing with a two-year-old, you are losing.

How to Not Argue with a Two-Year-Old

To understand the brain of a two-year-old, let's start with the concept of rapprochement. Rapprochement is not only a beautiful-sounding French word but a beautiful concept as well. Rapprochement is a concept invented by Margaret Mahler to describe the way babies between fifteen and twenty-four months begin to separate themselves from their caregivers.[76] The whole process of babyhood is a slow progression of separation. From the time a baby is in the womb, he is becoming increasingly more separate from his primary caregiver. Rapprochement is the phase in this separation where a baby begins to move away from the caregiver to explore his environment. The baby is only comfortable doing this because

---

76 Susan W. Coats, "John Bowlby and Margaret S. Mahler: Their Lives and Theories," *Journal of the American Psychoanalytic Association* 52, no. 2 (2004): 571-601. https://doi.org/10.1177/00030651040520020601.

he is constantly looking back to make sure his caregiver is there, and periodically going back to them. Feeling increasingly safe, the toddler further explores his environment. He is beginning to separate from the parent and become an individual being. The baby is both excited and horrified by this process. Remember the coyote from the chapter about sleep? The farther the baby goes from the caregiver, the more likely the baby is to be gobbled by the coyote. So, the baby is curious, but also nervous.

This push-pull relationship is what makes toddlers so crazy. They want to explore, but they don't want to be eaten by a coyote. They want to assert their independence, but they don't have the skills yet to do so. They want help completing the task on their own…but they don't want either you or them to see you helping. The toddler cannot accept that the puzzle piece is not a magnet, because this would admit to dependence on the parent and be a blow to the toddler's ego. However, the toddler needs the adult to help her operate the non-magnetic magnet. And this struggle between the two needs is altogether too much emotion for the toddler. So much emotion, in fact, that her body cannot sustain her weight and she falls to the floor in a fit of passion.

This kind of toddler behavior can be incredibly funny. When you recount these ridiculous stories later on to your friend, you laugh at them. But the behavior isn't actually that funny in the moment, especially if you are in the middle of a store. If another adult is standing there judging you. If it is the twenty-fifth tantrum the toddler has had that morning. It is a funny anecdote, though. "Yeah, she had a complete meltdown because the magnet wasn't a magnet." But in the moment, very few of us react with laughter. If we do laugh at the toddler, it only exasperates her frustration. The toddler demands to be taken seriously. In the moment, the most natural response to her rage is your own rage. It's so *frustrating* dealing with these moments. It's so *hard* to be patient, rational, gentle, and calm in the face of it. This seems especially true when the toddler in question is your own toddler.

It is easier to react reasonably to a child who doesn't belong to you. When it's your kid, you feel so connected to their rage that you can't respond to it rationally. You want to be able to alleviate their distress, but you can't because their distress isn't about something rational. The natural human response to someone with an elevated heartbeat and rising blood pressure is to mirror it. Our heart beats faster. Our blood pressure increases. When it is our own child, whom we love with our entire hearts and souls, our body functions are even more likely to mirror theirs. We match their volume and tone. It's the most natural thing in the world. Unfortunately, it is also counterproductive.

What are we teaching our toddlers when we scream at them? One day, my toddler was in the backseat of the car screaming her head off, and I turned to her and screamed back, "DON'T SCREAM in the CAR!"

My husband said, "You know, it probably doesn't make sense to tell her not to scream when you are screaming at her." Oh. Right.

When we get upset with our toddlers, nothing productive happens in our bodies. This is true not just for toddlers but for all human beings. When your heart rate is up, you are functioning from the fight-or-flight amygdala part of your brain. This is often called the "reptilian brain," because it's about as advanced as a lizard. This is the part of our brain made for running from tigers. When someone is screaming at you, whether that person is your own two-year-old or a sixty-year-old woman at the grocery store, you immediately go into the place in your brain made for running from tigers. Blood rushing to your thighs to help you flee faster. Your higher brain functions that control rational thinking shut down. Who needs them when you're running from a tiger? Hopefully, sometime before we destroy the planet through climate change, human beings will evolve to respond more rationally to perceived danger. Not many of us need these tiger-fleeing/fighting skills anymore. But until that happens, this is what we are stuck with at moments of heightened emotion.

When you yell back at your kid, you are showing her this is a good way to solve problems. You are keeping both of you in tiger-escaping mode when really, you want to get to a problem-solving-let's-move-on-from-this-non-magnetic-magnet-and-eat-breakfast mode.

Which brings us to my top five rules for arguing with a two-year-old.

1. Don't argue.

Easier said than done. Waaaaaaay easier said than done. In this book, I will give you several examples of times when I yelled at my kids. I don't want you to come away thinking I yell at my kids all the time. I don't. But I want you to know that despite all my best efforts, despite really, really, really not wanting to, I do yell at them.

The struggle is real.

To not argue, you need to ease yourself out of tiger-escaping mode. First, stop arguing. Just say, "Okay." You don't have to agree that the puzzle piece is a magnet. You don't have to give her whatever irrational thing she is asking for. You can just say, "Okay," or anything that will buy you a few moments to get yourself out of the argument.

2. Give yourself a moment.

What I am about to say is not intuitive. It's also not the usual advice you hear for dealing with toddler tantrums, but here it is. When your child is having a tantrum, don't focus on the child. Focus on yourself. The most important thing you can do is figure out how to calm yourself down. Give yourself a moment to think about what you are going to say before you say it.

This is where the mindfulness piece comes in. I have lived in the Bay Area for over a decade. I spent most of that time rolling my eyes anytime anyone said the word "mindfulness." Then I had kids and I realized I should take whatever evidence-based shit came my way. If mindfulness is something you already do or are good at, you are way ahead of me. I talk myself into using mindfulness in stressful moments. It works, but it can be challenging to talk yourself into doing it.

The most helpful thing you can do when you find yourself in tiger mode is to recognize you are in tiger mode. If you can get to that realization before you have completely lost your shit, you have mastered mindfulness. It is hard to do because it essentially goes against all of our evolutionary instincts. Having a mindful moment when you are in fight-or-flight mode takes a higher brain function, which you have cut off due to the possible tiger attack. For me at least, remembering to take a break from my child when I recognize I'm feeling elevated is easier than having that mindful moment

Sometimes, all it takes to get down from tiger mode is a few deep breaths to bring down your heart rate. Sometimes, you need to make a facial expression or say a few choice words to yourself to get them off your chest. I often recommend that parents excuse themselves for a moment and go to the bathroom and silently scream into the mirror before taking a few breaths and going back to their child. This is easy to do if you are at home. However, if you are in the grocery store when tiger mode hits and you don't have the luxury of stepping away, just remember, you are a human. It's okay to have your own honest reaction to being screamed at by an irrational tiny human. It's okay to feel that way. You aren't a bad parent. And it is cathartic and important to find some way of letting off steam. Just try not to do it in front of the child.

Once you have taken a second to calm your body down, it's helpful to be mindful of the reaction you are having and why. You can think to yourself, *I wish I had never had children.* And *then* think, *I'm having this bad thought because this little human is driving me completely bananas. I feel so angry and frustrated I don't feel like I can take it anymore.* Just noticing the emotion you are experiencing takes you out of the act of experiencing it and allows you to be the person watching the crazy person for a moment. It's nicer being the person observing the crazy person.

3. Help the toddler calm down.

When your little tiger is in the fits of a tantrum, she doesn't have access to the higher functions of her brain any more than you do. There is nothing to be gained by explaining to an upset toddler that she can't act this way, or especially that she can't feel this way. She is acting this way and she is feeling this way and she has little control over it. Toddlers have giant emotions and limited skills to manage them. They need to feel their emotions. Even though they suck to be around, tantrums aren't all bad all the time. Sure, they are frowned upon in restaurants, train stations and malls. People will give you some awful looks if you just let your small person have them in public.

FUCK THOSE PEOPLE, BY THE WAY.

But as often as you are able, let your toddler have her own emotional reaction. It's cathartic. Don't you wish you could roll on the floor in a violent rage every once in a while?[77] Just because toddlers should be allowed to have emotions doesn't mean you have to be standing silently by and listening. If you are at home, this is a great chance to scoop that little person up and let them have their complete meltdown in their room, or in a private space where you don't have to see them. The parenting program Nurtured Heart refers to these as "resets."[78] This is a great non-time-out word for them. You can just tell the toddler, "Okay, you need to reset in your room." *Always* give them a chance to do that themselves. And then, if they aren't capable of walking into their own

---

77 This does not apply to the President of the United States. I don't believe the person who holds that office should be allowed to have tantrums. For the record.

78 For more information about Nurtured Heart, visit https://childrenssuccessfoundation.com/about-nurtured-heart-approach/.

room, scoop them up and put them in there. Eventually, your toddler will want to reset on his own and will run to his room himself when he is upset, to cry, recover, and then rejoin decent society.

Hand-in-Hand parenting has another interesting notion they call "time-ins."[79] The program talks about staying really close to your toddler, coddling them and helping them to soothe themselves. It is a gentler approach and helps your children learn how to self-soothe when they haven't learned this skill yet. If this works for your child, this is a great alternative to resetting or time-outs. It works for some children. Other children prefer to be by themselves for a few minutes. What doesn't work for anyone is having the rational discussion of what happened and why, *while* the child is in the fight-flight part of his/her brain. Before that conversation can happen, the child needs to be in a rational place.

When the child is in a time-out, or a time-in, or a reset or whatever you call it, provide them with self-soothing mechanisms. Every child is soothed by something different. Eventually, you want your child to get to the place where they know what they find soothing and they can ask for it. In the meantime, you can make some educated guesses based on things others find soothing. Some kids like to hug a favorite toy or stuffed animal. You can even have a special stuffed animal that you keep stowed away to use only in stressed-out moments. Some kids like to listen to music or kids' guided meditations. Some kids like to take deep breaths or count downward from fifty. I recently met a little boy who did "wall push-ups" when he got stressed out. When your child is in a heightened emotional state, they will probably need help deciding what to do to calm down. You might have to force them to do five wall push-ups. Then all of a sudden, they will look at you, surprised that it works. Yeah, *I told you so*, you will be thinking but hopefully not saying.

---

79 Visit https://www.handinhandparenting.org/ for more information.

4. Don't argue. Litigate.

I'm not a lawyer, but I have watched a few seasons of *Law and Order*, so I feel qualified to talk about litigation. Once your child has calmed down, have a conversation about what happened. This is an important step because it helps the child put into words what caused such a big crisis. The child herself often can't remember what it was. Often because it was so unbelievably irrational. They are kind of like bad drunks in that way. The parent is like, "Why were you screaming about wanting to take my graduate school textbook to bed with you?" And the kid is like, "What? No! That doesn't sound like me." It's because toddler tantrums are so rarely about what the toddler claims the tantrum is about. They are about winning the goddamn fight, no matter what the fight was about. Despite their lack of willingness to discuss the crisis, press on. Try to explain the situation in words toddlers can understand. You need to wait until you are calm as well before you try to talk to them. When we are upset at toddlers, we tend to throw a barrage of big words at them, like:

"That doesn't make any sense! I already told you not to do that ten minutes ago and then as soon as I turn around, there you are, standing by the cabinet, doing the exact thing I told you not to do!"

That's a really long way of saying, "Darling. When I tell you not to do something, I need you to listen to me, okay? Please be a good listener."

Remember, these little people just learned to talk. And when they are stressed and we are stressed, there is a huge communication breakdown. We want to explain what happened to the child without arguing about it. We want to explain it in the simplest possible terms, remembering to include the family rules and norms we have already agreed upon. That's litigation, right?

"Remember what we talked about: you have to listen to mommy."

"Remember? We don't hit."

Make sure to use the exact phraseology they are familiar with. Don't say, "We don't smack our brother." If the family rule is about hitting, say "hit."

I tell families to have the conversation about the event at least twice with toddlers. Once, after the incident as soon as the toddler has calmed down. Even if you are in public, you can pull the child over and say, "Remember, this is what happened and this is why we were both so upset by it." You want to do this as soon as the child is calm, so they connect it back to the incident itself. Also, it's important your child knows you aren't holding a grudge against them. That's why I love the term "reset." Once the incident passes, let's quickly talk about it and put it behind us. Don't give your toddler the silent treatment. As soon as the incident is over, go back to your normal relationship. You were upset about the *behavior*. The crying, stomping around, hitting. You still love the child.

Later that day, you should have a second reminder conversation about the incident. This should happen that same day, while the incident is still fresh in the toddler's mind. Toddlers are basically goldfish, so if you wait too long to talk about it they will have absolutely no idea what you are referring to. It's important to remind the child once more about the incident, what happened, and why.

What we are doing by litigating this event for the child is moving the incident out of the reptilian part of his/her brain to the higher brain function where narratives are stored. We are creating a story that the child can make sense of, and thus, helping him to understand and manage his very strong emotions. The more we create these pathways for small children, the more they make sense of their emotions themselves, so eventually they can say to themselves:

"Oh. I'm frustrated because this isn't working. That is why I'm feeling this way. I should try something else."

5. It's okay to have feelings.

We never want to give our kids the impression that it is not okay to have feelings. It is easy to accidentally make children think it isn't okay to feel. When my daughter turned five years old, she asked me, "So, now that I'm five, am I not allowed to cry?" How depressing is that! Somehow in my messaging around not having tantrums anymore, she got the impression that she couldn't cry!

When children feel strong emotions and express them strongly, they face consequences. So, why wouldn't they naturally assume their feelings are the problem? Of course, it makes sense for them to think, *I'm in trouble because I am sad.*

We need to help small children separate their feelings from their actions. We should be explicit about this.

"I understand you are feeling sad because you didn't get a second cookie."

"I know you are mad because the boy didn't share the toy with you."

This kind of language helps toddlers understand they are not synonymous with the emotion they feel. The emotion is something *outside* of them. You are feeling sad. You are feeling mad. This helps them to feel some semblance of control. And toddlers absolutely love control. And then later, we can help them think about the emotion they felt in the past and they can begin to see the emotion in the rearview mirror. *Hmm, a hypothetical toddler might think. I was feeling mad and now I don't feel mad anymore. I was able to get over that feeling, so I can probably get over it again.*

Keep words about emotions super simple. For anyone who has ever tried to explain concepts like "jealous" and "annoyed," you might have noticed it's not easy. Mad. Happy. Sad. That pretty much covers it for toddlers.

As children get older, there are tons of resources and curriculum that will help them understand their emotions. The world of children's literature is filled with wonderful books that help kids verbalize their feelings. The Kimochis Social Emotional Curriculum teaches emotions through the use of characters called Kimochis.[80] I also love using the Social Thinking curriculum[81] with my clients on the autism spectrum, and it can be helpful for typical kiddos as well. Any curriculum or tool that externalizes and separates the emotional state from the child can be helpful. We want to help small children look at their emotions and understand that the emotions are separate from themselves. That feeling strongly is totally fine. We want to help them understand how they can make themselves feel better. If you don't have time to train yourself on a social-emotional awareness curriculum and start using it with your two-year-old, just show them the movie *Inside Out*. That should do the trick.

We want toddlers to be able to do what we do when we are at our best. The child equivalent of looking in the mirror and thinking, *I don't really hate having kids. I'm just feeling super frustrated because this insane tiny human is insisting that something is a magnet that is clearly a puzzle piece. Plus, I got three hours of sleep last night because the baby was up and I have to work full-time for almost no profit because childcare costs so much money because the middle class is dead in this country.*

But I digress.

---

80 Check out https://www.kimochis.com/

81 Check out https://www.socialthinking.com/

CHAPTER 15:

Magic

Despite what people tell you before you have kids, parenting a toddler rarely feels magical. There are more moments of oh-my-god-I-can't-believe-this-is-my-life-now than, "Wow, this experience is reminiscent of unicorns and rainbows." Especially in those difficult moments when you feel like you might lose it on your little angel, parenting can feel more like a horror movie than like Disney. By design, toddlers make us crazy. They have very strong, completely irrational opinions that they often do not understand themselves and can't explain. On more than one occasion, I have found myself in an argument with two-year-old Hazel about why her PB&J will taste the same whether or not it is cut in half.

It was during one of these PB&J-related arguments with Hazel that she inadvertently reminded me of something I had forgotten. Two-year-olds believe in magic. Unlike in the world of an adult, in the world of a two-year-old magic is real and it can be used to fix real problems.

On the morning in question, Hazel asked me to make her a PB&J. I made the sandwich in the kitchen, sliced it in half, and dutifully put it on a plate for her. As soon as I put down the plate in front of her, she started screaming. My blood pressure immediately rose as I asked her, "What, Hazel? What is it?" It was 7 a.m. I still had to wake and feed the baby, drop them off at separate daycares, and get myself a cup of coffee before reporting to work at 8:30. I didn't have time for toddler hysteria.

Hazel continued screaming, "You cut it! I don't want it cut! Put it back together!!!"

I weighed my options. Putting the PB&J back together, what Hazel wanted, wasn't possible. I could make her another one, but that would just encourage these kinds of outbursts in the future. I could tell her to eat it or get nothing, which would cause her to cry, wake up the baby, and set our morning on a terrible course full of drama, tears, and most likely time outs. My last option was to pose the problem to Hazel and see what she came up with.

"Well, Hazel, we can't put the sandwich back together because it's already cut. So, what do you suggest we do?"

Hazel thought about it, then went over to her toy box. "We could use my magic wand."

"Okay! So, what do we do?"

"Well, maybe you can use magic to put the sandwich back together?"

I took the wand from Hazel, waved it over the sandwich while reciting gibberish, and pushed the pieces of the sandwich back together, smoothing them hard enough against each other that it was almost as if they were never cut.

"Thanks, Mommy!" Hazel said cheerfully, and ate her PB&J.

Toddlers believe in magic and because they do, magic actually works.

Why does it work? We will never fully understand the two-year-old brain. Sometimes magic works to solve problems the two-year-old would really love to have solved. Hazel didn't actually care about her sandwich being cut in half. What she cared about was having her way. The developmental task of a two-year-old is to be as independent as possible. So, when she pictured a sandwich that morning, and then the sandwich appeared different from what she envisioned, that upset her. Two-year-olds live their lives like the world's worst bridezillas. They have a vision and they want reality to live up to their vision. The fictional character Hazel reminds me the most of is Meryl Streep in *The Devil Wears Prada*. In the case of the PB&J, the magic wand gave Hazel an out so she could still feel like her vision was being honored, even though the sandwich was still broken. Two-year-olds believe what they want to believe. And they want to believe in magic because magic is cool.

Another way to use magic with toddlers is to help them transition out of a funk. Sometimes they don't want to be mad anymore, but they don't know how to transition out of being mad without feeling like they have lost the fight. One morning, Hazel was upset about the amount of milk in her cereal bowl. She didn't care that much about it, but she had complained, so now she needed to stick to her guns and continue to be mad. The more indifferent I appeared, the more her anger escalated. It wasn't really about the milk. It's never about the milk. It was about her ego. Toddlers demand to be taken seriously. When they aren't, they get offended.

This particular morning, the whining escalated to screaming. Finally, I had had enough. "Hazel, we can't fix the cereal, okay!? Now, are you going to continue to be mad or can you be nice now!?" I asked.

Hazel stopped screaming and looked at me. She had had an idea. "Poof!" she said. "Look, Mommy, it's magic. I'm nice now!" She had found a way to transform her mood without the indignity of giving up.

Parenthood really isn't magical most of the time. But sometimes, it does involve magic.

Why Magic Works

The use of magic in parenting is not something I invented. There are a lot of fancy words for this and some science to back it up. The long and the short of it is that things work because we think they work. This is true for adults and it is even truer for children. Children have better brains than adults. They are plastic and flexible and full of possibility. They haven't become boring and insecure and stuck in their thinking. Children can get tricked into doing all kinds of things simply because you convince them they can do it, using magic. It is way more fun than screaming at them, and it usually works better too!

I know parenting books are (generally) the worst, but there is one I absolutely love. The book is called *Weird Parenting Wins* and it is a compilation of amazing, simple parenting tips that parents sent the editor, Hillary Frank, creator of the awesome podcast *The Longest Shortest Time*. I *love* this book because it is full of magical solutions to things. Hillary Frank explains in the introduction:

"In this book, you'll find all sorts of strategies that real parents use—but would never be in a how-to style parenting book. Actually, 'strategy' is maybe too strong of a word. Many of these wins were born out of trial and error; many are spur of the moment white lies; some began as what seemed like parenting fails but somehow, impossibly, turned into moments of wonder or connection or mutual maniacal laughter."

Here is an example pulled from turning to a random page:

"To get my boys to go to the potty, I bought a little gumball machine and put a jar of pennies in the bathroom. They would get one penny for peeing and two for pooping. They loved the excitement of operating the machine themselves." Lynne, Downingtown, PA[82]

The book is full of stuff like that! As I read through the strategies, I noticed a lot of them had something in common. Something I think of as "magic." The parents had found a way to get the child to do an

---

82 Hillary Frank, *Weird Parenting Wins: Bathtub Dining, Family Screams, and Other Hacks from the Parenting Trenches* (New York: TarcherPerigee, 2019).

unwanted task by making it fun, alleviating the power struggle, and making the child feel like they were already successful. Most of the strategies are specific to one particular child, and one particular situation.

And maybe that's what so many parenting books get wrong. It isn't the "strategies" *themselves* that people need to learn. Because so many of these strategies are so specific that they are only useful for one child. Rather than copying anyone else's suggestions, you can create your own magical solution by following a few simple principles:

1. Make it fun.
2. Make them think they already have the skills within themselves to do it.
3. Take away the power struggle.

Step #3 is the most important one. As you are no doubt already aware from having a toddler, or from overhearing a toddler in the bathroom stall next to you, power is everything to those little people. They are asserting their autonomy every step of the way, and being right, being in charge, and doing it themselves is how they become their own person, separate from their parents. It is *super* important to them. Way more important than wiping their butt "correctly."

If you dig into the power struggle, you will lose. The toddler has a secret weapon and they aren't afraid to use it. At any moment, they can start screaming at the top of their lungs if they don't get their way.

Anytime you are in a power struggle with a toddler, your first course of action should be to see if there is any way you can get yourself out of it. Your best tools here are distraction, misdirection, and magic. Always ask yourself, "Is there a rabbit I can pull out of a hat?"

Here are some examples of magic that I and others have used to trick small children into being/becoming better members of society:

Dreamcatchers

Dreamcatchers were invented by Native Americans to catch bad dreams and allow good dreams to travel down the feathers at the bottom of the dreamcatcher into the sleeper. What a beautiful, simple, and likely pretty successful intervention to prevent bad dreams in children! Many people believe dream catchers really do catch bad dreams that are floating around in the air. But also, what a brilliant way to help children relax before bedtime. Going to sleep not worrying about nightmares, and feeling convinced that you will have a good night's sleep, *does* decrease anxiety and increase healthy sleep. It works because the sleeper believes in it. Magic.

When Hazel started having nightmares at age three, I made a dreamcatcher and put it in her room. She immediately slept better and didn't have nightmares for the first few weeks the dreamcatcher was in her room. When she eventually did have a nightmare, I told her it was probably because the dreamcatcher was clogged and needed to be cleaned. For the next few months, I had to "clean" (a.k.a. poke my finger through) the holes in the dreamcatcher before bed.

Bad Thought Box

You don't want to tell kids not to have bad thoughts. First of all, it won't work. Also, if you do try to tell them what to think, you are entering into scary *1984* territory. But sometimes it is helpful for your child to be able to compartmentalize certain scary thoughts so they don't take over their lives. You can get a jewelry box that gives a satisfying slam when you close it. Make sure the box is totally leakproof before any bad thoughts go in it. You can do this by examining it closely under your child's watchful supervision. Then you can demonstrate its effectiveness by having your child imagine a bad thought in your presence, maybe something not too scary, like a bear or a tiger (because those animals are scary but also cute). Then, as she is imagining the animal, "pluck" the thought out of her head and drop it into the box, then quickly slam the box shut.

You will need to explain that the thoughts don't stay in the box; after they are left there for a few minutes, they disintegrate or disappear.

If your child isn't buying it, don't worry. That just means your kid is smarter than mine and she will probably grow up to be rich, so a few bad thoughts here and there can't hurt.

Magic Lotion

The use of "magic lotion" to get my daughter to swim was my single greatest accomplishment as a parent.

When she started swim lessons at age four, Hazel was deathly afraid of the water. She wouldn't put her face in the water without crying. My husband thought he could cure her of this by jumping into the water with her on his shoulders. You know, the old school "what doesn't kill you makes you stronger," "sink or swim" approach to parenting. Apparently, it worked for generations of children. It did not, however, work for Hazel. She didn't become stronger, and she did in fact sink. Her fear of the water became exponentially worse.

On her first day of swim class, I stopped by Walgreens and bought "magic pink lotion." I told Hazel it was bravery lotion that would make her feel brave when she rubbed it on her. She loved it because it was pink and smelled good. That day, she got into the pool and put her face in the water without crying. For the next four months, I rubbed the Magic Lotion on her every week before swim class and the little girl learned to swim. If I ever forgot, she would remind me to put on her lotion so she could be brave. After about four months, she stopped mentioning it and I stopped bringing it. She no longer needs the lotion because the bravery is now in her.[83]

---

83 I should say that I never mentioned this method to her swim school teacher… who would probably not appreciate me rubbing lotion on my child before swim class. For that I am truly sorry. I knew it was wrong but I did it anyway.

Band-Aids

Before writing this paragraph, I thought I would do a bit of background research on the history and usefulness of Band-Aids. Diligent investigative journalist that I am, I typed "Band-Aids" into Google. Apparently, there is an extremely emotional debate unfolding online about whether or not Band-Aids help wounds to heal faster. Ah, the internet…where dumb, pointless disagreements rapidly turn into personal attacks.

Whether or not Band-Aids help wounds heal faster is irrelevant. When Fritz puts his stool on top of the table and then attempts to jump to the couch, or when Hazel tries to cut the tag of her shirt and accidentally cuts her neck, I am going to be in trouble if I don't have a box of Band-Aids nearby. Some childhood injuries are real and require actual medical assistance. 99.9% of childhood injuries are totally overblown and require zero medical attention.[84] All they need is a Band-Aid.

Even if they don't need medical attention, they do need emotional attention. She needs someone to come over and give her a hug, ask her if she is okay, and show her you feel bad about what happened. Then, the child needs to feel something is being done to remedy the situation and take the pain away. The Band-Aid immediately makes the child think, *Okay, problem solved, I can go back to playing.* And because the child's attention then shifts away from their hurt knee, the knee (which wasn't that hurt in the first place) really does feel better. It's the placebo effect!

Mysteriously, Band-Aids are even more effective if they have pictures from *Frozen* or *Paw Patrol* on them. I don't know why this is. I'm just reporting the facts.

Ice packs, miraculously, don't just work for bruises. They work for cuts, unidentified boo boos, sunburns, and even hurt feelings. If an ice pack has a picture from *Frozen* or *Paw Patrol*, it also operates better.

---

84 That percentage is 100% well documented and correct.

Anything Your Kid Comes up With

The best magical solutions you will discover on your parenting journey won't come from you. They will come from your little one. Kids are better at magic than we are. As previously discussed, they have better brains. If you can't come up with a way to magic your way out of a predicament, see if they can. Invest in a magic wand and hope for the best.

One day when Hazel was acting like a little asshole, I asked her, "What can we do to change your attitude?"

She put her fingers in her mouth and said, "I'm going to throw my bad attitude away," ran across the room, and threw it in the garbage. Now, whenever she's acting like a total piece of shit, I ask her if she wants to throw her bad attitude away. It doesn't always work. But when she is kind of sick of having a bad attitude anyway, and is looking for a way out, this method is successful.

Again, children are better than adults. We can't just throw our bad attitudes away. We have to spend thousands on drugs and therapy and we are still whiney pieces of shit most of the time.

CHAPTER 16:

I'm a Better Therapist Than I Am a Mother

I sent this text to my friend Sara after the most challenging of mornings. Hazel would not stop throwing gigantic tantrums about the most miniscule of things. I kept trying to use "big deal or little deal" with her to get her to calm down. I asked her if something was a *huge* deal, like last night when she dropped a ladder on her foot, or a tiny deal like her baby stroller being sticky. But on that particular morning, none of it was working. I was tired, thinking about work, and it was incredibly difficult to muster sympathy when I tried to brush the hair off her face and accidentally poked her in the eye. There are times when that kid *triggers something* in me that is so deep and emotional and panicky, and there is nothing I can do to control my reactions to her actions. When I'm in a deeply calm space, thinking rationally, and have had a good long break from her, I can react in a sensible way. But so much of the time I am playing catch up. I am reacting to Hazel emotionally and then walking away, thinking about it with my rational brain, and then coming back and trying again.

Why is it so hard to respond therapeutically to my own kids?

After this incredibly exasperating morning, I dropped Hazel off at preschool. While washing her hands in the sink, she started to cry about her foot hurting. I knew her foot was still hurting from dropping a ladder on it the day before, but also, *enough already!* I was struggling with these dual emotions when Hazel's little friend McKenna came over and put a pink princess crown on her head. It was clearly a crown McKenna had picked out to wear herself that morning and with no thought at all, she took it off her head and put it on Hazel's in an attempt to cheer her up. Proving two things:

4. Girls are there for one another in truly remarkable ways, starting at the youngest age.

5. Thank god our children can grow and foster relationships outside of ourselves, because sometimes we as their parents suck at giving them what they need.

When I got to my car that morning I thought, *Why the hell am I working on a book about parenting when I often respond with so little patience to my own children?*

Luckily, I'm not alone. It is almost universal that those of us who work in the helping professions can't solve our own problems. This is a theme in almost every movie where a therapist is *not* the catalyst that leads to change in a character. The subtext of this plotline is, this quack can't even solve her own problems; how could she ever help anyone else?[85]

As I mentioned in the introduction to this book,[86] my parents are psychologists. When I was a kid, my dad worked as a family therapist, and published a fairly popular parenting book in 1990 called *Family Rules: Raising Responsible Children*. He was also my soccer coach. Sometime in the 90s, my dad was doing his usual coaching thing: standing on the sidelines and screaming at his two daughters as loud as he could. The coach of the opposite team, meanwhile, remained impressively calm throughout the game. After the game, my dad approached him and asked, "How are you able to watch the game without yelling at your daughter?"

The other coach replied, "I read your book."

The point is: I come from a long line of know-it-all hypocrites.

The difference between me and everyone else is, at least I know I'm a hypocrite. And that we are all hypocrites. I am incredibly patient with other people's children. My clients' tantrums don't trigger me at all. I can sit with parents while a child is screaming and calmly coach them on how to respond. I totally understand and empathize with the emotional torment of any child who isn't mine. When I hear another child cry, I feel nothing but sympathy for the child and their parent.

Everyone reacts differently to their own children, whether they are running down a soccer field or screaming about getting yogurt on their dress. It's very easy to react calmly and rationally when the child in question isn't the little monster you live with. We feel so much more emotionally

---

85 I could write an entire book just about the awful ways therapists are misrepresented by Hollywood. I don't get it… I thought everyone in Hollywood had a therapist. Why do they hate us?

86 You didn't read the intro, did you? I bet you skipped all the way to the section on sleeping.

connected to our own children that it is hard to react reasonably. We aren't in a state of non-judgmental, objective calm when we respond to them. We may feel sympathy for our child, but we also often feel judged by other parents, aggravated, and exhausted by the twenty things that happened earlier in the day, and unsure if reacting with sympathy is the right way to react. It is so much more complicated when you are responding to your own child. Because it isn't *just* the child herself you are responding to.

Everything you do or say to your child, you do or say within the context of the complicated relationship you have with the child and with parenting itself. How I respond to Hazel is complicated by my feelings about being a mom. Which is complicated by my relationship with my own mother, and how I want to be like her or not like her. As I'm responding to Hazel, I'm not just saying something to her; I am also watching myself saying something to her and thinking, *How am I doing? Am I fucking her up? Is this the wrong thing to say?* When I respond to a child who isn't mine, I'm responding as a professional, a role I feel 100% more confident with because I've been doing it longer and it isn't tied up with all my own childhood baggage and resentments.

Further complicating this is the fact that children act completely differently toward their own parents, with whom they have all their own baggage. Parents comment on this all the time. "She doesn't do that with me." "I wish I could see some of those manners." Children are both better and worse when they are with us, and as their parents we will never really see how they act toward other people…unless we install one of those nanny cams.

The best thing any of us can do is reflect on how we fucked up and try our best to do better. I spend most of my workdays talking to parents about their kids, and talking to other younger professionals who *aren't* parents about how to talk to parents. And what I find the most upsetting is what people *don't* admit to. Or what people who aren't parents don't understand. The lack of honesty about how often we lose our patience with our children is what makes it so hard for anyone to think of themselves as a competent parent.

I went to a party once as my friend Sara's plus one. The host was a mom from her kids' preschool. Most of the party guests were preschool parents, and so naturally most of the conversation consisted of drunken stories about our kids. At one point in the night, I was talking to a preschool mom and a preschool teacher. The mother explained to the teacher that when her kids start screaming at her for more milk, or less milk, or the same amount of milk but in a different container, or the same amount of milk in the same container but with a different spoon, or the same spoon and the same container and the same milk but placed on a different surface in the house…she calmly tells them, "I don't respond well to commands or demands!"

What a great answer. What a totally rational, unemotional way to respond to children without giving in to their demands but still being responsive to them and not making them feel scared or intimidated by your reaction.

I started cracking up. The mom looked at me quizzically for a few seconds before I realized I was acting like an asshole. The twenty-one-year-old preschool teacher nodded his head solemnly, approving of her fantastic parenting skills. A few minutes earlier, he had been lamenting to me about "those moms who send their kids to school with breakfast all over their faces and mismatched socks." I nodded in tacit agreement, even though that is literally how Fritzi shows up at school 90% of the time.

"Oh…" I said awkwardly when I had managed to stop laughing hysterically. "Oh, you're serious. You tell them 'you don't respond to commands or demands?' I'm usually like…GODDAMN IT, Hazel!" The preschool mom and the preschool teacher giggled awkwardly. My friend Sara, because she's hilarious and awesome, cracked up.

In the privileged, ultra-liberal bubble I live in, it's not okay to yell at your kids. It's gospel to the parents I surround myself with that the best way, the *only* way to parent is by listening to and validating your child's needs. You don't want to give in to their behavior, of course, but you need to validate their feelings.

I wholeheartedly agree with this approach. I do *not* think yelling at kids is helpful to anyone. And since 2014, my number one New Year's resolution has been to not yell at my children. Everything about yelling at kids is counterproductive.

Will I keep making this same New Year's resolution until Fritz turns eighteen in the year 2034? Probably.

The most badass thing I have *ever* seen a parent do was when I was working as an after-school teacher at my old middle school. I was playing with the after-school kids on the playground when my former gym teacher, Mr. Beck, stuck his head out the third story window of the school and whistled to his two sons who were playing on the playground below.[87] The boys immediately dropped what they were doing and ran to the parking lot. Whistling. That's some real power. Yelling at kids is a complete waste of time. They feel like shit. You feel like shit. You look like an asshole. And if you bring it up at cocktail parties full of parents, they may not invite you back.

In the spirit of that, I decided it would be useful for me—as well as for you, dear reader—to document a full week of my completely irrational kid-yelling behavior so you can see what a complete monster/moron I truly am. Also, in the glorious calm of the future, I will reflect on what I could have said were I not a terrible monster. Where you see "Mom" quoted, that is what I actually said to my child. Where you see "Therapist," you'll see what I would say if I were my own parent coach.

---

87 Mr. Beck, how did you do that? Please tell me.

Monday

Mom: In response to Hazel wanting to change pants for the third time this morning/five billionth time this week: "JESUS CHRIST,[88] Hazel! I can't deal with you and pants anymore! It's driving me crazy. You hate all your pants and it is actually making me lose my mind. This is the last time you are changing your pants *ever*!"

Therapist: Children can be very literal in their interpretation of things, so when you say, "You are never changing your pants again," she will not know it is an exaggeration and may worry you mean that literally. By saying this, you are giving a consequence that you can't actually live up to and if you continue to do this, she won't take you seriously.

Tuesday

Mom: "Whatever you are crying about doesn't *matter* that much!"

Therapist: Of course, what they are crying about doesn't matter to you, but it does matter to them. In the moment, to this child, it seems like a very big deal, and telling them it doesn't matter is telling them that *they* don't matter and their feelings don't matter. A better approach is to use the "big deal vs. little deal" framework developed by Michelle Garcia Winter's Social Thinking curriculum.[89] There are some amazing visuals you can use to illustrate the differences between a big deal vs. a little deal. The best time to roll this out is NOT in the middle of a tantrum, and you can spend time teaching your child these strategies during happy, content times and then refer back to them during meltdowns.

---

88 The only thing my children know about "Jesus Christ" is that it is something mommy says when she is mad.

89 https://www.socialthinking.com/

Wednesday

Mom: "JESUS Christ,[90] Fritzi! Whaaaaaat??! Stop crying!"

Therapist: In this elevated emotional state, Fritzi is not capable of controlling his ability to cry. Remember, this is a two-year-old. If you are getting frustrated with his feelings, rather than telling him to stop crying, you can leave the room and take a minute to yourself.

Thursday

Mom: I'm so proud of myself. I didn't lose it on the little people one time today. I'm an incredible mom.

I wrote the above words at 7:23 p.m. I should have known better. At 7:35, I started trying to put Fritzi to bed. Except, he wanted a cheese snack. Which he ate at roughly the speed of a Galapagos tortoise consuming its last meal. Then he wanted one particular stuffed penguin, which I had to spend ten minutes looking for. Then he wanted me to throw all the other stuffed animals off his bed, to which I muttered:

"God...mother...stuffed animals...Jesus[91]...fucking...of course this goddamn camel..."

Then I let out an incredibly deep sigh and lay down next to the beautiful two-and-a-half-year-old baby boy. And he asked: "Mommy? Are you still mad at me? I love you, Mama."

Therapist: When you respond to your son this way, he doubts your love for him. How does that make you *feel?*

---

90 I know...it is so offensive.

91 I'm going to get in so much trouble if anyone ever invites my kids to church with them

Friday

Mom: "Hazel, I do not have the patience today for the whole pants thing."

Therapist: Have you noticed that you have the same struggles with your kids every day? Getting your daughter to put on pants is clearly a trigger for you. Just leave the room, and give her all the time she needs to do it. Is it really important that she put on pants quickly? Slow down…be patient. It will happen. Maybe you need to give yourself more time in the morning to get ready. Even if it means waking up earlier, it will be worth it just so you don't have a fight every morning.

Saturday

Mom: "This is not a big deal! If you are going to have a fit, do it in your room. I don't want to hear it!"

Therapist: Having big deal/little deal conversations is not something you want to do in the middle of a tantrum. When someone is already having a feeling, the last thing they want to hear is that their feelings aren't valid. It was a great idea to have the child move their tantrum to their room. But you can suggest this to her calmly, without so much emotion.

Sunday

Mom: "No, Fritzi. No, *enough* with the *eeny meany miny moe*! GO TO BED!"

Therapist: Stop being such a dick.

How Can We Suck at This Less?

Let me paint a picture for you. A Lyft pulls up to a condo building in a small coastal town just south of San Francisco. A couple gets into the car. A middle-aged man with laugh crinkles on his cheeks and a *much* younger woman wearing very stylish clothing and jewelry. They are parents on their way to the city for a much-needed night out. What will they talk about on their twenty-minute drive? Their jobs? Their friends? Politics? Of course not. They will talk about their kids—what else?

Her: I got so frustrated at Hazel today. I feel bad. I totally lost it on her. She drives me crazy, though!

Him: Yeah, I know, that happens to me all the time. I hate it. She just makes me so mad when she doesn't listen.

Her: She won't listen! Why won't she listen?

Him: I don't know! She doesn't fucking listen to us!!!!

Silence. Sighs.

Her: She's the best though…

Him: I love her so much.

Her: Did you see that video I posted of her putting Fritz's clothes on?

Him: I miss them.

Her: I wish I didn't get so mad at her, because now I'm wrecked with guilt about it and I can't even enjoy my time out.

Him: I know. You'll forget about it once you have a cocktail, though.

Her: Yeah, that's true.

Why though? Whyyyyyyyyyyy? Why is it that I know so much about child development and behavior and yet I struggle so much? Every time I yell at my kids it ends the same way, with me feeling guilty. Then I talk my husband's ear off about how guilty I feel. It is a totally exhausting cycle for everyone, and that includes the poor Lyft driver. He's probably thinking, *Get your shit together! Or, if you are going to yell at your kid, just do it and stop doubting yourself!*

Is this just what modern parenting is about? Acting the same way we have always acted toward these little monsters who drive us nuts, but then feeling profoundly guilty about it afterward? In the years I have been trying to raise children while dispensing advice about how to raise children, I have gotten better at not completely losing my shit. But over six years into this thing, I really don't think I can ever bring my losing-my-shit meter all the way down to zero. Can anyone? As soon as I've gotten the hang of one problem, another problem emerges to take its place. This whole parenting thing will never go in the "case closed" file.

Rather than getting mad at Hazel, unreasonably yelling at Hazel, telling my husband how guilty I feel about yelling at Hazel, or swearing to do better and then fucking up all over again, I have started trying a new strategy. Admitting I fucked up. And guess what? My kids love it!

Here's an example.

Watching Hazel get ready in the morning is like watching paint dry after the paint you put on the house somehow managed to come off the house entirely and you had to reapply it seven or eight times before it fully dried. Almost every morning, I have the following thoughts:

6. Does this child have ADHD?

7. Is there literally something wrong with her?

8. Or is it just that she doesn't listen to me?

9. WHY DOESN'T SHE LISTEN TO ME!!!!!!!???????

When this last thought hits me, I am often filled with rage and all too often pose this question to the child who is sitting playing with her dollhouse, wearing one sock with her underwear pulled halfway up one leg.

"WHY DON'T YOU LISTEN TO ME???!!!"

Me posing this question to her in perhaps not the most understanding of tones almost always results in her either a) crying, b) whining, or c) ignoring me completely. What it *never* results in is her putting on her other sock and her fucking pink dress and getting out the goddamn door.

Following one of these completely irrational blow-ups, I had the foresight to talk to her about it. I gave her a hug, sat her down on my knee, and apologized for getting frustrated and yelling at her. I explained to her that it was very frustrating for me when she didn't get ready on time and I had to remind her over and over again. But just because I was frustrated didn't make it okay for me to yell at her. Instead, we would have to work together to find a way for her to get ready on time, and for me to be nice to her. This immediately solved both of our problems. Hazel got ready in thirty seconds every morning from then on and I never again yelled at one of my children.

AHAHHAHAHHAHAH. Yeah, right.

But we did both learn an important lesson. I felt so much better after apologizing to her and showing her my own vulnerability. Showing her that a lot of the time, I don't know what the fuck I'm doing and I'm just making it up as I go along, same as her. For Hazel, this reinforces her ability to see what is happening in someone else's mind. Adults get frustrated. They get mad and react as a result of their anger, just like four-year-olds. It's a normal thing that happens to anyone, but just because it's normal doesn't make it okay. Everyone, child or adult, can make amends and try super-duper hard to be better tomorrow.

We can teach our children about vulnerability and mistakes by pulling back the curtain for them. By showing our children that we too fuck up. We are helping them understand what it means to be human. We don't want our children to be afraid of failure. Afraid that when they make a mistake, there is no coming back from it. Showing our hand helps them understand what is in their own hands. They will fuck up too, and they can apologize and try to do better. They can learn from their mistakes; they don't have to hide them. They don't have to be perfect. That's a valuable lesson. So, it's totally no big deal to scream at your kids.

I'm just kidding. It totally 100% sucks. Don't do it.

CHAPTER 17:

Stop Being a
Judgmental Douchebag

Two eighteen-month-olds are playing together in a sandbox. The little girl is being carefully monitored by her loving and devoted father. The little boy is being left to his own devices. The abandoned little boy starts throwing sand at the little girl. The devoted father looks around thinking, *What an out of control kid! Clearly this little boy is spoiled rotten, and his parents let him watch TV all day and don't teach him rules and not to throw sand at people. I'm such a good parent. Where is this child's parent? No doubt staring at her phone instead of engaging with her child!*

After enduring a few more minutes of sand flinging, the father loudly says to his daughter, "Let's move away from this child," and starts to pick up his little angel to move her away from the offending child. But he is too late. His little girl has already been corrupted. She flings a little bit of sand in the little demon's face. Her father immediately removes her from the sandbox and puts her down on a park bench.

"Consequence," he tells his little girl. "You can't throw sand. Do you know why? Because it is hurtful." As he talks to her gently but firmly, he looks around thinking, *Hmm...wonder where that little boy's mother or father is. They should really see this; they could probably learn something.*

Meanwhile, across the playground, the exhausted mother of two grabs her three-year-old around the waist seconds before he runs out of the playground and into the street. She carries him, kicking and screaming, back to the equipment and looks across the playground to see what the baby in the sandbox is doing. Noticing that he is throwing sand, she yells, "Stop throwing sand!" but she can barely hear herself speak over the screams of her three-year-old.

Can we please just give each other a goddamn break?

Judgment. It may be the very worst thing about being a parent. And the playground is Judgment Ground Zero. God forbid your child throws sand, or grabs a toy from another kid, or runs in front of a swing set. Parents are so afraid of other parents judging them that they apologize to each other every five minutes.

Suzie doesn't wait for her turn on the tire swing. SORRY SORRY SORRY.

Little Billie throws sand in the sandbox (basically the most fun thing to do in the sandbox). SORRY SORRY SORRY.

One child gently touches another child's shoulder. SORRY SORRY SORRY.

And then after the sorrys, the parent of the offending child will always feel compelled to intervene. Loudly and publicly. To take the toy away from the child who stole it. To give the kid a consequence. Because, god forbid you don't react fast enough, you know there is going to be some dad across the playground thinking about what a terrible mother you are.

When I see other parents gently and firmly disciplining children in public, I always wonder, is this what they are like in private? Are they always this gentle and thoughtful and patient? Because I'm definitely not! Parents disciplining children on Bay Area playgrounds unanimously sound like something out of a training video in a co-op parenting class. "Ava, how do you think the little boy felt when you grabbed the toy from him? How can we make him feel better?" Is this all a big production we put on for the benefit of other parents, who are always watching us even when they pretend they aren't?

Fritz is obsessed with balls. When he was eighteen months old, his favorite activity wherever we went was to play ball with other adults. He got a thrill out of some adult he didn't know throwing or kicking the ball back to him. And he was insanely cute, so he was never without a willing playmate. One day at an indoor play space, he started his favorite activity with a nearby mom who seemed enthusiastic about playing with him. I hung back and watched, beaming with pride, as he threw the ball back and forth with this mom for five minutes before getting bored and moving on to another activity. A half hour later, Fritz circled back and threw the ball at her again. This time the mom turned to her friend sitting next to her:

"This little boy loves me! He came up and just started playing with me and I was like, 'Sure I'll play with you!' Meanwhile his mom is just over there staring at her phone."

WHHHHHHHHHHHAAAAAT!?

Okay. I stare at my phone as much as anyone else who spends multiple hours per week at playgrounds. But on this particular day, my phone wasn't even with me! The nerve! Judging other parents as being incompetent, uncaring, or phone-starers feels so good to us that we even make up complete lies just so we can feel superior.

It's easy to feel superior, and it does indeed feel awesome. It feels amazing to judge other parents at the playground, because then you get to feel like you are doing an okay job for half a minute. But we should cut it out immediately. Not just because it is super annoying to be labeled a bad parent when you are busy chasing around a second or third child, but also because it's creating a playground culture that is not helpful to our children.

I'm sure there are a bunch of moms and dads in the Bay Area right now who are convinced I am the worst mom in the world. And I'm cool with that. Because right around the time my second kid was born, I decided I was done with apologizing for non-heinous but annoying shit my kids do at the playground. Sure, if my kid smacks another kid on the face, I intervene. But I'm done sweating the small stuff. They are kids! They need to make mistakes. They need to mess up and suffer the social consequences that come with it. If they grab a toy, see what the other kid does. He's probably going to grab it right back, and the two of them will have to work it out amongst themselves. Our fear of judgment is creating a playground culture where we don't allow kids to suffer social consequences.

This past Christmas, I was standing with my friend Lauren at a tree lighting festival. Lauren has a six-year-old and an eighteen-year-old, and she's one of the least judgmental moms I know. We were standing there talking when this woman walked by us pushing a gigantic stroller through the crowd. I didn't have a stroller with me that year, because my kids had outgrown them, but the previous year I had brought my stroller and I was the one pushing it through the crowd, severely regretting the decision to bring it. When I saw Stroller Mom struggling, I explained this to Lauren, saying, "Man…that poor mom. I brought a stroller through this crowd last year and it sucked." Lauren nodded in agreement, also expressing sympathy.

Stroller Mom, seeing us watching her, left the stroller and marched up to us. "You know," she fumed, "you really shouldn't judge other mothers! It really isn't helpful!"

Lauren and I tried to explain ourselves, but it was too late. Stroller Mom had stormed off.

That moment stuck with me because it illustrates just how deep this issue of judgment goes, and how much it is fucking up the whole parenting universe.

Let's backtrack to our *Fish is Fish* metaphor for a moment. Poor Stroller Mom had a mentalization of two mothers talking shit about her. That wasn't the reality of the situation. But that is what she saw, probably based on her own insecurity, because so often other mothers *are* talking shit. I always feel like I'm being judged by other parents. Some of the time, I clearly am (like that annoying woman at the indoor play space), but a lot of the time, I'm probably wrong. It's probably just two moms looking at me and saying, "Man, that poor lady," or, "She's got really amazing style."[92]

In our world, we constantly feel like we are being judged. Often, that is not the reality of what is happening. But the point is, we feel that way. And it is extremely corrosive. I only live here and now, within the limited confines of my own brain, but I can't help but feel like this sense of judgment is a new phenomenon. Did parents thousands of years ago worry about being judged for their parenting skills? Maybe only if you refused to sacrifice your firstborn to the gods. Then the other moms were probably whispering to each other, "I can't believe she wouldn't allow the menfolk to slay her son in the name of Odin. What is wrong with that woman?"

In our own individual lives, we can fix this problem. We can smile at other parents, or roll our eyes conspiratorially. We can offer them help without being obnoxious about it. Like, if you have wipes and you overhear another mom swearing under her breath because she forgot wipes, give her some goddamn wipes. But you don't have to be obnoxious about it and make her feel guilty for forgetting wipes. Just give her the wipes. Remember, we all think we are being judged on our

---

92 Depending on how I'm feeling that day, I usually assume parents are thinking one of those two things about me.

parenting all the time. So, you have to act very non-judgmentally for other parents to feel safe.

One of the many, many, *many* things that suck about being a parent during COVID-19[93] is that it's now even more difficult to convey a sense of comradery to other parents while we are living in our masked, socially-distanced universe. My friend Yasmine had a baby at the beginning of the COVID-19 pandemic. She asked me how I navigated taking my babies in and out of the Moby wrap on my own when I was in public. I thought back to the Academy of Sciences, the zoo, and the playground and tried to remember how I got Fritz in and out of the Moby wrap on my own while Hazel was running around like the toddler terror she was. Here's how I did it: other moms. Inevitably, I would be struggling and another mom would come over and give me a hand. Gently, without judgment, often without even saying anything. As a mom during COVID-19, Yasmine doesn't have the luxury of strangers' help.

When we go back to that old world, let's commit to this. Silently, non-judgmentally helping each other. Taking off our masks and smiling to indicate that we are all there, judgement free and ready to help.

---

93 Here are some other things that also suck about parenting during COVID-19: everything is closed, school no longer exists, you can't see any of your mom friends, being stuck in your house for months on end with small children, no playdates…should I go on?

CHAPTER 18:

Monsters

When Hazel was two, she was afraid of monsters.

Hazel talked about monsters coming into her room at night, hiding under her bed, and hiding behind the curtains. As part of her bedtime ritual, we had to search her room for monsters. We told her that if a monster came into the house, Daddy would eat it. For some reason, she found this immensely comforting.

We don't know where this fear of monsters came from. We tried our best to shield her from anything scary. But at two and a half, Hazel's mind was a sponge. She absorbed information, and fears, from everywhere. She might have developed her fear of monsters from the kids at school, from the movie *Frozen*, or from an exaggeration of an animal at the zoo. When asked, she would tell us that monsters were just "pretend." But like all two-year-olds, the line between pretend and real was not a solid line. It blended, blurred, and often didn't exist at all.

Hazel is an incredibly lucky kid. To grow up here, to grow up now. All over the world, there are real monsters—in Aleppo, in the Sudan, and in countless other places in the world. Sadly, there are kids in San Francisco, maybe even in Hazel's school, who have real monsters to contend with. But for Hazel, when we tell her monsters are "only pretend" and that they "aren't real," we are telling the truth. At least for now, we can protect Hazel from the real monsters.

Because she was safe, Hazel was free to experiment with being afraid of monsters. She has played all roles in this game. Sometimes, she pretended to be a monster, and chased us around the house growling and scaring her baby brother. When she played that game, she was feeling and experiencing the part of herself that was indeed monstrous. At age two, Hazel had her share of monstrous moments. It was the monster inside her who grabbed toys out of her friends' hands. Who didn't want to share. Who pinched her baby brother when our heads were turned. When she acted like this, her father and I looked at each other, stunned. Were we raising a monster? But right after doing the bad behavior, little Hazel would always correct herself. She would say, "We don't pinch Fritz." "We share our toys, right, Mommy?" When Hazel displayed her monster self, she was just doing overtly what we as adults do subconsciously. We all want to grab things from each other. But because we are adults, we don't. Hazel was learning the art of self-control by being, and then correcting, the monster.

Hazel also liked to play the other side. The damsel in distress being pursued by the monster. She liked to test how much she could scare herself. There were many real things Hazel was afraid of at this age. Primarily, Mommy leaving her and not coming back. By pretending that a monster was pursuing her, she could experience this fear, and then the comfort that goes along with saying, "The monsters are only pretend, right, Mommy?" And then, "Mommy always comes back to get me."

In all of the many ways my children have been privileged, this is perhaps the most important one. My kids have had opportunities to understand their fears, to play with them, and to conquer them. For all the children throughout time and history who have had real monsters to contend with, this has not always been an option.

CHAPTER 19:

Screens—You are Destroying Your Child's Brain

The American Academy of Pediatrics[94] recently issued new recommendations around screen time. The previous recommendation of the American Academy of Pediatrics was no screens before three. However, after reviewing the evidence, the AAP now recommends no more than an hour of screen time for two to four-year-olds, and they still recommend no screens for children under two.

If you are interested in finding out more about the recommendation from the AAP, an article entitled "Media and Young Minds" is available online and gives some recommendations for educational apps like *Sesame Street*.[95] The AAP recommends that children between age two and four engage with media alongside their parents, and that parents help the child

---

94 In my head, the American Academy of Pediatrics looks exactly like the Council of Elrond from The Lord of The Rings.

95 Here's the link to the article: https://pediatrics.aappublications.org/content/138/5/e20162591

engage with the media and talk about the content with them. There are some good recommendations from the AAP about this. This article also highlights some of the well-documented issues stemming from children who have too much screen time, such as: impact on sleep, obesity, and development. The long and short of it is, they still recommend that children have interactive experiences with adults as much as possible, but an hour a day of screen time for your toddler has been determined to be okay for your little one's brain.

Thank. *God.*

Have you ever gone to a restaurant with a toddler? No? You are a smarter person than I am.

#justsaynototoddlersinrestaurants

Unfortunately for everyone, there are rare occasions when a toddler must be dragged into a restaurant. Or a work meeting. There may also be rare occasions in which you need to take a shower without your toddler squeezing all the toothpaste into the sink, or attempting to paint her nails but actually dumping a bottle of nail polish onto the rug, or dropping your glasses off the balcony. There may also be rare occasions in which a global pandemic forces you to quarantine in your house for months and then school closes for a year. On these very rare occasions, you may need more than one hour per day of screen time to get you through.

Call me crazy, but it is my extremely radical belief that your toddler will *still* have a chance of getting into AP Calculus even if you do this.

The long and short of it is this: we need screen time to get through our lives as parents. However, there is increasing evidence that extended screen time is terrible for kids. Children aren't learning when they are passively letting digital content wash over them.

A groundbreaking study by Dr. Patricia Kuhl looked at language acquisition in babies during the most critical period for language acquisition: six to eight months.[96] Dr. Kuhl divided the babies into three

---

96 Patricia Kuhl, Feng-Ming Tsao, and Huei-Mei Liu, "Foreign-Language

groups, none of whom had been exposed to any Mandarin. One group of babies was exposed to Mandarin by a native speaker sitting with them, playing with them and reading them books in Mandarin over twelve sessions. Dr. Kuhl described the experience of these babies as similar to "having a Mandarin relative move into their house."[97] Another group of babies received the exact same curriculum, but recorded and played for them on a video screen. A third group only heard the audio of the sessions, with no video or in person teaching. After twelve sessions of this, the babies exposed to Mandarin in person showed as much fluency in Mandarin as babies living in Taiwan. The babies who had watched video of the twelve sessions and the babies who had listened to the audio knew the same amount of Mandarin they knew before the study: none.

What happened in these babies' brains was that the part of their brains that processes receptive (understanding) of language was triggered when they watched the video and listened to the audio. However, the part of the baby's brain that processes expressive language was not triggered by the audio or the video. For the babies who engaged in person with the Mandarin speaker, both parts of their brains were triggered. When we learn language, we need the expressive language part of our brain to be firing as well as the receptive part, even though all we are doing is listening. The babies who received the audio or the video were just passively letting content wash over them. For the babies who had in-person lessons, even when they weren't talking, their brains were actively engaged.

Parents I meet like to brag to me about skills their kids can do on an iPad. They are very proud that their two-year-old can match shapes and colors on a screen. Parents tell me this when I attempt to have their child match colors using real objects. When I am testing this skill, I

Experience in Infancy: Effects of Short-Term Exposure and Social Interaction on Phonetic Learning," *Proceedings of the National Academy of Sciences* 100, no. 15 (2003): 9096-9101. https://doi.org/10.1073/pnas.1532872100.

97 Patricia Kuhl, "The Linguistic Genius of Babies," TED, 2010, https://www.ted.com/talks/patricia_kuhl_the_linguistic_genius_of_babies?language=en.

am not only looking for a child's ability to understand colors, but also how that child is engaging with me. Does the child look at me when I talk to them? Do they listen and learn from my example? These are the fundamental skills that lead to learning. Simply knowing that orange goes to orange doesn't help you with that. We need children to be in the world learning from the world. Engaging with adults and other children. Not just staring passively at screens. Which is why every time I see a commercial for Baby Einstein, I want to sue someone. These products trick parents into thinking that plopping babies down in front of a screen is *helpful* or, even worse, *preferable* to actual human interaction. There is simply no evidence to back this up. In fact, there is a lot of evidence pointing to the negative effects of prolonged screen time.

But I digress. Back to the restaurant. Have you been to a restaurant with a toddler? Yes? A plane? A car? Well, then you know exactly what I am talking about.

Sometimes, there is just no other option. If you want to stay at the restaurant and finish your meal, if you want to get through a ten-minute shower, if you need to call the insurance company, or if you need to put another child to bed, then giving your toddler a screen is most likely the best (or only) way to do this. I know that for hundreds of years parents managed these situations without devices. But these same parents also lost half of their children to polio, so they were more resilient than we are.

Many well-meaning professionals will insist that parents forego all screen time for their kids. But this ignores the fact that there are two people in the parent-child dyad. The child's brain is of course the most important thing of all. We don't want to do anything to harm it. There is no doubt putting a two-year-old in front of a screen for an entire day is not good for them. However, the other thing that is very likely to harm a two-year-old is a parent who is so stressed, overwhelmed, tired, and dirty from not showering that they can't function. Your mental health is *not different* from your child's mental health. Some days, you just plain old need a break, and an hour of *Sesame Street* is the only way you can get it. Sure, engaging alongside your child with digital content is the best practice. However, you also need to do the dishes and listen to a podcast for an hour. It's okay. Her brain will be okay.

Give yourself permission for a little bit of screen time. If you are able to find good educational content, that is the way to go. If you can engage with her on that content, even better. If you just need a break, that's okay too.

Screens in Places They Don't Belong

We know two things to be true: we want to limit screen time, and we also occasionally want to take showers and eat food. These things are nearly impossible to do with small children hanging around underfoot. For most of human history, we didn't have screens we could plop our children in front of. But for most of human history, we could tell our kids to go outside and come inside when the streetlights came on.[98] Anyway, the way I see it is that there is a limited amount of screen time children should be allowed every day, and the time they are allotted should be given to that child's primary caregiver. Which is why I am *so fucking* over screens popping up all over the place.

Later in this book, I will describe to you my fight to get movies out of my children's daycare. But in the time since that fight happened a few years ago, I have noticed how completely rampant the use of screens is in our children's lives. In places where they do not belong. They are taking over. Before the pandemic, I went to an indoor play place that we have been going to for years. They had recently installed a computer console for the kids to play with. So, instead of running around and expending energy so that they would sleep well at night, all Fritz and Hazel wanted

---

98 This notion shocks me because I feel like if I said this to Fritz, he would just move in with another family and I would never see him again. He's that kind of kid. He loves me. But he could love anyone.

to do was stare at the computer. Which means I was paying $20 for my kids to go there and stare at screens. We can do that at home!

During the pandemic, I sent Hazel to a six-week camp. It was her first opportunity to be around other children in four months. Overall, it was a great experience. She did projects, spent time with other kindergarten girls and teenage counselors, engaged in camp rivalries. You know, camp stuff. The camp was only four hours a day. Which is why I was enraged to find out that every Friday she was watching a feature film! This was her first opportunity to be around other children in months. I had spent four months trying as hard as humanly possible to minimize her time with screens. And these fucking people were using this precious social time to show her a movie???

Even before the pandemic forced school online, every classroom I visited in the Bay Area used screens in ways I didn't find beneficial. Kindergarten classrooms supplement teacher instruction by plugging kids into computers and having them complete lessons on a computer program called StarFall. I recently listened to a podcast[99] from the radio program Reveal about charter schools in New Orleans. A mother on the program kept asking her daughter's teachers for assistance with reading comprehension, and her teacher kept directing her to StarFall and not actually helping her!

I understand this interest and excitement about online learning programs. Kids love them and they help with simple academic skills like sounding out words and learning shapes and colors. The trouble for the mother in New Orleans was that her daughter struggled with reading comprehension, not sounding out words. Her daughter could read perfectly but didn't understand what she was reading. This is the pitfall so many educators and parents fall into when we start getting too excited about the use of screens for learning. We get so excited about the notion that we can plop a kid in front of something and they will

---

99 Take a shot.

learn. Sometimes we forget to ask, what are they learning? What is the most important aspect of their education?

Obviously, I want my children to read, but I care more about their social and emotional growth than I do about their ability to sound out words. Their school day should be full of rich, immersive opportunities to learn and engage with others. Think about the experience of a preschooler learning in a group with other children. They are not just learning how to sound out letters. They are learning how to sit and focus on what a teacher is telling them, how to respond and engage with their classmates, how to ask questions and have them answered. All of this is happening at the same time they are learning to sound out letters. We don't just want our kids to read for the sake of reading; we want them to read because that is how they will understand their world.

Sometimes, like in the case of Hazel's preschool putting on a movie when the kids are being too annoying, educators are putting screens in front of children because it is easy and they need a break. More often, however, it is because of a genuine belief that the screens are good for the child's learning. I totally understand this belief, because the internet is chock full of wonderful learning tools. When I worked for a private company treating young children with autism, I saw staff giving phones and iPads to children during therapy sessions. Sometimes they did it because they needed a break from the kid. Most of the time they did it because they believed it was the best way to teach something.

Many children with autism love music. So, using music during a session is a great way to get them to engage in a social activity. I love using the "Hokey Pokey" to teach imitation skills. To use music in session, therapists at my company would pull up the "Hokey Pokey" on YouTube and have it play while they danced with their client. Nine times out of ten, our clients would be staring at the YouTube video while they were singing and dancing, rather than watching their therapist's face. Screens are incredibly addictive for all of us, especially for small children, and *especially* for small children with autism who find watching faces aversive.

When I work with a child with autism to teach them the "Hokey Pokey," I don't really care if they learn that specific song. I mean, it's a cute song, but who cares, right? The "Hokey Pokey" is just a tool to get a child to learn about imitation, facial expressions, and reciprocal communication. When they are watching a video of the "Hokey Pokey," none of that is happening; it is a one-way experience. There is nothing reciprocal about it.

Screens also appear in schools in ways that may seem totally innocuous. I once spent time in a first grade classroom where the teacher was using an iPad projector to read a book to her class. For those of you who aren't familiar with what that is, remember the overhead projections we had when we were kids? Well, they use iPads for that now. Instead of the students in the classroom watching their teacher as she read them the book, they were staring at the screen while listening to her voice read them the story. Is this experience the same as having a book read to them by a teacher? No, not really.

When children watch someone reach them a story, their eyes dart between the person and the story they are reading. They watch as the adult's voice and facial expressions change. They notice subtle expressions such as a raised eyebrow or a furrowed brow. They aren't just listening to a story. They are experiencing a story being told to them. And their teacher, licking her finger to flip the pages, widening her eyes to express a character's surprise, is a part of this experience.

When they are staring at a screen while their teacher's voice narrates a story to them...none of this is happening. It is just one more screen.

Here's what happened to human beings: We got really excited about our amazing phones and we forgot that human beings actually learn from other human beings. Screens are great tools for distracting children on airplanes. They aren't going to kill them. But we should remember that the most important learning for children still takes place face to face.

Get Off Your Phone

I'll admit it: I'm totally addicted to my phone. I show all the signs and symptoms. If I don't know where my phone is in my house, I have to go find it before I can settle down. I instinctually check Instagram every five seconds even though I know intellectually that all of social media is complete garbage. I get that little spike of dopamine when I get a new "like" on a post. I scroll through my newsfeed and click on headlines like *Celebrities You Didn't Know Were Dead.* I will read them for a good five minutes before remembering I don't give a shit.

We are all on our phones all the time, and it is horrible. Old people like to talk about "kids these days" and their texting and their Snapchat and their everything. But we are all guilty. As parents, we love to use our phones to take pictures. We need them to text each other funny anecdotes or to bitch about something another parent at the playground said. Also, it's soooooooo boring at the playground. Before I am even conscious I'm doing it, I'm reading a Buzzfeed article entitled *Justin Bieber Wore Hover Shoes and Now I'm Worried He Is Going to Die.* Meanwhile, Fritz attempts to go down a firefighter's pole and almost breaks an arm.

Can you imagine if he ended up in the ER and the doctor asked me, "Where were you while this three-year-old was attempting to slide down a firefighter's pole?" Well, doctor...I was three feet away reading a Buzzfeed article about Justin Bieber.

One consequence of being around small children all day is that you end up feeling bored a lot. I was born in 1984. They were born in 2014 and 2016. We just don't have that much to talk about.

So, there you are, feeling bored. And there is your phone, full of viral content and social media posts from people you knew in high school and now are semi-cyber stalking. Boredom is the devil's playground.

Hazel has started demanding, "Mom, put down your phone!" When she does this, I am immediately consumed with guilt.

"You're right!" I reply, and plug it in across the room.

In a few short years, our roles are going to be reversed and I am going to be demanding, "Hazel, put down your phone and talk to me!" And I will complain to my husband, "Teenagers and their goddamn devices." Even though this is all my fault.

New research is emerging showing how detrimental this kind of "distracted parenting" is to our children. It interrupts the regular back and forth flow we have with them. We are sitting on a couch cooing at our baby. Our baby is laughing and babbling back to us. We stop to check a text message. We lose the rhythm, and this back and forth parental exchange that is so essential to early learning is lost. For older children, it means our three-year-old has to ask us, "Mommy, what do snakes eat?" five times before we respond.[100]

I try to think about playtime with my kids the same way I think about driving. I know my phone is going to distract me, so I purposely put it across the room. When I'm driving, my phone helpfully puts itself in "Drive Mode," so I can't get any texts or calls and I have to click "Not Driving" before I can do anything on it.

Apple engineers, if you are reading this, here's a suggestion. Make a setting so that when iPhones detect the sounds of little children playing, they set themselves to "Playing with Kid" mode and no activity can be done. Then the user will have to click "I Am Not Playing with a Child" before they can access their phone.

Our phones are too addictive, and we are too weak to resist them. This is really the only solution.

---

100 And when we do respond, our answer is, "I have no goddamn idea. Let's ask Siri."

CHAPTER 20:

Don't Go There

It seems like a million years ago, but a former world leader was known for quoting, "The definition of insanity is doing the same thing over and over again and expecting different results." Not sure what world leader I am talking about? Hint: his name is not Trump.

When it comes to parenting, this is very good advice.

Sometimes, we are so determined that something is going to work that we try it over and over and over in the exact same way. And yet it still doesn't work. Shocker.

I went to see a lactation specialist when Hazel was two months old. That little baby was an amazing breast feeder, but she *refused* to take the bottle. I read that moms shouldn't give babies bottles, because then the baby will begin to prefer getting a bottle from mom and refuse to breastfeed. So, my husband was trying to give Hazel the bottle instead of me. However, for her first four months, Hazel would start crying every time my husband (or anyone else) even looked at her, let alone gave her a bottle. Clearly, this wasn't working. And yet, that was the advice my parenting books, Google searches, and friends were giving me, so I kept trying it.

The first thing the lactation specialist said was, "Well, that doesn't seem to be working, so let's try something else."

Oh, I thought, *you mean if the conventional parenting advice doesn't work, I can try something else?*

Yes. Yes, you can.

If it isn't working, just stop. Try something else. If your kid has a tantrum every time they go into a particular grocery store, what about not going there? If there is a way around it, take it. Because most likely, this problem won't last. Remember the key thing about development? It develops! So, maybe just wait until he decides to freak out about something completely different.

When I was a kid, my mom let us quit whatever activities we wanted. She was the opposite of one of those moms who always make you follow through when you make a commitment. My mom was more like, "I honestly don't care if you learn how to sculpt clay houses. Just don't do it if you don't feel like it."

The consequence of this is that I have a lifetime distaste for being scheduled to do things that don't seem mandatory. I have no problem going to work or to the gym, but I'm the last person you will see at, for example, a PTO meeting at Hazel's school to plan Fall Fest. My husband is the same way. Basically, neither one of us will ever voluntarily start a hobby or activity that involves meetings. Why go to a meeting? By choice?? We hate meetings.

I'm sure my propensity to quit things will affect my children in some terrible way. Hazel will no doubt complain to her friends in college, "I wish my mom had forced me to keep up with ballet. I would have been so good!"

I have no doubt future Hazel would have been an incredible ballerina had I not let her drop out after the third ballet class. But here's the thing.

That teacher was super mean! She yelled at the kids, she yelled at the parents, and no one wanted to be there. I had to rush from work to pick up Hazel in time to get her there, and then we had a terrible time. Why would I do that to myself?

Earlier in this book, I referenced the book *Stumbling on Happiness* by Daniel Gilbert. In it, Gilbert explains that basically we all suck at determining what decisions are going to make us happiest. When you decide to have your three-year-old suffer through a ballet class they hate, you are making the bet that it will be worth it because they will have learned ballet, or at least they will have learned the value of sticking to commitments. However, there is a good chance you will be wrong in this bet. The chances that they will grow up to be a prima ballerina are extremely low.[101] Even the chance that the child will stick with dance is low. So, you are sacrificing your and your child's current happiness for something that may or may not happen in the future. Being a parent is hard enough; you don't need the additional stress of dealing with the Cruella de Vil of dance instructors.

I'm not advocating that you drop out every time you have a bad experience. A few years after the ballet class referenced above, Hazel started dance with an amazing teacher. Even with this amazing teacher, she had a few days when she wasn't into it. I still made her go because I had faith in the teacher and the class, and I had faith that Hazel was just being lazy but would have fun when she got there.

Give yourself the allowance to drop out once in a while. I'm telling you, it's liberating.

---

101 Also, do you really want this for your kid?

CHAPTER 21:

Sometimes Toddlers Make Sense

I know this is a controversial thing to say, but: sometimes toddlers make sense. They are illogical so much of the time that it takes us by surprise when they act like rational human beings. I have a useful metaphor. Let's say you live with a terrible roommate. This roommate never does any dishes, leaves her stuff all over the house, and basically treats you like a human dish towel/vacuum cleaner. You do everything for this roommate and the only time she thanks you is when you demand a "thank you" from her for a service already rendered. Not only that, but when you mess up even the slightest in this service, this roommate screams at you, and often loses control of her muscles and limbs in the process. Sound familiar? Oh, yeah, and did I mention this roommate doesn't pay rent?

Then one day, out of the blue, you ask your roommate to explain her completely insane behavior, and she gives you a completely logical, well-thought-out answer. All of a sudden you think, *Oh my god, you mean there may have been a method behind this madness?*

Toddlers are so full of irrational, overwrought reactions that it can be hard to imagine some of them may come from a thoughtful, rational place. When you are having a particularly difficult day with your little hell raiser, it can even feel like the point of their behavior *is* to irritate and frustrate you. If you think about the toddler as a completely out of control roommate, it can help you understand why you find your child so frustrating at times. Our emotional reaction to our small children is understandable, when we view their behavior through the lens of a roommate. If an adult acted this way toward us, they would be out on the street within a month. Of course, the reason we still continue to house and feed our little children is because they are more than our roommates; they are our most loved and cherished creations. We know that logically. However, in the moment, it can be easy to forget this and feel just as frustrated, if not more, than you would feel about a terrible roommate.

My roommate, Hazel, likes to react to me like this whenever I ask her to do a chore:

Me: Hazel, can you please clean your room?

Hazel: Mooooooooom, it's not fair! Me and Fritz have to do everything for you.

The way we understand the behavior of our roommates and children all comes down to something called Theory of Mind. Theory of Mind is a mental health term that refers to human beings' ability to understand (or guess) what is in the mind of another person, and what thoughts and feelings might be driving their actions. This is a skill most human beings develop around seven to eight months. In babies, Theory of Mind is demonstrated through skills like pointing. When a baby points at an object he finds interesting, he is indicating not only that he is aware of the object, but that he is able to draw your attention to the object. One of the early indicators of autism is a lack of pointing. People on the autism spectrum struggle with Theory of Mind because they have a difficult time understanding other peoples' intentions. Similarly, Theory of Mind is difficult for people with mental health issues and personality disorders.

Everyone struggles with Theory of Mind sometimes. Our own feelings and reactions get in the way of us making good guesses about others' intentions. Let's pretend you say hi to your coworker in the morning and she doesn't respond right away. If you are a remarkably well-adjusted person with impeccable Theory of Mind, you might say, "I doubt Sandy is angry at me. She has no reason to be. Most likely, this is not about me. I know she has been struggling to get her son off to school in the morning, so she is probably just tired and frustrated. I'll check in with her later."

Depending on your level of confidence, your own personal feelings about Sandy, and the amount of sleep you got the night before, you might not be so well-adjusted in your response to this. You could easily feel hurt and assume the entire thing was about you. Many people who really struggle with Theory of Mind always think it is about them and *often* react irrationally as a result.

Let's say you immediately snapped at Sandy and said, "Why are you being so rude to me? It is *not* okay!" It isn't that your emotional response was that different from the person with good Theory of Mind. It would be normal for anyone to be upset about Sandy's rudeness. What was irrational was that you responded right away, rather than taking the time to think about it, or saying nothing because you were unsure. The better you are at Theory of Mind, the more you will be able to understand what is in the mind of another and also understand that you may *not* understand what is in their mind.

Which brings us back to your toddler. If you understand development and have good Theory of Mind, you know your toddler isn't acting up *because* she despises you and wants to drive you insane. You know her responses are those of an emotionally immature person who is less independent than she so desperately wishes to be. However, when we are in the moment with these small people, it is often difficult to access our own Theory of Mind about what they are going through and feeling, and how it might be affecting their reactions.

Which is why it is important to leave alive the possibility that sometimes toddlers make sense.

I know you still don't believe me that there is any logic to the madness of these little people. So, allow me to give you another example.

Hazel loved her preschool. She went every day, loved her teacher and her friends, and often asked to go on the weekends. Which is why I found it so frustrating when, for a period of about a month, she made it so difficult for me to leave her there in the morning. Hazel had a best friend called Lani. Every morning, Lani would come running across the room to see Hazel, shouting, "Hazel! Yay, you are here! Let's play!"

Hazel would then respond by hiding behind my leg and saying something terrible to Lani like, "No, Lani! I DON'T want to play with you!"

Terrible, right? Also, so weird, because the teachers told me that she and Lani played together all day every day, and every time I picked Hazel up from school she and Lani were giggling and acting like best friends.

This went on for months! Hazel would yell at Lani, and I would tell Hazel not to be mean to her friend. I would suggest ways they could play together. I would linger for an extra ten minutes each day, not wanting to leave until my little person was acting more normal. For months, we went through the same frustrating ritual every morning. I couldn't understand where Hazel was coming from. I have a pretty good understanding of how kids' brains operate, so I knew she wasn't actively trying to hurt Lani's feelings. But I didn't understand why she was doing this. It was starting to get on my nerves.

Then one morning on the way to school, I did the completely obvious thing I hadn't thought of doing in three months: I asked her about it.

"Hazel," I asked, expecting nothing, "why are you mean to Lani when I drop you off?"

"Because then mommy stays," Hazel answered without hesitation.

It all clicked. My reaction to the behavior was the cause of the behavior. When Hazel first started at that school, she would run up to Lani and give her a huge hug and they would run off together immediately. So, I would leave. But when she was mean to Lani, I lingered to resolve the situation. Logically, Hazel thought, *If I am mean to Lani, Mom stays. So, I should be mean to Lani.*

It is wonderful when your children can explain their logic to you. What I learned from this incident was always to just ask. Because who knows? Sometimes, a toddler will give you a completely sensible answer.

But of course, this is rare. Younger toddlers aren't verbal enough to explain themselves. Even the ones who are very verbal often don't understand their own reactions well enough to explain them. Most *adults* don't understand their reactions well enough to explain them. Which is why Theory of Mind is so important.

All behavior is communication. What is this child telling us with this tantrum? What is this behavior intending to show? This is really hard to do in the moment. Which is why sometimes the best immediate intervention is just to separate yourself from the child, so they can react and you can regain your sense of calm and avoid introducing your small child to a string of new four letter words.[102] When you do have the time and patience to do so, take a minute to ask your child why they were acting so crazy and see what answer you get. If you don't get a satisfactory answer (or any answer), use your Theory of Mind to put yourself within their world. Remember, this is not a grown-up with bad manners (like our imaginary terrible roommate); this is a person who

---

102 These words are not new to my children because I fucking suck at not swearing in front of them.

has only been on the planet for basically ten minutes. What could this person be experiencing?

The biggest gift we can give to the little irrational beings we live with is to assume they are indeed rational. Let us assume their behaviors and reactions are tied to actual feelings and the ways in which they understand the world. Then no matter how misguided their reactions are, we can help them to behave in ways that will solicit the reactions they are hoping for.

For Hazel, I ended up staying at her school a few more minutes in the morning, and starting our day sooner in order to do this. But instead of just staying there out of exasperation and annoyance, I told her I was staying purposefully to help her settle in. Gradually, she stopped being mean to poor Lani in the morning.

Making Sense to Toddlers

There is a phrase that people in the mental health field love to use: "Name what is in the room." It is useful in therapy and also, as it turns out, when you own a tiny human whom you don't want to turn into a psychopath.

Name what is in the room. If a client walks into your office angry and frustrated, rather than launching in to talking about whatever you talked about during your last session, name what is in the room: "I can't help but notice you are upset." It's an effective tactic. For one, it is jarring. People aren't used to being called out for their emotions. In our daily lives, we give off all sorts of vibes that no one ever calls us out on. Imagine if you were on the phone with someone from T-Mobile, just to pick a random example. And imagine the person is telling you that you cannot contact the fraud department because the fraud department doesn't have a phone number, email, or fax, and that if you need to get in touch with them you should write out a physical letter, put it in an envelope with a stamp, and hope for the best.

Okay, I lied. This is not a random example. This actually happened to me! T-Mobile's fraud department only communicates through snail mail!!!! There are two entities left on earth that operate this way: T-Mobile and Santa Claus.

Anyway, let's say you are on the phone with the customer service agent, getting increasingly agitated, and they say, "I can't help but notice you sound upset right now. Can we talk about that?" It's extremely jarring and also refreshing. Now, you can speak about the emotions you are experiencing. By talking about the emotions, you remove yourself from feeling them for a second and then you can take a step back and analyze them.

Turns out, this tactic works for children too. Naming what you think the child is experiencing is validating for them. This is a very common technique suggested by parenting coaches. It works well.

Babies start developing Theory of Mind at seven months. They are able to guess at the intentions of the adults around them. In a typically developing child, Theory of Mind develops like this:

Baby cries.
Parent says to the baby, "Oh, you are crying because you are hungry."
Baby begins to understand, "Oh, I am crying because I am hungry."
Baby feels hungry and knows that if she cries, the parent will provide food.
Baby sees another baby crying and thinks, *That baby is crying because she is hungry.*

Toddlers are constantly making guesses at why people are displaying the emotions they are displaying. Sometimes these guesses are really good: "The baby is crying because she is hungry." Sometimes the guesses are not so good: "The baby is crying because she wants to watch *Frozen*."

Young children do their best to understand the world around them using guesses based on their past experiences. There is no other way for them to learn about the world. Unfortunately, for toddlers, sometimes the way they make sense of their world can make them feel sad and scared.

Small children are actually very good at noticing emotions. They would have to be, right? It's a very basic survival instinct to know if someone is a nice person who is going to give them snacks, or a mean person who is going to withhold snacks...or worse. Children know when you are angry almost immediately. The trouble is, they sometimes don't understand why you are mad or how mad you are.

Irritation with small children often builds slowly over time. Let's say for example that a child wakes up and demands to have her hair put into pigtails. As soon as you are done putting pigtails in said hair, the child insists that you have done it incorrectly and demands to have her hair put in a ponytail instead. Then she demands cereal for breakfast. But you are out of cereal. She throws a fit about this. As soon as this fit is over, she starts demanding she wear her fancy princess dress to school, the one her younger brother spilled milk on the day before, which is still in the wash. Finally, you convince her to wear a suitable (if slightly less desired) princess dress. On the way to the car, the child begins whining that she forgot to bring her dolly with her and demands she be let back into the house to get it. When you finally make it into the car, this child drops her doll on the floor and wants you to pick it up before you start driving.

That is when you lose it. Not about the dolly, necessarily, but just about the entire frustrating morning. The problem is, the small child isn't aware that your frustration with her has been building for an hour, because you've been attempting to remain calm and use your I'm-a-rational-adult voice. So, to her, it appears as if you have suddenly become irrationally angry about her wanting you to pick up her dolly. She doesn't consider that you might be feeling frustrated because of the whole annoying morning. Instead, she is focused on who the anger is directed at: her. More often than not, small children tend to internalize these negative emotions and imagine that there is something wrong with them as people. They think, *Mommy hates me,* instead of, *I was a pain in the butt this morning.*

This way of thinking is referred to in the world of mental health as the "internal working model." This term was coined by the psychoanalyst John Bowlby to describe the way children see themselves and the world around them. For children who grow up in healthy circumstances (with love, attachment relationships, and their basic needs being met), their internal working model is that the world is a good place with good people. However, for children who experience trauma, abuse, and neglect during their early lives, their internal working model is very different. These children often unconsciously internalize feelings that the bad is within themselves. The psychoanalyst Ronald Fairbairn wrote: "It is better to be a sinner in a world ruled by God than to live in a world ruled by the Devil."[103] For small children, it is often less scary to feel that they are the bad ones who are causing bad things to happen. For better or for worse, small children are extremely egotistical by nature and assume they are the cause for the circumstances around them, whether these circumstances are good or bad.

Getting frustrated with a kid who has been a pain in the butt for an hour is not going to traumatize them and change their entire worldview. Children are resilient. However, it is important to think about Bowlby's work on attachment when thinking about how small children's brains work. To have accurate Theory of Mind about a two-year-old, you need to remember that the brain of a two-year-old is not going to operate like

103 W. Ronald and D. Fairbairn, "Theoretical And Experimental Aspects Of Psycho-Analysis," *British Journal of Medical Psychology* 25, no. 2-3 (1952): 66-67, https://doi.org/10.1111/j.2044-8341.1952.tb00794.x.

the brain of your terrible roommate. The two-year-old is most likely not going to think, *Ah, I'm being a little terror this morning*, or even, *Mommy is really losing her cool about nothing right now*. The two-year-old sees the emotion and reads it as anger directed at her. But she may not understand that the anger is about her actions, not the person she is. Without an explanation of this, the two-year-old is likely to internalize this emotion and think she is bad. She may get upset right back at you and set off a cycle of anger and frustration. Or even worse, she might just internalize the feeling that her mother doesn't like her or want to be around her.

So, what can we do? We can help our small children make sense of us and our emotions. We can explain to them right away what happened that made us mad, reiterating that the emotion is not about them but about their actions. We can end this interaction by reminding our child that we love *them*...even if they are annoying the living shit out of us.

The more we model this for our children, the more they will do it for us. If we can remember to ask them questions about why they are having the reactions they are having, eventually they will learn to answer those questions. Nine times out of ten, you will get some mindless answer that makes absolutely no sense like, "Bananas!" But on the tenth time, they may explain to you what they were thinking and why.

Will this work? I don't know. You will have to wait fifteen years and ask Hazel.

CHAPTER 22:

The LAAT (Little Asshole Assessment Tool)

A big part of my career has been learning, utilizing, and training people in developmental assessments. I have been trained to use about a dozen of these things and am familiar with a dozen more. They all have one thing in common: acronyms. So, when I set out to develop my own assessment tool, I knew the first thing I had to do was come up with a name and an easy to pronounce acronym. Therefore, I present to you the LAAT, pronounced LATE. The Little Asshole Assessment Tool. This easy to use, evidence-based[104] assessment tool was developed following over a decade of experience with Little Assholes (a.k.a. children). It is easy to administer, quick to score, and can help you determine if you have a normal child on your hands or a super compassionate and well-spoken Hollywood actress posing as a child.

---

104 By "evidence-based," I mean there is a lot of evidence to support the fact that young children are assholes. Have you ever been to a water park? Case closed.

Asshole behavior in young children is our collective dirty little secret. As parents we are all mortified when they do it, and yet we are dimly aware there is really nothing we can do about it. The truth is, asshole behavior isn't just a shitty side effect of being four years old; it's kind of the definition of being four years old. Developmentally, early childhood is a process of moving from a tiny, tiny little sucking nothing to a fully grown being who can walk out of a car, walk into a school carrying a backpack, and proceed to sit at a desk and learn how to read and write, all while using the bathroom independently, eating when hungry, drinking when thirsty, and knowing how to sneakily get away with all kinds of shit. It's pretty amazing, actually. And it only takes five years!

I would argue that one of the crucial ways in which a small speck of a human being goes from sleeping 80% of the time to functioning independently is through acting like a total asshole. Small children first have to figure out what their needs are (eating, sleeping, being snuggled) and then they have to figure out how to get those needs met. Then they have to figure out how to communicate to get those needs met, and then they need to figure out what other people's needs are and how to get other people's needs met (or if they even care). And they do all this while being smaller and less powerful than almost everyone else in their lives.

The behavior of small, spoiled children pisses us all off. Watching a two-year-old scream about wanting a banana peeled a specific way makes all of us think about the end of civilization. You don't have to be a crotchety old man to listen to that and think, *My parents would never have put up with any of this shit.* We all have that little voice in our heads pointing out that the screaming child is lucky just to *have* a banana, let alone to have it peeled. When my children demand snack after snack, I can't help but think how lucky they are to be so picky. If they had ever experienced genuine hunger in their lives, they wouldn't reject gummies because they don't have a picture of Scooby Doo on the front.

How many times have you heard this?

Child: Mom, I'm starving!

Mother: Okay. Do you want strawberries?

Child: No.

Mother: Granola bar?

Child: No.

Mother: Yogurt?

Child: What flavor do you have?

Mother: Cherry.

Child: No.

Mother: Apple Sauce?

Child: Is it in a container or a pouch?

Mother: Container.

Child: No.

Is that the behavior of a starving person? Or someone who has ever experienced genuine hunger? Absolutely not. It is the behavior of a Little Asshole.

Yes. Their behavior is completely irrational and intolerable. But also, what the fuck else are they supposed to do? Can you imagine living in a world where you were forced to eat shitty food you didn't like for every meal? Where you were denied access to the fridge because of some arbitrary rule called "bedtime"? Where you were forced into a bath even though you didn't *feel* dirty? Most of us wouldn't tolerate this shit for even a day. And small children put up with it for *years*! Think of the two-year-old standing in the middle of the airport screaming for his banana to be peeled correctly. He isn't a spoiled brat. He is a protester finally standing up to an evil regime. You are the regime! He is the resistance!

Another reason for the prevalence of asshole behavior in young children is that they don't yet know we are supposed to lie to one another. This is something my clients, many of whom have autism, have an even harder time with. A big part of living in society is lying. We either lie by omission (e.g. pretending we don't notice the big scars on other people's faces), or we lie just to make people feel better ("You look exactly like you did ten years ago!") For my clients with autism, this takes a very long time to teach. For typically developing young children, it starts to emerge around four or five but doesn't fully develop until way older... just before they turn into little assholes again when they hit puberty.

Hence, I created the LAAT, so you can see how your child is measuring up compared to his peers in terms of developmentally appropriate, evolutionary necessary asshole behavior.

Give one point for each positive answer:

1. Does your child refuse to share toys with another child unless coerced, threatened, or bribed?
2. Has your child ever loudly proclaimed in a public place, "Wow, Mommy, that lady is *fat*"?
3. Has your child ever told a grandparent that she liked a different grandparent better?
4. Has your child ever thrown a fit in public because you wouldn't buy them a stupid plastic toy?
5. Has your child ever told another child, "You can't play with me"?
6. Has your child ever told another child, "That shirt is ugly"?
7. Has your child ever told another child, "My mom is better than your mom"?
8. Has your child ever told another child, "You are not my friend anymore"?
9. Has your child ever bitten, pushed, kicked, hit, sat on, or put another child in a headlock?
10. Has your child ever responded to getting a present with "I don't like this"?

Scores between 8-10: Congratulations! You have a Little Asshole on your hands. The good news is that your child is completely normal. The bad news is that this behavior sucks and they will need to outgrow it if they want to be able to lead a normal life. On the other hand, if they *don't* outgrow it they will probably be rich and/or president. So, either way…good news!

Scores between 5-8: Your child has a few asshole tendencies but overall sounds like a pretty chill kid. Monitor closely.

Scores under 5: Beware! You may not have a real child on your hands! Is your child secretly reciting lines from a movie script written by a childless twenty-eight-year-old man?

So, what do you do if you have a Little Asshole on your hands? Just because this behavior is totally normal doesn't mean it doesn't suck. It does suck. You can build compassion in your child. You can ask your child questions like, "How do you think that made him feel?" Most children don't want to hurt other people's feelings. The goal isn't to hurt the person's feelings; it is just an unwanted side effect. You can build compassion by getting their brain going. Hopefully, at some point in the future, you won't have to do this and they will think on their own, *I don't want to say that because that will hurt his feelings.*

Name the behavior you don't like. Explain why you don't like it. Talk about it ad nauseum, but talk about it when your kid is listening, not when he's throwing a tantrum. "You sound spoiled when you scream at me to buy you a toy." What is it that you don't like about the behavior and why? You can explain this to a four-year-old; you just have to put it in four-year-old-friendly language. If you don't have the language, someone out there does. I guarantee you, there is a children's book about it, and it most likely features a llama.

DO NOT BUY HIM THE TOY WHEN HE IS SCREAMING! I cannot emphasize this enough. Do not give a screaming child what he wants. Ever. Even once. They are like elephants that way. A child who has screamed and gotten what he wants will remember that scream and that reward forever. That same child won't remember what he ate for a snack that day. But he will remember that he screamed and Mom gave in.

Lastly, wait. The child will change. Do not stay up worrying about this for hours. Do not talk to your partner about this behavior until he's ready to shoot himself. Don't do internet research until four in the morning. The Little Asshole will grow up. Hopefully not into a Big Asshole.

CHAPTER 23:

Five Non-Annoying Things You Can Do to Help with Development

One of the most annoying things you can do to parents is giving them extraneous tasks to help their young children learn.[105] Like you don't have enough going on, now you have to bend over backwards to ensure your two-year-old will get into Harvard. First of all, Harvard doesn't even accept two-year-olds.[106] Secondly, you don't need to reinvent the wheel. Helping young children with their development is about doing less rather than doing more.

To make this easy on you, here are five non-annoying things you can do to make your child smarter.

---

105 FYI this is why 2020 was the fucking worst. STOP SENDING ME LINKS TO VIRTUAL LEARNING OPPORTUNITIES!

106 haha

1. Get rid of half the toys.

Toys are fruit flies. One day, you only have a couple. Seemingly overnight, your house is filled with eighty-five million. How does this happen? Simple. Your child has, what, three aunts, four uncles, four grandparents, two teachers, and three complementary aunties? That's already sixteen people who give them a toy when they were born, at every birthday, for Christmas, Chanukah, and on and on and on. And then the only way you can get out of Walgreens is by buying them that stupid pink unicorn.[107] And goodie bags!

The issue is that your child has a terrible attention span. When they are in a room with eighty-five toys, their natural inclination is to jump from toy to toy in a matter of seconds. They are literally a kid in a candy shop. They want to look at *everything*. But the result is that they only look at each toy for a few seconds without playing with it. You want to encourage your child to pay attention to one activity for at least five minutes before moving on. That way, the child has time to figure out what the toy is supposed to do. Fewer toys means your child has to be creative with what they have. It encourages combining toys and problem solving.

Find a day when you have no children with you and nothing else on your agenda. Yeah, I know, when has that ever happened? Well, you might have to schedule it! When the day arrives, take every single toy in your house and put them on the floor. Sort them by type of toy. If you are anything like me, you will suddenly find you have nine plastic cars, four play phones, five princess wands, three tiaras, and eight million tiny plastic unicorns. Sort out two or three of each of these. It is probably a good idea to have at least two of each if you have two kids. Then take the most undesirable ones and either chuck or donate them. Take the remaining items and put them in a storage bin. So, it should look like this:

-Two cars for the toy room

---

107 Didn't I just tell you not to buy them the stupid plastic toy?

-Two cars to donate

-Two cars for the storage bin

Obviously, some hard choices will have to be made. But you can do it! Remember, you are the grown-up. Not that little person who makes all the decisions in your life. At the end of this project, you should have half as many toys as before. The toys you put in storage should go where the kids can't have access. Then a few months from now (you know, when you next have a day off), you can take those toys out of storage and swap them out with the toys in the toy bin. And wow! Brand new toys! This keeps things fresh and exciting without promoting that kid-in-a-candy-store craziness.

Here's another thing you can do while you are sorting: put all the puzzles and games on a shelf. If the kid needs help to play with it, don't put it in the toy bin. This will just lead to strewn puzzles pieces everywhere. You want to encourage more deliberate and purposeful play.

WARNING: be careful what you throw away. During one of my purges a few years ago, I threw away Hazel's pink princess Ariel phone. If I'm being diplomatic, I will say that it was a total piece of crap. It was some cheap piece of plastic she had gotten at Goodwill. When you pressed a button, it played "Part of Your World" in a terrible high-pitched tone. It was the kind of toy that makes my husband go, "What is that noise and how can we make it stop immediately???!!" So, I chucked it. I didn't think anything of it at the time, because Hazel had about four other plastic phones. Well…it was a bad move. That happened four years ago and she still brings it up. I'll be like, Hazel, make a wish on your birthday cake. And she will whisper, super soft and sad, "All I want for my birthday is my Ariel phone back…"

Also, I may or may not have indirectly blamed the disappearance of her Ariel phone on President Trump. I didn't *exactly* say that he took her phone…but I didn't deny it either.[108]

108 Unforeseen benefits of living in the Trump era.

2. Get rid of all the buttons and batteries.

I know this is going to shock you, but people are trying to make money off of your kid. One way they do this is by creating these dumb, gadgety, talky, button-pushing, battery-requiring toys. They are cool, sure. But what makes them cool comes from the toy itself, not from the child. Hazel has a dollhouse with a million of these dumb buttons in it. You press a button to hear the bathtub running, another button for when the "cookies are done," etc. When she plays with it, she just plays all the games the house wants her to play. It doesn't encourage her own imagination and creativity. The house is the thing being creative and interesting, not Hazel.

Kids don't need much to create a game. Small children have limitless imaginations. When Hazel decides her dolly needs to take a nap, she finds the closest dish towel, book, shirt, whatever, and pretends it is a blanket. She usually doesn't rush into her room and grab her specific "dolly blanket." Adults are the ones who are literal and boring. We want to put the cute doll-sized blanket on the doll. Small children don't have this need. They just want to imagine the baby is sleeping with a blanket. It works for them.

To encourage imaginary and explorative play for your kids, simplify their toy chest. Get rid of all or most of the talky-battery-buttony toys and replace them with simple toys. Stuffed animals and dolls. Toy trucks that don't make noise. A simple toy kitchen. LEGO bricks and magnet blocks. Play-Doh. Those are all toys that rely on the child to make up a game. And your child will! The more you can give them the tools rather than the answers, the more they will create things rather than just press buttons.

3. Sit them at the table.

Some small children seem to have a motor attached to them. These are generally the kiddos whom we see for early intervention services. All two-year-olds are active, but some of them are *very* active! These kids especially benefit from being sat at a table a few times a day to play. Obviously, don't strap down your wailing eighteen-month-old and force him to complete a puzzle. That's just mean and pointless. But when he is ready and interested, maybe when he is finishing a meal, leave him at the table and introduce an interesting activity. This encourages him to play with one toy or game for longer and more in depth, rather than running from toy to toy.

4. Let them do a terrible job.

What is the most common phrase you hear your toddler say? I mean other than "Ha ha! Poop!" I'm guessing it is, "I want to do it myself!" Toddlers' desire to do things on their own vastly outweighs their abilities. They are the least competent, most confident people on the planet.[109] Every day they can do new things, and they find this incredibly exciting and rewarding. They become more competent every day. However, they still pretty much suck at everything.

Especially when you are rushing out of the house, rushing to get ready, rushing to leave the museum, and rushing out of the car, their suckiness at everything can really get to you. Watching paint dry is a more rewarding and less frustrating experience than watching Fritz walk down the street by himself when we are trying to get somewhere. Most of us live such busy lives that we get used to going through life that way. Then all of a sudden, it is Saturday and we have nowhere at all to be but we are still acting like if we don't get out of the house in the next five minutes the whole place will burn to the ground. And the toddler wants to put on their own shoes, or butter their own bread, or pour their own juice. But they are so bad at it that it is frustrating to watch.

---

109 Not exactly true. One politician in particular comes through as a shining example of confident incompetence.

When I let my kids do things on their own, I feel like I'm doing the task three times. It goes like this:

I buckle Fritz's car seat. "NO!" he yells. "I want to do it myself!"

I unbuckle it. I stand there watching him attempt to buckle it.

Two minutes later, I say, "Okay, Fritz, you tried but you couldn't do it. Now I will do it." And I buckle it again while he screams at me.

It isn't that you actually did the task three times, but your brain just ran through it three times.

After this brief exchange, I have completely forgotten where we are even going in the car and I'm asking myself if I should just go back inside and give up on the day.

When it's Saturday, when you have the time, let them do a terrible job. The juice will spill everywhere. The shoes will go on the wrong feet. They will pee on the floor. You will buckle and unbuckle the car seat. They probably won't do any damage that a roll of paper towels can't fix. By making mistakes, kids learn how to do things better. By showing them you believe in their competence, you are demonstrating your faith and trust in them.

5. Use visuals.

One of the most important things I have learned from working with children with autism is the importance of using visuals to teach things. Visuals are great to use for non-autistic kids as well. Children under five have a difficult time with executive functioning and with understanding time. They struggle with figuring out how to do a task they want to do. They struggle with understanding how long it will take, or when it needs to happen. Giving kids visual schedules helps them manage this.

"You will be going on an airplane in two weeks" is meaningless to a young child. They will likely hound you every day for the next two weeks about when they are going. My brother and sister-in-law solved this problem with my niece Maggie by never telling her information ahead of time. The last time she came to California, she found out the night before the trip.[110]

For some kids, though, not knowing the information ahead of time creates anxiety. Rather than telling the child "two weeks," you can take out a calendar and mark the days off with X's. That gives the child a visual understanding of what "two weeks" means.

A task like getting ready in the morning is often too complicated to be done without cues. Using a visual schedule helps to break down all the steps. Ideally, you won't need to use these schedules forever. You can just use them until they are no longer needed and then phase them out.

Of course, there are plenty more things you can do. Should you enroll your child in a reading class before she starts kindergarten? Should you reduce screen time to twenty minutes per week? In the age of the internet, we can find a million tips about what we should be doing to help our children. There are think pieces about think pieces about this.

Here's what you need to remember: your relationship with your child is the most important thing in his life. If you are killing yourself to drive him to swim class and then once you get to swim class he whines and cries and still doesn't know how to swim even after months of trying? Maybe you don't need swim class. You should be able to help with your child's development within the natural routine of your life. Because if you are stretching yourself, and it isn't fun and enjoyable to you, it probably won't be for them either.

110 My brother Lev has three kids and he's boss like that.

CHAPTER 24:

Children's Books I Despise and Ones I Love

There is a difference between bad children's books and good children's books. Some children's books are pieces of garbage that you should throw out immediately. Others are fine. Some are masterpieces that you and your child will read over and over, and that you will remember into adulthood. I have dedicated this chapter to helping you decipher between these two categories.

It is hard to write a good children's book because it is for two audiences. You have to create a book that adults will want to read without wanting to bang their heads on the table, and you have to tell a story that is stimulating to children.

I have in front of me a children's book called Sewing Stories: *Harriet Powers' Journey from Slave to Artist*. When I first received this book in the mail, I thought to myself, *Oh, cool, an inspiring story about a historical figure who gets no recognition in traditional history textbooks.* Then I started reading it to my four-year-old. Here's a snippet:

"Strong-limbed Harriet helped the women sew. Afterwards, she danced at the frolic. Horsehair fiddles, cheese-box tambourines, and sheep-bone drums formed the band. If Armsted Powers could capture Harriet beneath a quilt, he could claim a hug and a kiss! Harriet slowed her pace, just a bit. Sure enough, Armsted caught her with a story."[111]

Keep in mind: this is a children's book. You know, illustrations with limited text on each page. It's for CHILDREN WHO CAN'T YET READ. Children who ostensibly live in the twenty-first century. What the hell is a cheese-box tambourine? Also, what is going on with this non-consensual-seeming encounter between Harriet and Armsted?

I'm not trying to pick on this well-meaning children's book; it just happened to be the one in front of me when I started to write this. It is an example of an entire genre of children's books that drive me completely crazy. There are several categories of such books.

Bad Children's Books

The "Who Is This For?" Bad Children's Book

These are books that pretend to be written for children but are actually written for adults. If you think you have one of these books on your hands, ask yourself this question: "Does my child like or understand or enjoy this book?" If the book uses the phrase "cheese-box tambourine" or is titled *A is for Anarchist*, then the answer to that question is probably no.

These books are often written and illustrated by people who think a certain person or topic should be made into a children's book because the topic doesn't get enough attention, or because they think the children's parents will think it is cute. These books are generally bought "for the child" by the child's parents, aunties, or grandparents for the purpose of

---

111 Barbara Herkert and Vanessa Brantley-Newton, *Sewing Stories: Harriet Powers' Journey from Slave to Artist*, (New York: Random House Children's, 2015), 4.

being cute or teaching the child something "important." For example, that the word Zapatista starts with a Z. The books are then read to the child once…or maybe not even once if the child has exceptional taste. These books are always well-meaning, but that doesn't stop them from annoying the hell out of me. I find it insulting that anyone would write children's books for an audience other than actual children. Is nothing sacred?

The Nauseatingly Cute Bad Children's Book

Stop trying to be so goddamn cute. I have one book on my shelf that is about a little girl trying to find the perfect gift for her mom's birthday. The little girl in this book looks about three years old. Like every three-year-old girl, she is totally consumed with the needs and feelings of others. Right? Because that's normal. Anyway, she has a dream in which she is abducted by the sun and the moon. Which sounds horrible, but in the book, it is a good thing. Being with the sun and the moon inspires her to pick beautiful flowers for her mommy's birthday. I hate this book and whenever my daughter picks it out (by accident—she won't admit it, but she also hates it), I try to talk her into something else. It is just so trite and unrelatable. It is a book about a totally sweet and uncomplicated little girl having no complicated feelings at all about her love for her mother or her mother's birthday. Don't waste my time with that crap. A normal three-year-old is just wondering if there is going to be cake and will most likely ask if she is going to be getting any presents.

The 1,2,3 or ABC Labeling Book

There are roughly two million children's books that involve counting and the alphabet. Counting and alphabet books have an important role to play. We need children to learn the alphabet and learn to count. Otherwise, how will they ever be able to read a menu and pay for an espresso! But there are just too many of these books. And they are soooooooooooo boring.

Any parent will know what I am talking about. One duck, two ducks, eight fucking ducks. A is for Apple, B is for Banana, C is for I'm going to Crucify myself if I have to go all the way to Z. There are tons of books that make counting and learning the ABCs super fun, silly, and enjoyable for everyone. So, we really don't need all five billion of these boring ones. Parenting is a tough enough job. We don't want people to feel damn near suicidal while going through the alphabet for the ten millionth time.

Children's Books by Famous People

Celebrities love writing children's books. And publishers love to publish them. Here is an incomplete list of famous people who have written children's books: Madonna, Jay Leno, Barack Obama, Dave Eggers, Jim Carrie, John Travolta[112], Chelsea Clinton, Ricky Gervais… and literally everyone else who has ever become famous for anything.

I understand why celebrities do this. It's a lot easier to write a children's book than to write an adult book, or make a podcast, or a new movie, or whatever else celebrities do. I imagine these self-indulgent people sitting around their houses, maybe with children and maybe without, and coming up with an idea for a bear who is looking for a picnic basket. The celebrity thinks, *That would make a great children's book!* They scrawl it down on a piece of paper, call their agent, and a month later they have made money off it because for some reason people like buying children's books by celebrities. Not me. I refuse.

My mom used to illustrate children's books. Which is probably why I find the whole celebrity children's book author thing irritating. It's an insult to people who do this for a living. Mo Willems doesn't try to be president or host the Emmy's, does he? Stay in your lane, celebrities.

112 Creepy, right?

Just because you are good at doing stand-up doesn't mean you are good at creating literature for children. It isn't the same skill set. Also, it takes literally no effort to come up with a mediocre children's story. I make up stories for my kids while answering work emails. It isn't hard to write a bad children's book. And I'm sorry to say this, but most of these celebrities' books are bad. Not all of them, though! Keep reading to find out which celebrity wrote a fantastic children's book.

Good Children's Books

Despite how unnecessarily cruel I was in the above pages about bad children's books, I really love children's books. Reading books to small children is one of the most important things you can do as a parent or educator. Eventually, we want these human beings to read, so they can go to college, have jobs, and most importantly, text each other witty anecdotes about encounters they had at Trader Joe's. Even more important than reading are the lessons that children's books can teach us. Really good children's books teach crucial lessons about human behavior and what is happening in the minds of other people. Children relate to the characters in these books, their feelings, the situations they are in, and how those characters responded to those situations. Through interacting with these characters, children think about how they can act when they encounter similar situations. The good books do this using subtlety and wit. The really good books are entertaining to parents as well. And the great books also have cool pictures.

The classic children's books have already won tons of deserved awards and received accolades. This includes everything by Dr. Seuss, Maurice Sendak, and Margaret Wise Brown. Here are some of my favorites that you may not have heard of:

***Llama Llama Books* by Anna Dewdney:** The best thing about these books is that Llama Llama is an imperfect child. He throws a tantrum at a grocery store. And his friend is a bully who never truly redeems himself. Llama Llama has complicated emotional reactions to situations that all kids find themselves in. His mom is perfect (which is annoying), but he is anything but. The pictures are beautiful and the books rhyme.

I Want My Hat Back **(and the other Hat books) by Jon Klassen:** These books are hilarious to children and adults. The books do something interesting where they include visual information that isn't in the text. In *I Want My Hat Back*, the rabbit is wearing the bear's hat, but the text doesn't talk about it. This gives the child the opportunity to say, "Hey, there is the hat!" Not only is this fun for the kid, but it also encourages them to engage with stories by looking for visual clues that are subtle and aren't named. That's a skill that will help them interpret real life situations as well.

This Is a Ball **by Beck and Matt Stanton,** *The Monster at the End of This Book* **by Jon Stone,** *The Book with No Pictures* **by B.J. Novak,** *Splat!* **by John Burgerman, and** *Press Here* **by Hervé Tullet:** I said I would give a celebrity credit where credit is due and I have. *The Book with No Pictures* is by the actor and writer BJ Novak. Mr. Novak, you have my permission to write children's books. His book and the rest of these listed here are awesome for the same reason. They put the children listening to the book in a powerful role. *In The Monster at the End of This Book*, the child is flipping the pages even though Elmo, and the adult reading, are telling the child not to. *In The Book with No Pictures*, the adult pretends they are in the helpless role of having to read things they don't want to read. *This Is a Ball* has a similar shtick. These books are hilarious and joyful and fun, and this is the #1 reason they are awesome, because everyone reading is having a good time (and no one is suicidal). *Press Here* and *Splat!* allow the child to engage with the book physically by pressing the pages together to move the story forward. In these books, the child is the one driving the reading experience. They feel powerful!

***A Day in the Life of Marlon Bundo* by Jill Twiss, *Rosie Revere Engineer and Sofia Valdez, Future Prez* by Andrea Beaty**: Children's books that are designed for the sole purpose of teaching a child an important life lesson are terrible. Children see right through them. They *know* they are being taught something valuable and they don't like it. However, there are some incredible children's books out there that promote women in leadership roles (like the Rosie Revere and Sofia Valdez books) in fun, playful, powerful ways. They teach valuable lessons, but they are also smart and funny and well-illustrated. I cannot possibly explain the backstory to the book *A Day in the Life of Marlon Bundo*, so I will just say briefly that it is a funny, tender children's book that promotes tolerance through the narrative arc of a gay bunny.

***Pig and Elephant and everything else* by Mo Willems:** These books are simple, funny and have only a few words on each page. Mo Willems books taught my daughter how to read. He also created weekly online content for kids during the first few weeks of the pandemic, where he read to them and taught them how to draw. For both of these things, I am entirely grateful.

How to Read a Book to a Child

Not to brag, but I am amazing at reading books to children. Some people are great at chemistry, some people know how to calculate a tip without using their cell phone, some people can change a tire…some people know the difference between a tire and a wheel![113] I can't do any of those things, but what I can do is read books to small children. What most grown-ups don't realize is that it isn't actually about *reading* the book. The kid doesn't care that much about hearing every goddamn

---

113 A man working at a Tire Repair Shop once asked me if my wheel was broken or my tire. Up until that moment, I had thought they were the same thing.

word. Have you ever read *Peter Rabbit* to a child? Like, actually read it? Two-thirds of those stories are words no one has spoken out loud for a century. She spends whole paragraphs describing the geometry of how a bunny got into the back of a chimney. Best to skim some of that. But the stories in *Peter Rabbit* are timeless.

Feel free to summarize. Feel free to go off on a tangent. Feel free to discuss "where does rain come from?" for twenty minutes in the middle of a story. Reading books to children shouldn't be about reading. It should be about storytelling. Use silly voices. Summarize. If the kid can't read themselves yet, skip. Feel free to do whatever you want except be boring. *Please* don't be boring. And you really need to throw away all your stupid pointless children's books, because I guarantee that book will be the one your snotty little two-year-old is going to grab for story time.

CHAPTER 25:

Strangers Taking Care of Your Baby

Dr. Bruce Perry is a psychiatrist and giant in the field of infant-mental health. His work on child trauma is revolutionary and is currently helping to reconstruct how society thinks about the brains of tiny humans. I went to see him speak a few years ago and was blown away by almost everything he said. Almost.

At some point in his lecture, Dr. Perry went off on a tangent criticizing childcare in this country. He wasn't only criticizing the quality of childcare in the US, which as a whole is subpar; he was criticizing the *existence* of childcare for little children. Dr. Perry argued that the practice of having three to eight tiny people cared for by one adult is fairly new. He ruminated about how for thousands of years, little human beings existed in societies where they had lots and lots of adults around, and therefore got lots of attention from several adults, rather than having to share one adult with seven other toddlers. Dr. Perry alluded to how the destruction of the middle class is partially to blame for this, as parents need two incomes to survive.

I sat in the audience for this lecture, nodding my head in almost total agreement with him except not quite. I agree that the destruction of the middle class in this country is to blame for families needing two incomes. The high cost of childcare prevents most people from being able to afford a one-on-one nanny or even a small quality daycare experience. When unveiling her plan for universal childcare during the 2019 democratic primary, Elizabeth Warren[114] pointed out how the dilemma with the contemporary childcare system is that most families can't afford quality childcare and most childcare workers aren't paid a living wage. So yeah, the whole system is fucked up. I agree with Dr. Perry about that. But still, as I sat there pregnant while my two-year-old was in preschool, I couldn't help thinking, *Thanks, Dr. Perry, for making moms feel even more guilty than they already do.*

Every parent I know who has their child in daycare feels guilty about it. Additionally, every parent without childcare is convinced that their child is missing out on valuable learning opportunities. And when everyone's childcare disappeared in the Spring of 2020, we *all* felt like shit. Moms and dads who stay home with their little ones are often stressed about money and about what kind of effect taking a few years off will have on their future job prospects. These parents often feel almost embarrassed when they say they aren't working, like their lives are boring and meaningless. On the other hand, parents who have their children in daycare feel guilty for missing out on meaningful moments and feel bad because they would rather work than play with dolls all day.

The ideal solution to this problem is what Senator Elizabeth Warren experienced. Her great aunt came to visit and stayed for twelve years to take care of her children. In a lot of cultures, this is standard practice. I semi-jokingly asked my mom to do this and her answer was basically,

---

114 In a just world, it would be President Elizabeth Warren.

"Hell no." I work with a lot of families where the grandparents take care of the kids. There are issues with this too! Parents feel guilty that Grandma doesn't have the energy to be doing this and that she isn't providing the children with all the stimulating activities they should be getting at that age. Or they feel guilty because Grandma completely uprooted her life. Or families love the shit out of Grandma...but she also drives them completely insane. And so, they live in a constant state of guilt about that.

Let's talk about the price of childcare in the United States in the 21st Century. When we had two kids in daycare, and Fritz only going three days a week, we spent $2,000 a month on childcare. That's $24,000 a year...JUST ON CHILDCARE! Yes, this is in the expensive Bay Area, but childcare prices aren't that much lower in other parts of the country. When I was in Germany, I casually asked someone how much Germans pay for state-subsidized childcare. They pay between 100 and 150 euros a month. That's around $2000 a year!

We have state-subsidized childcare in this country, mainly through Head Start programs. However, this is only available if you are extremely low income. A friend who worked for Head Start explained to me roughly how the income qualification for the program breaks down in San Francisco. For a family of three, only one parent can work making minimum wage to qualify for Head Start. If the parent makes more than minimum wage, or if both parents work, the family is too high income to qualify. What this means is that in the state of California, we don't provide free childcare for families where two parents make minimum wage.

I hate it here.

You are damned if you do and damned if you don't. Modern parents are fucked. And I agree with Dr. Perry; we could be doing a lot better as a society by providing our little ones with quality, affordable childcare. But I also want to point out that the need for two incomes isn't the only reason more kids are going into daycare. More kids are in daycare now than a hundred years ago because of *options*! Because there are many, many moms out there who *want* to work. Who have the opportunity to work. And we need to remember this and not take it for granted. Because you never know when we are going to overthink ourselves into a *Handmaid's Tale* sort of reality. So yes, more adults per child. But also, our moms fought really hard to have the opportunity not to stay at home. Let's not take this for granted.

So, should you stay home with your child? Should you go to work? If you do work, who should look after your kid? Is it worth paying three times as much for a better preschool? Or is an okay preschool going to be fine for your kid?

Here's my answer to all of this: it depends.

I have been doing clinical work with families in San Francisco for over a decade. I see kids wherever they are: homes, playgrounds, afterschool programs, malls, and schools. Sometimes I feel like I have visited every preschool in the Bay Area. To save you the trouble of doing this too, I'll share my findings.

The Best Preschool in the World

If I were to design the best preschool in the world, what would it look like? It would have a huge outdoor space for kids to run around in. The day would have a regular schedule so kids knew what to expect. The toys would be imaginative and promote creativity. Reggio Emilio preschools do a great job with this. I visited a Reggio Emilio preschool in San Francisco where all the toys were essentially rocks and sticks. It was awesome! Small children can do anything with a stick. What they don't need are a bunch of plastic things with buttons that you press. Kids thrive when they have a lot of space and time to play. Small children shouldn't be stuck inside for six hours at a time, sitting at tables doing worksheets and writing their names. They will learn to write! They don't have to do it when they are two. I love schools that have organized short circle times throughout the day. Children should get lots of experience with sitting and focusing and listening with a group of kids. There should be a clear behavioral plan and a system for following it. The worst thing you can do to a three-year-old is say, "That behavior is unacceptable," but then do nothing about it. At a lot of preschools, children are required to get each other ice packs when they hurt one another. I love this! The offending child takes care of the child they injured. This builds compassion and accountability.

The Best Preschool Teacher in the World

I have met the best preschool teacher in the world. Her name is Teacher Phoenix. She has red hair, rosy cheeks, and she is the best at what she does. I first met Teacher Phoenix when she was my daughter's preschool teacher. I was anxious about Hazel transitioning to a new school. Hazel was nervous about it too. But then Hazel *fell in love* with Phoenix. She was warm and loving and always ready to give a hug. She was creative and energetic. When I dropped Hazel off on St. Patrick's Day, the kids ran over to Hazel yelling, "A leprechaun came! A leprechaun came! And he used the bathroom!" Phoenix had shown up early to work and painted little green footprints leading into the bathroom and on the toilet seat. What a hero.

After meeting Phoenix, Hazel started saying she wanted to be a teacher when she grew up. Whenever she made Fritz play school with her, she pretended to be Teacher Phoenix. Hazel was devastated when Phoenix left for a new job. She talked about Phoenix for a year after she left. I didn't know where Teacher Phoenix went, and I wanted to thank her.

A year later, I walked into a preschool for a child observation and there was Teacher Phoenix! She was working as a mainstream preschool teacher in a classroom that included kids with special needs. Once I watched her in action at that school, I knew it was official. She was the best preschool teacher in the world. In addition to being warm, energetic, friendly, and sweet, Phoenix was firm. She was never mean. She never raised her voice. She never sounded exasperated or frustrated or tired. But from the tone she used with the four-year-olds, they knew that whatever she was telling them, that was what they had to do. When she gave an instruction, she expected it to be followed. She would wait patiently. She would provide additional instruction. If needed, she would acknowledge the child's feelings. But one way or the other, if she told you to clean up the blocks, you were cleaning up the goddamn blocks. My client thrived in her classroom, the same way my daughter had.

Phoenix's boss, if you are reading this, please give her a goddamn raise. Whatever you are paying her, it isn't enough.

How to Find the Perfect Preschool for Your Child

Preschoolers respond best to that magic combination of warmth and firmness that teachers like Phoenix have mastered. Most young children respond well to structure, and flexibility within that structure. They respond well to routine. They like to know what the day is going to look like. But the school doesn't have to be rigid to the point of inflexibility. Children benefit from the morning circle, snack, tabletop, and outside time routine of a typical preschool. A school with warm but firm teachers, with plenty of fun indoor/outdoor activities, structure, circle time, and some focus on numbers/letters/animals is probably going to be a good fit for most kids.

Within these adequate preschool programs, there is a scale of most structured to least structured. In typical preschoolers, there is also a scale between needing more structure and needing less structure. Kids struggle when their tolerance and need for structure is out of alignment with the school they attend. Here are some examples:

Co-ops

In case you don't live in the Bay Area, let me explain to you what a co-op is. A co-op is a "school" where instead of paying teachers to teach, they use parents as indentured servants. Instead of "teaching" children, they let them run around stabbing each other with sticks. Instead of telling them to stop, they encourage them to make better choices.

I apologize for the above paragraph. That was rude.

I have visited lots of co-op preschools and known lots of families with kids at co-op preschools who are very happy with their children's experiences. Preschool is insanely expensive, and co-ops are a low-cost way for parents to get a little free time and for kids to have some social time. They are wonderful for building communities, for teaching parents new skills and for giving children space and time to meet each other and socialize. For typical children, who don't have developmental delays or need lots of structure, these schools can be fantastic.

They aren't for everyone. The co-op model means that most of the "teachers" at these schools are parents, with no teaching or childcare background whatsoever. Being a parent to your own child does not qualify you to teach other children around the same age. In fact, it may *disqualify* you because you may make the logical fallacy of thinking that because your child behaves a certain way, so do all the other kids. Of course, a lot of the parents who teach at co-ops do have their own professional experience with children. But that is just a coincidence, and not a prerequisite to running circle time or pushing kids on the swings or whatever else they do when they are supposedly teaching. Most co-ops have a few actual teachers and then use parents instead of hiring more staff. This works out fine for a lot of kids who just need play time. For kids who require structure or additional pre-academic instruction, this is not the best fit.

I have seen a lot of children struggle in these settings. These are kids who need a Teacher Phoenix to give them an instruction and stick by it.

Or kids who need extra help joining in with a group of kids playing. Not just children with developmental delays, but any children who thrive with structure have a hard time with this unstructured model. When this happens, it is challenging for parents who believe in the co-op model, who can't afford anything else, or who had their heart set on being a part of the co-op community. Co-ops generally believe in more relaxed rules and discipline, and are slow to say that a program might not be a good fit for every child. I have gently suggested to many families that they look for a different school. Some kids will thrive anywhere, but some kids need a bit more.

Worksheet Schools

Worksheet schools are the opposites of co-ops. These are the schools that believe in the drill and kill model of learning. Those. Kids. Will. Learn. To. Read. These are preschool programs that are heavily academic, where children spend most of their day engaging in structured activities: circle time, worksheets, etc. These schools teach children how to follow directions, how to follow through and complete a task, and how to read and use beginning math skills. For some kids, this is a good fit. These are generally smart kids who aren't that defiant in nature and don't struggle with following directions and learning new skills. These are good schools for kids who don't need to run around like puppies for half the day.

My son Fritz needs to spend most of his waking life jumping off things. My daughter is very independent and self-directed. Both of them would probably hate schools like this. If kids are self-directed, stubborn, natural leaders but not good followers, they will probably struggle. Let them play for a few years. They will get there.

What to Do When Your Kid's School Sucks

Get them out. Obviously. Find a better fit. Pay more money. Move across town. Move out of town. Quit your job. Sell your house. Get them out of there.

But what if you can't? Obviously, if you are taking the time to read this book, you love your kids and you want what is best for them. And if your instinct is telling you their preschool sucks, you should take them out. When Fritzi was three months old, we put him in a home daycare that seemed fine at first. Then I showed up a few weeks into him being there and realized it was terrible. He never went back. I took a week off work, my mother-in-law helped out, and we found a place that was great for him (where he learned to love spicy food!).

Unfortunately, this is not always an option. Maybe the only childcare in town is the one your child goes to. Or you feel like it isn't the best fit in the world but there isn't another option. Or there is another option, but it costs twice as much. The school where Teacher Phoenix teaches costs three times as much as the one my kids go to. On the one hand, I know how important early education is. 80% of brain development takes place in the first five years! On the other hand, $4000 a month!!!

If leaving isn't an option…there's another option. Talk to the school. Tell them about your concerns! The worst feeling in the world is dropping your child off somewhere that sucks, or where they aren't happy. It sucks for everyone—for you because you feel like an asshole, and for your child because they are miserable. But also, it sucks for the childcare provider that they are failing to satisfy you. Taking care of children is a thankless, low-paying job. It's very challenging for childcare centers to retain quality workers. Teachers are underpaid, undertrained, overburdened, and overstressed. The last thing they need is to be told by a parent that they are sucking at their job.

Therefore, as soon as you are unhappy with the childcare being provided, you should rush into the director's office unannounced and berate them aggressively in front of their staff. That usually goes over well.

No! Don't do that!

People don't change because someone yelled at them. If they did, we wouldn't have so many stickers stuck to our walls, and the floor of the bathroom wouldn't be leaking through to the garage because of the amount of bath water it has endured. Also, my husband's dirty socks wouldn't be on the floor in the living room. People make changes within the context of relationships. Whether in our children, in ourselves, in our husbands, or in the teachers and professionals we interact with every day, change is built on a platform of respect and collaboration. People make changes in their behavior when they feel understood and sympathized with. If people are under attack (i.e. a parent has just barged into their office accusing them of child abuse), their brain immediately goes into fight or flight mode. Either they are going to yell back at you or they are going to cower under their desk until you go away and then complain about you to their coworkers. Either way, your kid isn't going to get a better outcome.

Remember, even if you are right, you are still an asshole.

I recently worked with a parent of a child with autism who was attending a summer camp. The child was very high functioning but struggled with social dynamics in new environments. The parent showed up on the first day of camp and without introducing himself, he marched up to the camp director and began telling her everything she had to do to make sure his daughter had a good experience. Later that day, his daughter was having a rough time, and he got a call to go pick her up. He showed back up at the camp and started banging aggressively at the front door until they let him in. He started screaming, "You need to keep her busy!" and, "You can't expect her to follow transitions easily!" He started berating them without any conversation of what they could do to help her within the structure of camp. For this father, all that mattered was his own child's happiness. But a camp has sixty kids' happiness to worry about. The camp staff wanted to help her, but they were stumped on how to do so without more constructive guidance.

I have over twelve years of experience working as a social worker, and I can tell you—angry, rude, disrespectful parents do *not* get the best treatment. To be clear, I have not seen providers give parents subpar treatment because of their behavior. Most providers care too much about the children to do that. But here is the reality. The parents who are super sweet and respectful, those are the ones who get the icing on the cake. As a social worker, you can meet the expectations of care or you can go above and beyond. There is always an extra email you can send to that amazing speech therapist in Half Moon Bay who usually doesn't take new clients but will maaaaybe make one little exception. There is always that extra twenty minutes you can spend with a new behavioral therapist to make sure he really understands all his new client's goals. All providers who work with children (teachers, social workers, camp counselors) are extremely busy and overworked. Who gets the little bit of extra time at the end of the week? The parent with the very nice manners who wrote them an extremely polite email.

How to Write That Extremely Polite Email

My kids have attended a local childcare since they were two years old. I like most of the teachers, they have a lot of free time to play outside, and it is super close to my house. Maybe it isn't the most amazing preschool in the universe (see above where I explained that I'm not a fucking millionaire), but they are happy there. I have no intention of removing them from the school. However, a few years ago, there was one thing that really bothered me: movies.

It started out as "Movie Friday." It was something the kids looked forward to all week and was probably a good way to bribe them into behaving. Obviously, I would rather have my kids play catch, read books, or cut stars out of paper, but still, movies on Fridays was not a big deal. Then I started noticing the kids watching movies at other times during the week. Once I went in the middle of the day and heard an exhausted teacher say, "All right, guys, I'll put on a movie for you." Putting a movie on because you are exhausted is a right reserved only for parents and teenage babysitters. No one else! I know two-year-olds are annoying and exhausting...but literally your one job is to play with them. The research is in! No one is learning anything from a Mickey Mouse DVD from twenty years ago.

I mentioned my concern to the site director, but she wasn't particularly receptive. So, I decided to write an email. What follows is the email I wanted to write and then the email I actually *did* write.

The Email I Wanted to Write
Dear Daycare,

Are you fucking kidding me? Have you had your head buried in the sand for the past ten years? Screens are bad for children's brains! 80% of brain development happens in the first five years, and you want my kids to spend half of that precious time watching *Spiderman* on DVD? Come on now. At the very least, try to find something educational like Dora. At least Dora speaks Spanish!

I work all day and when I get home, I have to make dinner, clean up after everyone, do laundry, give the kids a bath, clean up again, respond to some work emails, respond to 700,000 texts from my mom, and then put the kids to bed. I don't want to stick my kids in front of the television, but sometimes, I have to. You have no excuse! Your one job is to make sure these little people don't kill each other when they all try to get Mr. Potato Head at the same time. Why can't you just do a circle time where you read a few books and then talk about the seasons? Then have one child volunteer to check the weather outside and come back to report that it is cloudy and windy. Then do an art activity where you make clouds out of cotton balls. Then do a sensory motor activity where children pretend to run through the wind using a fan and long colorful ribbons. Is that so hard!?

I'm paying you people to form neural connections in my child's brain that will determine their ability to reason, regulate, and think for the rest of their life. And you are wasting time showing them the original *Dumbo* (racist depictions of black people and all.) I'm pulling my kid out of this goddamn school on Monday if you don't stop this shit immediately.

Respectfully,

Michelle

The Email I Actually Wrote

Dear Daycare,

I am a parent of a child at your school, Hazel, who has been attending since she was two. For the most part, we have been happy at your daycare. Hazel loves her teachers and we are thinking of sending our son Fritz there when he turns two.

I haven't turned in his application yet and did want to check in about one thing before we did. I know they have "Movie Friday" at school, but I have noticed teachers putting on movies for kids at other times as well. We try to limit screen time for Hazel, so I have been disturbed by this. I have actually checked in with a few other families about this as well, and they were also concerned. I mentioned it to the teacher, and she said they put on movies after parties when the kids are riled up. But this isn't written as part of their curriculum. I'm wondering if this is part of the daycare structure and if it is happening at the other sites? We would think about moving Hazel to a different childcare site if this doesn't happen there. We love Mrs. X and the other teachers and this is the one thing that upsets us. I would like to suggest that movies only be shown on Friday afternoons as written in the curriculum.

On an unrelated note, I actually work in the field of child development and have worked in early childhood mental health for ten years, so I would love to offer my help for free in any way I can to help the daycare with staff training or consultation.

Respectfully,

Michelle

What Happened Next

A happy ending. The Director wrote back almost immediately telling me they did not want children watching screens all day and would discuss it with the teachers. It has been over a year since the incident occurred and now they only watch movies on Friday afternoons...much to the dismay of Fritz, Hazel, and probably all the other little ones.

I thought the fight was over and I had won. But as always, I had only won that particular battle, to benefit that particular child at that particular time in her life. A few months later, Hazel started Transitional Kindergarten and went to a new after-school program. On the first day, the teacher handed me a copy of the weekly schedule. I read: "Mondays: Screen Day." Every Monday the kids were expected to bring in their iPads and watch them for, I guess, the entire day. I work from home about half of the time, and so if I wanted Hazel to watch an iPad for half the day, I could just leave her at home. Do teachers think they are the only ones who have discovered that if you put children in front of screens you don't have to deal with them? This is somehow a revelation. Yes, I *know* if you tell my child she can have a screen in an hour she will behave like a total angel and then once you give her the iPad you won't hear from her for the rest of the day. I am also aware of the existence of YouTube. We are trying our damnedest not to turn our children into the cowboy kid from *Charlie and The Chocolate Factory*. You would think that a city-run after-school program would agree with that.

I did my absolute best I-am-a-reasonable-parent-and-you-can-work-with-me song and dance for them. I went and met with the Director and stated my case. Screens are bad for children's brains. Can you please not ask my child to bring an iPad to school? The Director assured me that she totally agreed with me and that the Monday Screen Day was only for the summer and not for the fall. She said she would open up a discussion of screen time with all the childcare programs during their next team meeting. I left the office feeling hopeful.

For the next two months, every time I showed up, Hazel was playing with a few other kids in the classroom while half the kids huddled around video games. It would be a sunny day and the kids would be inside watching each other play video games. Hazel wasn't usually participating in this activity. She was bored and had nothing to do. One day, I picked her up and she was painting with watercolor on a piece of computer paper. The paper was totally soaked through and the table was wet.

I recognize that this wasn't some expensive after-school program for rich kids (which in the Bay Area is anyone with an annual salary of over a million.) This was a city-funded program. But still. Come on, people. I had tried my best to do the reasonable parent thing and it didn't work.

I moved Hazel to a new program. She was bummed for one day. The new after-school program was great. They spent all their time outside playing. Everything was going great until the global pandemic came and ended childhood as we know it.

You should try to negotiate. You should try to be reasonable. But sometimes, you just have to get your kid out of there.

The Most Important Thing

When parents ask me about my kids preschool, I sometimes don't know how ot answer. I can't give them a glowing answer. I know more than the average Jo about preschools, and I know their preschool isn't the best school in the world. The do a lot of dumb worksheets. They watch movies on Fridays. They bribe the kids into napping. Some of the teachers are old school and yell at the kids. As mentioned, I've been to 99% of the the preschools in the Bay Area,[115] so I can say unequivocally, it isn't the best. I have a lot of moments in the past four years when I have thought to myself, should I find a new school? I'm an *expert* on child development for God sake, shouldn't I be finding the best possible school, even if it does cost $4000 a month.

But then something will happen. Something like, Fritz's teacher will tell me how much she loves Star Wars just like Fritz. Or Hazel will come with to pick up Fritzi and his teachers will coo over her, "Hazel, you have gotten so big! We missed you so much!"

COVID-19 restrictions do not allow parents to enter preschools. Parents are in the bizarre position of not being able to see inside the classrooms their children go into everyday. Now, more than ever before, trust is a crucial ingredient in my relationship with my children's care. I know these teachers and I trust them. I trust them to love my little Fritzi, who they have known for two years. I know that as human beings, beyond even their capacity as his teachers, they love my little guy.

That is the secret ingredient to quality childcare. Find people who love your children. The rest will come.

---

115 Give or take.

CHAPTER 26:

A Love Letter to Childcare

Disclaimer: A version of this was originally published as a blog post on San Francisco Bay Area Moms[116]

During my local school board meeting in the summer of 2020, a representative of the teacher's union spoke emotionally about her fear of returning to in-person teaching. "I want to go back into the classroom more than anything...but it is not safe to do so," she lamented. "In what other profession are people being asked to stay indoors, for eight hour a day, in close proximity to others?" Safely muted over Zoom, I answered her rhetorical question, "Childcare."

I agreed with the decision of my school district not to reopen. But it was impossible to ignore a glaring inconsistency. Schools weren't safe for teachers...and yet childcare centers were safe for workers? Schools throughout the Bay Area started the 2020 school year in distance learning. Meanwhile childcare centers reopened in July 2020.

---

116 The blog post can be found here: https://sanfrancisco.momcollective.com/childcare/a-love-letter-to-childcare-workers/

The pandemic drew attention to so much glaring inequality in our society. This was just one of many examples. Childcare workers, who are primarily low-income women of color, were forced onto the front lines of this pandemic even as K-12 teachers stayed home. For those of us who work in the childcare industry, this wasn't particularly surprising. If anything, it was expected. The devaluing of this workforce is rooted in sexism, racism and classism. The pandemic shone a spotlight on our preconceptions of these workers and this work. It also spotlighted something even more basic. Our devaluation of a word embedded in the name for this work force: "caring."

There is a push in the world of early childhood to take the world "childcare" out of circulation. Instead, we use terms like "early education" and "preschools." The words "education" and "school" in and of themselves hold power. We automatically respect the notion of "teaching," and "educating." Meanwhile, words like "caring" "tending" and "babysitting" intrinsically hold less value. The push towards high quality early education is important. But also, we cannot let this language overpower the far less glamorous--and I would argue more important--job of childcare workers.

75-80% of brain development happens in the first five years of life. By the time children start Kindergarten, their brains are essentially complete. Young children are social beings and they learn through *positive adult relationships*. Many children spend up to fifty hours per week in childcare. Those facts alone should convince any rational person that working in a daycare is the most important job in the world. And yet the work of a childcare provider is largely invisible. Because the work of these (mostly women of color) looks exactly like the work that has been considered valueless for most of human history.

So I want to say, to the teachers at my son's childcare, who have loved and cared for him for two years already: I see you. I see the way you tenderly hold his hand and lead him inside when he's feeling nervous.

How you joke with me about his Star Wars obsession. To the teachers I work with, I see how well you know these children. How you tell me, "I don't think that strategy will work for her...she only likes to transition outside when she gets to be the leader."

The quiet, beautiful, invisible, unassuming everyday work of childcare workers is this: blowing bubbles in anticipation of a child having a difficult time at drop off. Celebrating when an eleven-month-old takes her first steps. You *know* these babies. You rejoice at their victories, delight at their mischief, problem solve around their challenges. The children see themselves reflected in your eyes and they know that they are cared for and loved. Your students blossom within this love. Everyday their brains grow and shape *within* a relationship with you.

Our society doesn't value this work because this is the work of caring. We don't value this work for the same reason that most Americans don't get paid maternity leave. That nurses are paid less than doctors. That social workers are paid less than police officers. We don't see "caring" as valuable.

Ten years ago, I was a new social worker full of big ideas but without a lot of experience. I sat with a wealthy tech executive in his mansion in Palo Alto talking to him about his child with special needs. "Thank you," he told me, his eyes watering, "for helping us with the most precious thing in our lives...our little boy."

I was new to this work. I was underpaid and overworked, and I was still learning my job. Most of the time, I felt like I was learning as I went. But I cared about the children on my caseload and their families. I cared about them deeply, and they could tell. My caring was everything.

In 2020, our childcare workers are putting their lives at risk every day. A lot has been written about how much our economy relies on childcare. But it is more than that. These workers aren't just important because they make it possible for Americans to go to work. Childcare centers are not storage units for America's children. They are growing the brains of the future.

To all the childcare workers on the front lines: thank you for caring for our most precious thing: our children. My hope is that as a society, we will also care for you.

CHAPTER 27:

How to Feel Guilty While Also Sucking at Your Job (a.k.a. Being a Working Mom)

For a check in at a work meeting, a manager asked everyone to go around the room and say one thing they have been excelling at. Almost everyone I worked with at the time was in their 20s and didn't have kids yet. My coworkers said things like, "I've been doing a lot better with my progress reports," and, "I've been better at creating effective Behavioral Support Plans."

When it came to me, I said, "I basically feel like any day I get to work on time after dropping off two children at two separate locations, I should be given a medal before I even open my laptop."

Man…if there were any justice in this world, every working parent would get a standing ovation when they walked through the door of their office.

The above visual is a picture of my kids "eating breakfast."

I have worked for most of the time I have had children. I've had times when I was on leave and other times when I worked only a few days a week. I've had times when I worked from home once or twice a week while caring for my kids. And then 2020 happened and I found myself working from home full-time with zero childcare. This involved putting myself on mute during a conference call so I could pry a pizza cutter out of a chubby little hand. This involved conducting a Zoom training and a backyard scavenger hunt *at the same time*. This involved forcing my children to take two-hour baths so I could complete a work project. This involved screaming at my husband at 3:30 p.m. every day when he got home, "Okay!!! Your turn!! I have supervision calls!"

During the four months that I did this, I kept thinking two things:

.   1. I cannot believe how hard this is. This is so incredibly, incredibly difficult, how am I pulling this off? How is ANYONE pulling this off?

And....

.   2. This is crazy hard...but actually...it has always been crazy hard.

Being home with my kids for four months and working simultaneously was crazy-making. But it also wasn't new. As a working mother, I have had to do this insane balancing act since day one. In a way, it was nice to have society finally acknowledge it. Suddenly, it was acceptable and normal to work from home, to have children in the background on Zoom calls. People knew I didn't have a choice. I will always treasure those months when it was just the three of us, all day every day, even though it was breathtakingly insane.

What made the quarantine work + childcare mash up so challenging was that my brain had to do two completely different things at the same time, so I ended up doing them both badly. I like working. And I like being with my kids. But working at the same time as being with my kids is like trying to drive and cook simultaneously. Actually, that's a bad metaphor because cooking and driving are both things I am terrible at. It was like writing and running simultaneously. You end up being a slow runner, and the writing isn't that great either.

When I was home during my second maternity leave, I felt like brain cells were leaking out of my ear holes. If this is your life, you will know that if you spend all your time with small children, you genuinely forget how to talk to adults. I love my children. They are the silliest, most fun people in the world, but after day three of hanging out with them, I can no longer fake an interest in knock-knock jokes. I found that after a few days of non-stop kid time, I wasn't having fun anymore. I wasn't being the mom I wanted to be. I was turning into the cranky, distracted version of myself.

When things are normal and I'm not involved in some sort of state-wide quarantine, I work during the week and Saturdays are preserved as my day to take my kids on adventures. When Saturday rolls around, I'm excited to be with them. I can tell knock-knock jokes without audibly groaning and I can push them on the tire swing for up to ten minutes without completely losing my mind. The most important thing in my life is the quality time I spend with my kids. It is better for me and for them to have one hour of super engaged adult play time than eight hours of me checking my Outlook and telling them I have to go into a Zoom Meeting. After months of quarantine, Hazel (and the rest of the nation) has become extremely triggered by the words, "I have a Zoom meeting."

I like working. I like using my brain to figure things out and using my mouth to have conversations that include words like "reflective practice." Also, our family doesn't have a choice. We live in the Bay Area, where a square of sidewalk rents for $1500 a night. Unless someone in your family invented an app that schedules your dog's massage for you, most families here need two incomes.

Because being a working mom is right for me, I'm going to go ahead and assume it is right for everyone and that if you choose to stay home with your kids you are lazy, boring, and stupid.

JUST KIDDING!

I know plenty of men and women who stay home with their kids and are amazing, intelligent, wonderful people who made a decision that works for them. Do I judge them? No.[117] Do I kind of envy them? Yes. Do they make me feel guilty about my life choices? No. It isn't their fault I feel guilty about my life choices. I'm sure that would happen no matter what I did.

So many mornings as we are all getting ready for work/school, one of my children has said, "I don't want to go to school! School is terrible!

---

117 Kind of.

I want to stay home with you!" Having your child tell you they don't want to get dropped off somewhere and would rather stay home with you is the working parent's worst nightmare. There are countless times that one little person or the other little person has thrown a tantrum as I walked out the door of their daycare or preschool. Then I spend half my day guilt-ridden, trying to decide if I should quit my job. Inevitably, when I go to pick up this child at the end of the day, she is perfectly happy playing princesses with her friends and refuses to go home.

Working and having children felt like being on a daily emotional rollercoaster even before COVID-19 hit. That feeling when you drop your kid off at daycare on July 5th and they are the only one in the classroom because every other parent has taken their child on vacation or let them stay home? That feeling sucks. And it will never go away. I'm sure Hazel and Fritz will include it in the memoir they write about me someday: "I was always sitting there on July 5th and December 26th with one other lonely child and a half-empty cup of broken crayons with the papers torn off."[118]

Now that my kids are back at school, I'm in the same emotional rollercoaster I have always been in. I love being with my kids and I hate the thought that I'm missing out on so many amazing, hilarious moments with them. But it is quality and not quantity that matters. Sure, Hazel probably says some truly hilarious shit at school that I will never hear or know about. Fritz probably has some adorable giggle fits. Even though I adore kids more than basically anything else (Broadway musicals are a close second), there is only so much I can take. When they were with me all day, I missed out on magical moments because I was too bored or stressed out to listen.

Rather than focusing on how much time I spend with my kids, I consider what I'm doing during the time I have with them. It's so easy

118 Hazel's memoir about me will either be titled *Where Is the Cap to That Goddamn Marker?* or *Please Wipe That Schmutz Off Your Face.*

to slip into a trap where I come home from work and immediately start doing dishes, laundry, making dinner, giving them a bath, and putting them to bed. Then their entire experience of me is equivalent to a voice in a loudspeaker saying, "Take off your shoes. Brush your teeth. Don't draw on the table. Don't throw a ball at my head. Don't, don't, don't, don't." Even I get sick of hearing myself. Most nights, I don't have two hours to spend building a magnet blocks castle. Our lives are busy. But what I do have is forty minutes, each day, to sit and play with my kids. That forty minutes of completely engaged play is more meaningful than the six hours of distracted, annoyed, bored time I would be spending with them if I were home with them all day. I know myself. I know that I can only take so many demanded and then half eaten and then discarded snacks before I completely lose my mind.

When I talk to working parents about spending time with their kids, this is the suggestion I make. Do you have forty minutes a day for uninterrupted child-directed play? What are you, Oprah? Of course, you do! Spend forty minutes completely, totally, fully immersed in a princess tea party, in throwing a frisbee, in drawing a unicorn, or in making a house out of a cardboard box. And then you can go back to doing the dishes or watching Rachel Maddow explain the end of democracy (or whatever it is you like to do in your spare time).

CHAPTER 28:

Teaching a Child How to Swim/Do Anything

One of the most amazing experiences I have had as a parent was watching Hazel learn to swim. Before we had children, my husband and I assumed we would teach her ourselves. You know, teach her to swim, puree our own baby food, take her on hikes.[119] All those notions expecting parents come up with. Adorable!

Naturally, growing up across the street from Ocean Beach in San Francisco, Hazel was terrified of water until age four. This fear was only intensified by Jeff jumping into a swimming pool with her on his shoulders in an attempt to show her that being underwater wasn't that bad.

So, at age four we enrolled her in swim classes at our local swim school. Hazel marched up to her swim teacher on that first day and announced, "Hello, I'm Hazel and I'm not going underwater."

---

119 After four months of quarantine, my kids are traumatized by the word "hike."

Her swim teacher reacted immediately, saying, "Okay, Hazel. No problem! We're going to have so much fun today."

Two weeks later, Hazel was putting her face in the water. Four weeks later, she was holding her breath underwater. Two months of once a week, half-hour swim lessons later, that little girl was swimming.

How did this happen? First of all, that swim school has that shit dialed in. I was extremely nervous about signing Hazel up for classes. Mostly because I didn't want to pay $30 a week to have her sit around splashing her feet in the water. When I talked to the site director about this, he basically told me, "Chill, lady. A strong-willed four-year-old who is afraid of water? What, you think we haven't seen that before? Please."

I spend my professional life thinking about how children learn. So, I found the process of Hazel learning how to swim fascinating to watch. The children start off wearing inner tubes and floating around the pool. Then they float one by one under a foam tunnel with holes in it. Then the swim instructor pours water on top of the tunnel while they are going under it so water splashes over their heads. Then they spend some time without their inner tubes on, kicking and experimenting with putting their faces in the water. If a child refuses to put their face in the water, they are encouraged but not forced. The child who refuses to put his face in the water watches his or her peers getting lots of praise and encouragement. Eventually, he decides he may as well do it too. As soon as he puts his face in the water, he is applauded like he won an Academy Award.

Within a few classes, all the kids have mastered that first step to swimming. The process continues like this, with children being gently encouraged through play and fun to move one more step forward, every step of the way. When a child gains a new skill, they receive a sticker. When they get to the next swimming level, they get a ribbon. Parents applaud every sticker and buy ice cream for every new level.[120] Gradually, children go from not swimming to swimming.

Watching it felt like watching a miracle. But the process is incredibly simple. Children learn to swim when they see the steps broken down into smaller steps (scaffolding) and when each step is reinforced with tangible reinforcement (stickers and ribbons) as well as intangible reinforcement (social praise). Children are further reinforced through the spoken and unspoken praise of their peers. New skills are taught through fun and play, rather than through terrorizing them (i.e. the old "sink or swim" approach). The swim teachers are all young, dynamic, caring adults who are skilled in their craft (i.e. they know how to swim). It is so simple that it seems silly to be amazed by it. And yet, it was breathtaking to watch.

One of the reasons I found the process so amazing to watch is that it is a super simple version of a problem I face in my work and personal life every day. How do you teach a child a new skill? How do you teach a new skill that is more complicated and invisible than swimming? The skills I teach the kids I work with are harder to see, harder to examine, and way, way harder to teach. Like joining in a group of kids playing on the playground. Or recognizing when you hurt someone's feelings. But watching Hazel learn to swim reminded me that is actually the way children learn. So, why don't we teach the harder, squishier, more emotional things using this simple method?

If we taught a child to regulate their emotions the same way we teach them how to swim, what would that look like? Right now, here's how most of us attempt to teach our children to regulate their emotions:

"FRITZ, STOP CRYING! USE YOUR WORDS!"

Which is essentially the emotional equivalent of throwing him into a freezing cold pool. Right now, he doesn't know how to regulate his emotions. He doesn't yet have that skill. But we don't think about

---

120 I don't think the ice cream part is an official part of the program. But it's pretty obvious that this is what should happen. Isn't that the sole reason that ice cream exists? To celebrate children's accomplishments?

children's emotions the same way we think about learning how to swim. We generally don't think about these skills as something they have to *learn*. We think about them as something they have to *stop*. This would be like if instead of teaching Hazel to swim I tried to teach her how to stop drowning. It is easier to teach someone to do something than to teach someone to stop doing something.

What if we used the same principles that work for teaching a child how to swim, to teach them how to do something much more nuanced? Like regulating their emotions, or sharing a toy with a sibling, or explaining their feelings instead of throwing a tantrum.

Remove the Power Struggle

The best way to win a fight with a child is to not have it. If they know they are in a fight with you, they will want to win it. Of course, they'll win! They are little and you are big and you want something from them and they know it. Of course, they are going to withhold, because then they have all the power. Have you ever gotten into a fight with your significant other about something that you knew you were *totally* right about? When they text you to apologize, do you text them back right away? Or do you make them sit and stew because you have all the power? You let them sit there and wait for your text! Of course, you do! That's our kids; they have the power, and they know it.

So, how do you win a fight with a three-year-old? Make them think you aren't fighting with them. We spent a year trying to get Hazel to put her face in the water and she wouldn't. On her first day of swimming, she announced to her teacher that she wasn't going under the water and her teacher responded with a shrug. It totally threw Hazel off her game. She was ready for a fight. But her teacher responded as if the last thing she wanted was for Hazel to go in the water. That "okay, whatever" paired with a shrug was incredibly powerful for our little warrior. When she realized there wasn't going to be a fight, she decided she may as well just have fun.

Make Learning Fun

Before we took Hazel to the magical swim class that actually taught her how to swim, we took her to a bad swim class that didn't teach her how to swim. The main problem with the first swim class was that the water was freezing cold. From the moment she got into the water, she was totally miserable. Of course, she wasn't going to swim! It wasn't fun!

This issue of things being fun comes up all the time in my professional life. Therapists will complain to me about their clients not making progress with their goals, or being unfocused and whiny during sessions. So, I will observe the sessions. And I will spot the problem within the first five minutes. I'm always extremely diplomatic with my feedback, but what I want to say is: "James. You aren't fun! I am so bored sitting during your sessions. Look at your client! He's losing his mind. Of course, he isn't following one-step directions. He wants to kill himself!"

Adults are able to learn a lot from very un-fun situations. I just watched a three-hour-long PowerPoint about the Assessment of Functional Living Skills and I have never been so bored in my life. However, I did learn a lot. For children, especially young children, play is their work and you are going to have far more success teaching them something if it is fun.

Hazel's swim class has figured out how to break down every single little skill into its core components and teach it in a fun way. They have a little song or a dance or a toy that goes along with every little part of learning how to swim. No wonder she learned so quickly!

Scaffolding

I was about to explain what scaffolding is to you. Then I realized that I didn't know the exact definition, so I Googled it. Then I was going to type what I had just Googled onto this page, but make it sound like I was super familiar with the definition and its origin, and not like I just Googled it and plopped it on the page. Then I decided to just cut and paste it here so you can see for yourself:

I am not exaggerating when I tell you that I was shocked that this came up when I Googled "scaffolding." I am so immersed in the world of early childhood I forgot that "scaffolding" has a meaning outside of education. I know this makes me sound like a woman in *The Stepford Wives*, but my husband is out of town right now and I'm waiting for him to come back to change a lightbulb for me.[121] I know a lot about a few things...and very little about a lot of things.

Turns out, "scaffolding" is a helpful metaphor. Scaffolds hold up a structure before it is strong enough to stand on its own. That is what we are doing with our children when we teach them a new skill. In swimming, you should *not* throw your child into the pool. Instead, you should gradually give them more and more freedom in the water, while holding them to make sure they don't sink, until they are able to hold themselves. When you are teaching a child to read, you shouldn't hand them an entire book and say, "Go for it." Instead, read to them, and have them read a few words on their own, until over time they are good enough readers to read on their own. A skill should be taught bit by bit, gradually loosening the support until the child can do it independently.

---

121 If you marry an electrician you never have to change another lightbulb, right? That's the deal?

Most people don't hand four-year-olds *War and Peace* and most people (other than my husband) don't dunk two-year-olds in the pool. But most of us *do* tell our children to stop crying, to calm down, to stop freaking out, without putting scaffolding up to support this skill they don't yet have. When you give your child a hug, that is emotional scaffolding. When you make guesses about what is wrong—"Is it because you are feeling shy?"—rather than telling them to go play, that is emotional scaffolding. For some reason, we expect these emotional skills just to blossom in children. Like one morning they will wake up and realize, "Oh yes, my syrup touching my pancake before I have dipped my pancake in my syrup is a normal part of human existence and definitely not worth screaming about."

But that isn't going to happen. They will get there. But the more you can support them along the way, the less likely it is they will collapse in a pile of bricks on the sidewalk...that metaphor really fell apart in the end.

Positive Peer Pressure

Young children respond extremely well to positive peer pressure. That is why they are willing to put their faces in the water after they have seen other kids do it. That is also why they are more likely to follow directions at preschool than they are at home. Positive peer pressure is a force you can use as leverage to teach your child better emotional functioning skills. This process happens naturally when they start school. It is a sad fact, but second graders are less likely than third graders to wear a pirate costume to school. Kids tend to make each other better. And they also make each other less interesting.

How can positive peer pressure help you teach your child emotional skills? Kids handle difficult situations like pros all the time, and they don't usually get credit for it. Give them credit! When you see children in books and movies using their words instead of throwing tantrums, point that out to your child. When you see this behavior in a classmate or friend, make note of it. You don't have to say to your child, "Wow, Henry didn't even cry when his mom left. You would have had a complete meltdown." Instead you can say to Henry, "Great job saying goodbye to Mom without crying! I could tell you were upset but you handled that really well!"

You can elicit your child's help in noticing positive behavior in their peers. You can have them comment on each other's behavior: "Tell Fritz he is doing a great job listening!" It isn't that helpful to turn your child into a snitch[122] who notices every time another kid is crying. But helping them to notice and encourage good behavior in peers can be helpful.

Tangible and Intangible Reinforcement

Tangible reinforcement is when you give a child an object or food after they exhibit a wanted behavior. In Hazel's swim class, the kids get ribbons and stickers when they learn new skills. If you have potty trained a child, you have probably used tangible reinforcement. If you have gotten a child to eat a vegetable, you have probably used tangible reinforcement, saying something like, "If you eat two bites of broccoli, you can have ice cream." Tangible reinforcement in parenting is extremely common. Sometimes it is referred to as bribing. Same thing, fancier phrase.

Tangible reinforcement gets a bad rep sometimes. We want children to want to behave well. For the sake of it. Not just because they get something in the end. I understand that in principle. Adding tangible reinforcements doesn't mean we don't ultimately want the child to do the behavior without the reinforcement. Most adults will eat broccoli even if they aren't getting ice cream after dinner.

Tangible reinforcement can build habits that eventually are reinforced by themselves. This works. I have seen this happen with clients and with

---

122 Jeff taught Hazel "snitches get stitches" and now every day I live in fear that she will say that to someone at school.

my own kids. It works for potty training and doing chores. But it can also work for social behavior.

Give me a break, you're probably thinking. *I'm not going to bribe my kid into being a good citizen. That doesn't sound like a good idea.*

Hear me out:

We eventually want children to do all kinds of skills, from using the bathroom to helping out a friend in need, without receiving any tangible reinforcement. We don't want eight-year-olds to expect an M&M every time they help us carry something in from the car. Eight-year-olds help us in part because of the intangible reinforcement they receive. Intangible reinforcement is any kind of praise the child gets, or even just the feeling of satisfaction they receive. Intangible reinforcement is the reason any of us do anything. We don't need to be complimented anytime we help someone (although it is nice); sometimes it is enough just to feel that warmth of knowing we did the right thing.

Fritz and Hazel have a "helper jar." Every time they help me with anything, I put a pom pom in the jar. When the jar fills up, I buy them a small toy. The helper jar allows for both tangible and intangible reinforcement. Every time they do a chore or something helpful, they get a pom pom to hold for a minute and put in the jar. That in and of itself is rewarding, because my kids are very small and get excited about things like pom poms. I also make sure to provide them with intangible reinforcement. "Great job with emptying the dishwasher, Fritz!" When they receive this intangible reinforcement, they experience the warm feeling inside of having done a great job.

Sometimes, I ask them to do a chore and then reward them. Sometimes they offer to do a chore because they want a pom pom. Sometimes I "catch them doing good" and see Fritz picking up toys without being asked.[123] So, I surprise him and give him a pom pom as well as lots of

---

123 This has literallt happened once.

praise. Then they receive another tangible reinforcement every time the jar is filled by getting a toy.

We have been doing this for a year and I have seen amazing effects. They have gotten used to helping. They like how it feels to help. They sometimes clean up without being told. When I ask them to help me, or to help each other, they will do so without saying, "Where is my pom pom?" The tangible reinforcement helped to build a desire for the intangible. Hopefully, they will eventually be people who help old ladies cross the streets without asking for money.

Back to swimming: I cannot disclose the name of this magical swim school because what is this? Some kind of #sponsored Instagram feed? But I will say that whatever exorbitant amount of money I ended up giving them to teach my kids to swim, it was probably worth it. And if there was an emotional school I could send them to where they could learn other life skills that quickly, I would pay those people too.

CHAPTER 29:

I Was Curious and It Was There

For most people, most of the time, we have to get to know a kid before we care about them. Not a baby. I can see a baby in a grocery store for two seconds and completely fall head over heels in love with him. I may even hide behind a bin of avocados so I can take a picture to send to my sister. Creepy, right?

The same is not true of kids. When you see a kid at a grocery store, they usually seem annoying. Unless this is Hollywood and you overhear them imparting precocious wisdom to their mothers, they really don't seem incredible from far away. It's when you get to know them, ideally when they aren't around their parents (all kids are more annoying in front of their parents), that they show their incredible-ness. I meet new kids at work every day. Once I get to know them, I love each one for their own simple, weirdo ways. That's the best thing about kids. Their unique weirdness.

Most of what kids do is completely weird and random. When I started doing clinical work with children a decade ago, I would interpret their every move with significance. Parents would ask me, "Why does she drink out of a straw when it is the yellow cup and not the red cup? What does this mean?" I spent hours with parents trying to puzzle out what was behind a specific behavior. A word to the wise: that's how therapists are when they first start providing therapy. They are looking for meaning in every interaction. But the more time you spend with children, the more you realize: kids are just weird.

Non-kid people do this too. They make meaning out of a child's every action. A kid will start rolling on the ground blowing spit out of their mouth. A non-kid person will ask: "Oh no, why is she doing that? Is there something wrong with her mouth?" 90% of what kids do can be attributed not to some grand agenda but simply because 1) they were curious and/or bored, or 2) it was there. This is why it's so funny when I hear myself and others ask children: "Why did you do that? What were you thinking??"

I ask my children this all the time, like when I find them jumping around on top of my husband's work truck, or pouring a bottle of my contact solution into the sink. As soon as I hear the words leave my mouth, I think, *Wow, that is the dumbest question.*

My kids look at me with blank expressions, because the truth is, they weren't thinking. They were curious and it was there.

At this point, you are probably wondering where I am going with this. I'm assuming you bought this book and immediately flipped to the end because you figured, "I don't have time to listen to this lady's whole argument; I'll just see if her thesis is going to help me with my five-year-old's tantrums. Only then will I read this book." Here it is, the big reveal.

Here is how you can be the best parent in the world, at least for a few minutes a day, every day. Live in that curiosity with them. Most of us live extremely busy lives. We work; we take our kids to swim class at 10 a.m. every Saturday morning; we have three birthday parties to go to every weekend.[124] We feel like we have no time. We get so used to the rush, rush, rush that even when we have no reason to rush, we are rushing. How many times have you rushed your kids to the playground just so you could stand around bored for three hours? Why are we always rushing them from one thing to another? Like, is the playground really that important? What is there that is so valuable?

One Saturday morning, I needed to find an excursion to take my kids on, so I drove them to a toy store in West Portal. We parked the car and started to walk down the street. As usual, Hazel was walking at the speed of paint drying, stopping every few steps to stare at something. I was a few paces ahead of them going, "Come on, Hazel. Let's go, Hazel!" The toy store hadn't even opened yet. Why was I yelling at her to hurry up? Because grown-ups suck.

Hazel stopped in front of a window and peered in. I watched her little face transform to delight. I went to see what she was looking at. She had stopped in front of a dog groomer and was watching three dogs of different sizes getting haircuts. The groomer waved us inside. We ended up spending fifty-five minutes there. That happened two years ago and Hazel still brings it up.

She was curious and it was there.

Many of the most amazing moments of childhood happen in the spaces between scheduled activities. We don't always have time to be in the moment with our kids, but we *do* have time for that *sometimes*. I'm not a patient person. It takes a lot to get me to slow down and not think about all the places I should be, and all the things I should be doing. I hate being late. If a birthday party starts at 3 p.m. it is extremely hard for me to get there at 3:15. But every day I consciously try to give

124 Unless there is a global pandemic and then birthday parties, swim lessons, and everything else that brings our lives any semblance of joy are all cancelled.

myself time to be curious with my kids. To try something because it is there. The best thing about children is how incredibly curious they are about things we couldn't give less of a shit about. They think the most insignificant things are fun. Yesterday, Fritzi wanted to be the one to take a hot dog bun out of a bag. He had never done it before and he didn't know what it would feel like to do it. Adults never get as excited about the big things as kids get about the little things.

Letting a child do something on their own that you could easily do for them is one of the most annoying parts about being a parent. I could buckle Hazel into her car seat in five seconds, but instead I have to do it myself, have her try (and fail) to do it herself, and *then* do it for her. Most mornings, I don't have time for it. I'm rushing; I'm tired; I'm already sick of the bullshit and it isn't even 9 a.m. But some mornings, I do and I can. And it is worth the headache just to let them take the time they need to figure it out.

It often feels like these times in the car are the spaces between things. These are the spaces between the activities that make up our day. We went to the park; we went to a party; we went to the grocery store. These are all the things we have to do, and the journey between those places is just me rushing them. Them feeling rushed. Us being mutually annoyed at each other.

When you can, allow a little wandering to slip in. A little window watching or exploring or just trying things out. It ends up being the best part. They have been to ten million birthday parties. But have they rolled a traffic cone down a hill?

Almost every Saturday, I pack my kids into my messy little Prius and take them on an adventure somewhere. We like to go to museums, playgrounds, play spaces, festivals, birthday parties, beaches, farmers markets, and libraries. We seek out places that the kids like, but that I will enjoy as well. Now that I have a school-aged child, I feel more pressure to sign her up for organized activities. I find myself in more and more excruciatingly boring and uncomfortable waiting rooms (at swim class, at dance class, etc.). This can't be helped. Hazel asks to do these things, so I want to encourage them. But I hate spending my Saturdays there, and avoid it as much as I can.

There are so few Saturdays left where my kids will be little enough to go wherever I tell them we are going. When they have no agency to refuse. I call them Adventure Days, and most Saturdays, it is just the three of us. Sometimes my husband or someone else comes with us. I prefer it to be just the three of us. Every time another adult joins us, especially an adult without their own child in tow, they change the adventure. They start with the "Come on, Hazel!" and "Put that down, Fritzi!" and "Let's go check out this exhibit" shit that I'm so tired of.

Here is what I want to say to all these other adults, whom I love dearly and would never want to hurt. You are the annoying ones. Because they come in with so much of their own adult energy and their own adult expectations, wanting my kids to go along with their program. It is natural and I do it too. But on Saturdays with my kids, I consciously try to turn that "hurry up, let's go over here, okay one last time" part of my brain off. I can't ask another adult to do that; it's unnatural for them.

When an adult is in a museum with a child, even an extremely well-meaning, loving adult, they are naturally trying to get the child to go along with their predetermined museum agenda. They want to see certain things, go to certain places, take certain pictures of the child playing in a certain way, and leave the museum at a certain time. So, they are constantly diverting the child's attention toward what interests the adult, and trying to get the child to spend as long looking at something as they want them to. When the child doesn't go along with their plan (i.e. by running away to an entirely different part of the museum), the adult I am with inevitably looks over at me with a sigh, a laugh, a smile, and an eye roll. They might say, "Man…kids, am I right?" The implication here is that the kids are annoying. They totally understand and excuse their behavior, knowing my kids are acting like every other little kid in the world. They aren't so annoyed that it is ruining their day, but they are slightly annoyed because the kids won't follow their plan. They expect me as the parent to get my kids to go along with the plan they have in their heads of how the day should go. Like I'm supposed to chase the kids down so we can go to the exhibit we meant to go to. Why?

What I want to say (but would never say, because again, I love these people)[125] is, "You are the annoying one. Not them." My kids spend all day everyday being rushed around in the adult world. This is their one opportunity the entire week to follow their own curiosity wherever it leads them. Children are these tiny, vulnerable people who are so much more interesting and fun than all of us adults. And yet they spend all their time being bossed around by a bunch of bigger, dumber, less fun and interesting beings. Just give them one day. Give me one day to follow their agenda.

I once conducted an observation in a second-grade classroom at a Catholic school. It was an extremely hot day by San Francisco standards: 80 degrees. San Francisco schools don't have air conditioning, so the poor second graders were sweating in their totally impractical long-sleeve uniforms. They were sitting on hard wooden desks listening to their teacher drone on for an hour about sentence diagramming. Six and seven-year-old children sat at hard wooden desks in a hot stuffy classroom for an *hour* listening to the most boring lecture I have ever heard in my life. I could barely pay attention.

I came away from this experience with one question: "Why do we do this to our children?" Children are full of exuberance, energy, and

---

125 By "these people" I am referring to my mother, father, husband, stepmother, and literally every other adult who has been generous enough to spend a day with me and my kids. I love you all enough never to say anything about this to your face but instead put it in a book that hopefully you will read.

curiosity. As a society, we systematically squash this out of them with years of sentence diagramming.

You don't always have to be the boss. You don't always have to dictate what they do and how they do it. You don't always have to be the teacher, or the drill sergeant, or the lifeguard. Sometimes you can be just another delighted face, watching a dog get a haircut.

CHAPTER 30:

Why Children are Better Than Us

Disclaimer: A version of this chapter was previously published on the San Francisco Bay Area blog, in my blog post titled "How Our Children Transport Us."[126]

The thing about having small children and working full time is that you never have time to do the things that are important but not that important. Like going to the dentist or getting your car smogged. Or eating dinner. I drove around with one hundred books in my car for two months, waiting until I had time to stop by Green Apple Books on Clement to sell them. I waited for an occasion to arise where I was in Richmond with no children, and that day never came. So, one afternoon, when the kids and I were headed back from The Discovery Museum, I

126 Read the original post here: https://sanfrancisco.momcollective.com/parenting/how-our-children-transport-us/

thought, fuck it, let's do it right now, and I tried to find a parking spot by Green Apple.

For those of you who aren't familiar with Clement street in San Francisco, or children, let me explain a few things. You really can't find a parking spot on Clement street on a Saturday. And small children are incapable of walking more than one-fifth of a block without whining, so after circling the block five times, I probably should have given up. But I still hadn't scheduled a teeth cleaning, or found a time to get my car smogged, or done anything productive (other than keeping two humans alive and making money). So, again I figured fuck it, and found a spot on California Street, one very long uphill block away.

"Okay, Fritz and Hazel, let's do this!" I told my kids, as I lifted five bags of books out of the truck of my Prius. "I'm going to need your help!" The kids looked at me like I had lost my mind, because the concept of "being helpful" was foreign to them. Despite their resistance, I loaded them each up with as many books as they could carry. For three-year-old Fritz, that was one very large hardcover entitled *Neuroses*. Five-year-old Hazel managed to drag one small tote bag behind her. That left me with four bags to carry. The kids looked at me like, "Are we really doing this?" Fuck it, I told them. And we were off.

The walk between California Street and Clement is 0.2 miles long. In this 0.2 miles, Fritzi had a tantrum because his shoe got stuck in the mud. He lay down on the sidewalk in protest and I had to carry him, in addition to the four bags of books. Hazel said it wasn't fair both because Fritzi was carrying fewer books than her *and* because the book he was carrying looked bigger than any of her books. We passed ten people, none of whom offered to help me even though it was goddamn obvious I needed help.[127] Finally, three years later, we made it to Green Apple.

By the time I had dropped my books on the floor of Green Apple, my reservoir of patience had completely run dry. I was annoyed that we

---

127 Also this was pre-pandemic so they really had no excuse.

don't live in a society where people offer to help a mom carrying books. Also, aren't there cultures where five-year-olds are actually helpful? Not just "oh cute you are helping mommy" helpful, but like, you can give them shit to do and they can do it? Also, when was I supposed to do all these adult things that other people have time to do? Before I had kids, this task would have felt fun. An excuse to go to Green Apple and spend money on books. An excuse to get lunch on Clement Street. A fun chore. Not an epic errand that drained me of my will to live.

Green Apple Books is a San Francisco treasure. One of those quirky, crowded bookstores that have everything you want and where the staff is way too cool and busy to waste time being in any way pleasant or helpful to customers. I dropped my books off with a small, bearded employee with a squeaky voice. He told me he would call me when he was ready. I then spent twenty minutes reading Fritz and Hazel a book of shark facts. When the man called my name, I was relieved that we would be out of the store soon and I could go home and put them in front of the TV while I did something that brought me immense joy: folding laundry while watching the 1990s *Buffy the Vampire Slayer* spin-off show *Angel*.

Fritzi followed me up to the front. The small, bearded man with the squeaky voice started to go through the small stack of books Green Apple was going to buy. Fritzi stood nearby, gazing up at him with a confused expression.

"Mommy," Fritz asked quietly, gesturing to the employee, "is that a baby?"

The man kept talking and I ignored Fritz.

"Mommy!" Fritzi repeated, tugging at my shirt. "Is that a baby?"

Again, I ignored him. The employee glanced over at Fritz briefly, then continued talking.

"MOOOOMMMY!!!" Fritz yelled, pointing directly at the employee, "IS THAT A BABY????"

At this point, the employee let out an uncomfortable laugh. "No, Fritzi," I told him. "Of course he isn't a baby. He's a man."

"Hmm," Fritz said, looking the employee up and down suspiciously. "He sounds like a baby."

The employee smiled and said, like the total good sport that he was, "Well...I do get called 'ma'am' a lot on the phone."

I grinned at the employee. And I grinned at Fritz even harder. It had been an annoying afternoon. The traffic coming back from Marin followed by completing this errand with the kids had left me feeling exhausted and irritated by the little people who dominated my life. Everything had been so much easier without them around. Trips to Green Apple, teeth cleanings, it had all been effortless in a way I didn't appreciate at the time. People without children do not appreciate the ease with which they live their lives.

But then I looked down at little Fritzi's face and remembered that according to his worldview, it would not be out of the question for a baby to be working at a bookstore. In Fritz's world, this was just as possible as anything else. I had been focused all afternoon on how difficult it is to have these little people exist in my world of errands and to-do lists. The world that Fritz exists in is magical and unpredictable. Being with Fritz and Hazel during this tiny window of their childhood allows me to live in that world with them. What a gift.

Maybe my car won't get smogged and my teeth won't get cleaned very often. But fuck it. It is so much more fun to live in this world these little people create for me.

CHAPTER 31:

What Quarantine Taught Me about Parenting

As I write this, the COVID-19 pandemic is far from over. Our lives aren't back to normal yet. They may never be. Still, Part One of the pandemic is behind us. Part One was when the stores were out of toilet paper and we were rescheduling meetings to mid-May "when this is all over." Part Two of the pandemic is where we are now. When most of us have figured out how to match our masks to our shoes and plans are being rescheduled to mid-2022 "when this is all over…hopefully." The "new normal" is normal. It fucking sucks. But at least we are used to it. And we have enough toilet paper.

The pandemic triggered something within me. It triggered a lot of things actually: fear, panic, hopelessness, a new appreciation for expensive whiskey. But also creativity. I wrote a lot during those months. What I wrote started out as notes jotted down on the notepad app on my phone.

A lot of this writing ended up being published in blog posts on the San Francisco Bay Area Moms blog.[128]

I spent the first four months of the pandemic working full time while at home with my small children. Everything was closed, no one was available to help and it felt like our full and colorful world had been reduced to the size of our living room. Fritz's preschool reopened in July 2020. In August 2020 I put Hazel in a full-time "Kindergarten pod" with three other Kindergarten girls and the most amazing teacher in the universe, Teacher Helen. My husband and I were incredibly lucky. Neither of us got laid off. In fact, I got a promotion. We moved to a new house. I felt grateful, and incredibly sad and incredibly desperate and incredibly hopeful (depending on the day and moment within the day.)

During the COVID-19 pandemic, I learned a lot about myself as a mom. There is no "bright side" to this horrible virus that has killed so many people and decimated whole communities. There is no silver lining. But there are lessons.

I Learned How to Be Bored

Before COVID-19 destroyed our lives, there was a hefty accusation people loved to throw on parents called "overscheduling." We were told to lay off the swim and dance lessons! Let children be bored! It's good for them!

Well…

March 2020. Swim and dance, school, yoga, play dates, museums. Cancelled. Playgrounds closed, parking lots closed, this patch of grass open, that patch of grass closed. No longer a risk of over-scheduling. Parents were afraid of getting a deadly virus and of society collapsing, yes. But they were not afraid of over-scheduling.

128 Read the original posts here: https://sanfrancisco.momcollective.com/author/michellekaye/

I have always been skeptical of the "let children be bored" argument that uncles are so fond of. When my children are bored, they tear holes in the couch. They pick fights with one another. They fill nothing spaces with mischief and mayhem. The best way to stop a child from whining is to give him an activity. It's my number one intervention, and it's effective. I've always thought nostalgia for the Tom Sawyer childhood was misplaced. Remember: Tom Sawyer got into a lot of trouble. He almost died, more than once! And that Huck Finn character was bad news.

But then the pandemic hit. With everything cancelled and days laid out in front of us like blank canvases, something shifted. And it wasn't my children who changed; it was me. Before quarantine, I was always just a little bit distracted. Watching the kids bike ride and thinking about what my friends should bring over to barbecue. Going to the playground for just an hour before rushing off to a birthday party. I always felt the urge to fit as much as I could into a day. This feeling of needing to keep them as busy as possible, to keep me as sane as possible. Parenting is most fun when you are parenting with others. Before quarantine, I would find any opportunity to meet up with other parents and kids. It was constantly, "Let's play for ten more minutes then we're going to the beach!" My brain was always rushing them along from thing to thing. There was always a greener, more interesting pasture to get to.

During quarantine, there were no greener pastures. No plans in sight. They could ride bikes on the driveway for two more months if they wanted.

During the first few weeks of quarantine, my brain was restless. I was filled with anxiety and dread. But I was one of the lucky ones, who had food on the table and enough toilet paper. So, my brain stopped its constant chattering and just sat still.

Before quarantine, I was always coming up with new activities. To keep them entertained…but really to keep myself entertained. During quarantine, the goal became to make every activity stretch out for as long as possible.

"Mom, how far can an owl see at night?" my daughter would ask me.

"I don't know, Hazel. Let's do research on the computer. Let's draw a picture of an owl. Let's write ten owl facts and show them to Daddy when he comes home."

My brain became quieter. When my kids showed me a ladybug, the only thing on my mind was the ladybug. I was in the present moment for them in a way that I used to find challenging. Quarantine helped me accept boredom. I still don't know if boredom is "good for kids." But it might be good for me.

I Learned How to Teach What Matters

During the pandemic, I have been inundated by emails about "distance learning." An educational website where my five-year-old can practice reading and counting skills. Videos sent by their dance teacher with steps they could follow at home. Everyone who normally worked with my children was reeling, trying to stay connected to their students. As someone who works in early childcare myself, I understand. We weren't just providing this content because we had too much time on our hands. Teachers were lost without their students. They missed them terribly. They missed singing songs, dancing with them, teaching them to read and count. You don't become a teacher for the money. You do it because teaching brings you joy. Across the world, teachers were desperately reaching for the joy they feel from teaching.

But we need to be careful, both as parents and as educators of young children. *There is no such thing as distance learning for preschool.* Small children learn through experience. Circle time cannot be emulated by sitting cross-legged in front of a screen. The best video of the best preschool teacher in the world is still just a video. It is wonderful for our children to stay connected to their teachers, but it is not a beneficial way for children five years old and under to learn.

Here's the thing: we cannot expect parents to become preschool teachers. Even parents who are preschool teachers cannot suddenly be preschool teachers to their own children while also cooking and cleaning and working and FaceTiming with their parents and binging Netflix shows and keeping themselves from going insane. There are millions of parents who lost their jobs during COVID-19 and are worrying about how they will feed their children. We cannot keep sending them Play-Doh recipes and home school schedules with the expectation that they can set up a preschool in their home.

In my work life, I tell parents and providers that the best thing you can do for kids is just to play with them. Get down on their level, join in with their activities, and expand on the themes they present. Join in their imaginary world. Be an active part of their learning by playing their games with them. That is how small children learn—through play and exploration. Through being shown by the adults in their lives that their ideas are interesting and valid, encouraging them to have more.

Learning in early childhood is not only about matching colors or learning the difference between big and small. It's not that these concepts aren't important, but they are just skills. For children five years old and under, all learning happens within the context of relationships. You don't have to designate fifteen minutes of "academic time" per day for your child to learn how to draw a triangle. She can learn about triangles when she is playing with magnet blocks. Or by going on a walk and looking at the shape of a roof. Standardized testing has pushed these academic skills earlier and earlier. Children used to learn how to read the alphabet in kindergarten. Now they are generally expected to have this skill *before* kindergarten.

The real, important learning tasks for children five years and under are social-emotional skills. They will learn how to read. They will learn how to count and spell and tell you if something is bigger or smaller. Our true job as parents is not to teach them these things. The real teaching is happening in the moments that seem small. The spilled pancake batter. The impromptu puppet show.

I Learned How to be Joyful

There was one distinct day during quarantine that was a gift. It doesn't take away from how stressful the first few months of quarantine were, when it was just me and my children each and every day. Or how horrible everything was with society collapsing and so many deaths and no movies being made in 2020 and the California Academy of Sciences closed and no bars and everything else. But that one day was a gift. It wasn't just the best day I had during quarantine; it was a day I will always remember. When my kids are grown up, I will grieve for that day.

I woke up to Fritz and Hazel coming to cuddle. Hazel reminded me that I had said yes, they could have the purple Peeps in the cupboard, but just not after dinner because it gave Fritz too much of a sugar rush. That was why we started our day by microwaving Peeps so we could watch them blow up into chicken balloons before deflating into melted marshmallow mush.

After the marshmallow breakfast, we did an hour of Cosmic Kids Yoga. The first few weeks of quarantine, I forced them to do homework at the breakfast table. After a few weeks, I stopped even opening the home school calendar. I adored Hazel's Transitional Kindergarten teacher, and Hazel worshipped her. But the assignments were tedious, and I found it frustrating to sit there and force her to complete them. I taught Fritz to write his name and then decided that was good enough for a three-year-old. A month into quarantine, the one and only morning routine we became diligent about was yoga.

After yoga, we put our bikes in the car and started to drive to Golden Gate Park. Fritz asked to go through the car wash across the street from our house. I put "Car Wash" by Rose Royce on the stereo. We went through the car wash twice in a row. Because we had nowhere we needed to be. Until maybe August.

Fritz insisted I play "Booty Man" by Tim Booty Wilson three times on the way to the park. The sun was shining; it was warm with a slight breeze. I had gotten enough sleep last night. I was wearing my favorite sunglasses and having a good hair day.[129] The kids were cracking up in the back seat. Laughing whenever they heard the word "booty." The world felt brighter than it had in weeks. Quiet. But calm, not apocalyptic.

We fed the ducks at Stow Lake. We biked downhill through the park. We sat outside the California Academy of Sciences, and I showed them how to make ants on a log with celery, peanut butter, and raisins.

They rejected the ants on the log. Instead, they ate peanut butter right out of the jar. It felt amazing to be in Golden Gate Park, this place where we have always been so happy. A new Ferris wheel had gone up without us knowing about it. It stood there, representing the dream of

129 The best my hair has ever looked was during the first three months of quarantine when my husband and kids were the only ones who saw me outside of a Zoom screen. Life is cruel that way.

what things would be like one day. I wasn't filled with sadness about what we were missing. I was filled with joy at what we had.

We biked back to the car and drove toward home. I blasted the Moana soundtrack with the windows open. Singing along. My arm outstretched in the cool breeze. I spontaneously pulled over at Stern Grove. We walked into the park and spotted a small grassy hill. I asked the kids, "Do you want to roll down?" They looked at me skeptically. Somehow, they had reached the ages of three and five without ever rolling down a hill. What a travesty.

"Here, I'll show you." I rolled down the hill, the kids rolling after me. After rolling down twice more, I felt nauseous and dizzy and realized there is a reason most thirty-five-year-old women don't roll down hills.

We raced down to the bottom of Stern grove. We looked for tadpoles in the pond. We found a dead mouse. Hazel asked if we could "dissect it to see what it looked like on the inside." Fritz burst into tears.

A man was on the stage juggling. Hazel asked him, "What are you juggling?"

"Balls," the man said.

Fritz asked, "What kind of shirt are you wearing?"

"White," the man replied.

"Noooooo" Fritz clarified, "what *kind* of shirt like Star Wars shirt, sporty shirt, you know."

"Oh, I guess just 'juggling shirt.'" This seemed to satisfy Fritz. The man handed Fritz a business card:

Clyde Always
Author/Illustrator
Fine Artist
Vaudevillian Storyteller

Oh, San Francisco…

Hazel ran through a sprinkler. She was soaking wet and it was time to go home.

It was a perfect day. Full of adventure and giggles. Full of joy. Their joy and my joy. I was happy because it was sunny and I had gotten enough sleep the night before. I had enough patience not to get upset when they fought with each other. Work was slow, so I didn't have to be on my phone. All my attention was on the kids. I was having fun because we were doing things I like: biking and hiking and doing yoga. And they were having fun because they like those things too. Also, because they were enjoying me and my good mood. I didn't grumpily tell them, "Just roll down a hill or something." I rolled down a hill. Three times![130]

There is a joy cycle that exists when things are going well with small children. You are happy. They are happy. You are happy they are happy. They are happy you are happy.

This joy cycle is how small children learn. They learn through relationships. They learn through the positive feelings they get from your positive feelings. These face-to-face positive interactions are vastly more effective in teaching small children than the passive experience they get through screen learning. That isn't to say children don't learn through screens, because they do. Hazel can explain how Coronavirus germs spread because of an episode of *Storybots*. But what is way more impactful on her learning is the daily, positive face-to-face interactions that she has with me and her father. Even when those interactions are about marshmallows exploding in the microwave.

Not every day of quarantine was like this. There were some terrible days. And most days were a balance of good and bad moments. During quarantine, my priorities shifted. My basic needs were met. I am lucky enough to have food, water, shelter, and toilet paper. Therefore, my only goal for the day was to find joy. Many days, this goal seemed out of reach. But then there were also days like this.

---

130 Don't try this at home.

Children need joy. They need food and water and safety and shelter, and after those needs are met, they need joy. Joy is created through these joy cycles. When you are enjoying your child and they are enjoying you. Sometimes, we find joy in helping them with their homework, even when it is hard. But when we are cranky and exhausted, they are cranky and exhausted too.

During quarantine, parents were told to "forgive ourselves" for the homework we didn't do with their children. But I don't think parents should have to be forgiven for not doing something we should never have been asked to do.

That was our home school. Rolling down hills. Making ants on a log. Looking for tadpoles. Talking to quirky strangers from a distance. We cannot be everything to our children. And we shouldn't try. Our goal is only to keep them safe and bring them joy. And when we don't have the mental capacity for that, there is Netflix.

CHAPTER 32:

The Most Precious Thing

When I was just starting out in the field of social work, I didn't know what I was doing. Like we do when we start off, I was pretending I knew more than I did and learning as much as I could in the meantime. But I was trying my best. I cared deeply about the children on my caseload. I cared about their parents too. I listened to their concerns. I listened to their ideas about what solutions they thought would work. I tried my best to give them the help they needed. When I look back at some of the things I said, I recognize that they weren't always the best. I was wrong a lot. But I tried really hard. And the families I worked with could tell.

In one of these early years, I sat with a couple in their gigantic house near Palo Alto, discussing their three-year-old son with autism. The father had an important job. He had been challenging to work with over the past few months, questioning my every decision and disagreeing with his son's diagnosis. I didn't know it then, but I would see this pattern often in fathers of children with disabilities. When they found out there was something wrong with their kid, their grief manifested in anger and outrage.

But in that moment in their living room, this father wasn't angry with me. It was our last visit together before his son aged out of our program. Tears streaming down his face, he told me, "Thank you for helping us with the most precious thing in our life: our little boy."

At that point in my career, I was considering doing something else. I loved living in San Francisco, but we weren't making enough money to stay in the city and start a family. I knew people who were making three times as much as me designing user interfaces for apps that delivered energy drinks. I was wondering if I had made a mistake going to social work school. Maybe I would be happy working in the technology industry and buying a beautiful mansion on the Peninsula.

But that dad's words changed something. He was a powerful man who had everything he wanted: a beautiful house, a full-time nanny, a devoted wife. And yet I was able to make such an incredible impact in his life. Simply by showing up, listening, and trying as hard as I could. I had helped him with the most precious thing in his life. That felt like real power.

He wasn't thanking me because I came into his life with all of the answers. It wasn't because I knew everything there was to know about autism (I knew very little.) I was a novice. Trying my best. Muddling through. Asking questions when I didn't know the answers. Listening and really trying to understand his experience.

This is what new parents do. We don't know what we are doing. It doesn't matter how many friends with kids you have, or how much advice your mother gives you. When it comes to being a parent to your kid, everyone starts off as an amateur. You can't shadow someone else and slowly take over when you are ready. When it's your own kid, you're in charge from day one. You learn on the job.

What really matters isn't having all the answers. It isn't about knowing exactly what you are doing. You don't need to know everything about child development, or everything about parenting.

What matters is trying as hard as you can. And acknowledging to yourself, to your partner, and to your kids that you don't have all the answers. That you are going to be here, living in your relationship with them, for as long as you can. You will muddle through this together. And hopefully, one day, if you are lucky, they will thank you.[131]

This week, my daughter said something that made me feel like the best mother in the world. We passed a library and she said to me, "Mom, I'm afraid of librarians."

"Why are you afraid of librarians?" I asked.

"Mooooooooom," Hazel answered, "think about it. Rules…getting in trouble…of course I'm afraid of librarians. You know I hate getting into trouble."

I'm not happy that Hazel has a fear of librarians. I really hope she gets over that! I wish she had less anxiety about everything in her life, because that would make things easier for both of us. But that just isn't who she is. Hazel is a worrier. She lays in her bed at night unable to sleep because she's thinking about that time she accidentally referred to a classmate's mom as her grandmother. She didn't eat her lunch for the first two weeks of Transitional Kindergarten because she was afraid someone sitting near her would be allergic to something in her lunchbox. This is the person she is. And although I hope she learns to manage her anxiety, it is probably the person she will always be.

I know what kind of person she is and I can usually guess at the kind of things that will make her anxious. She isn't living on an island alone with her anxiety. I'm sitting on that island with her, knowing her, guessing at what she is thinking and feeling and trying my best to come up with solutions.

131 Does this happen? At their wedding? At your retirement? God, I hope so.

And the best part is, she knows that I know her. She isn't alone with all her worries. She knows there is this person in the world who understands her. I don't think there is a more important gift you can give to a person than that.

So, all those days when I yell at her for not getting ready fast enough, I just think of that moment in the car when she told me she was afraid of the librarian and I feel better.

I'm the best parent in the world. And now that you have finished this book, so are you.

Acknowledgments
(But Interesting)

When I get to the end of a book I love, I read the acknowledgements section because I'm hungry for more of a window into the author's world.[132] I'm almost always disappointed. Because acknowledgements usually read like this:

I would like to thank my editor, Linda, my agent, Andrew, and also Pierre Glasstone, Diana Hendrik, Susan Cleary, and Alan Weisman for help with this book.

BOOOOORRING! Who the hell are those people? Did Alan give you the clever idea about the character hiding the weapon behind the bookcase in Chapter 3? Did you and Andrew have a little thing going? Give me more!

It is in this spirit that I bring you…acknowledgments. But with personal details!

Stephanie Diaz (editor)

You sent me a proposal on Upwork and I hired you immediately because your response to me was funny and you had a science fiction background. When we talked on the phone my questions to you included "what is a copy editor?" and "how do I use this website I signed up for?" Thanks for all your citation help, and your "lols" in the comments. I'm going to include your website because other people should pay you money to read stuff because you're awesome: https://www.stephaniediazbooks.com/

---

132 Jeff reads the acknowledgments section of every book as well as the copyrights section because he has very strange neuroses about it. As if there is going to be a test after. It's bizarre.

Erica Murach (Book Designer)

I wanted my friend Erica to design this book because she has the best style of anyone I know. I figured if my book looked anything like her wardrobe, or her store, or her child then people would want to read it. I assume she designed this book the same way I wrote it: in fifteen minute intervals while her daughter was distracted with a toy, during naps, while breastfeeding, with one hand while the other hand mashed up a banana into bite size chunks. Thank you Erica, you fucking rocked it. If you want to hire this badass or buy things she made find her on @establishsf on Instagram.

Hope Kaye (sister)

Thank you, thank you, thank you for all your editing assistance. You put a lot of commas where they needed to be and took a lot of semicolons from places they didn't. The commas and semicolons of this book thank you. Also, when I asked if you would do another copy edit, thank you for suggesting I hire an actual pro (see above for pro.)

You are the best aunt in the world. When you have kids, I'm going to have to do fucking everything for them to try to make up for how much you have helped us and it still won't be enough.

Jeff Smith (husband)

Thanks for taking the kids to your parents so I could work on this book during July 4th weekend. Also, sorry for not letting you read early drafts, I knew you would remember things differently and I didn't feel like having to change my anecdotes. You're an awesome dad. You work your ass off. You tell them super long stories about bunnies and do light saber battles with Fritz. You taught them to ride bikes during quarantine. Unlike most men, who just think they can fix things, you actually can. Thanks for putting up with all my weird quirks such as tearing open cereal bags like a rabid racoon, always fucking up mac and cheese, throwing out the instructions to new appliances, and slamming the shower door. I know I drive you crazy. I love you.

Ken Kaye (father)

Dad. You wrote parenting books back in the day and contributed to research in the field of infant mental health before "infant mental health" was the hot buzz word it is today. You have been incredibly supportive of this project. Also, my desire to make you proud of me was a huge motivator to finish this thing. Thanks for all the invaluable parenting advice, such as, "Pushing children on swings is excruciating, I always just refused," and, "Kids usually don't notice when you skip pages of books. They notice when you skip words on the page, but they won't notice if you skip whole pages."[133] I'm sorry I didn't let you edit this book. You would have cut out too many uses of the word "fuck" and I wanted to leave them all in. Each and every one was 100% fucking necessary.

Rosalind Kaye (mother)

Mom. Thanks for always supporting me and teaching me that it's okay to not follow through with stuff when you're just totally over it. Even if I never finished this, you would still be unquestionably proud of me. So much of who I am as a mother is because of you. I will never be as good at homemade cakes and Halloween costumes as you were. But I have Amazon Prime and you didn't.

Nick and Lev Kaye (big brothers)

Thanks for being awesome dudes, amazing brothers, super fun brothers-in-law to Jeff and killer uncles to Hazel and Fritz. Thank you for always loving and supporting me.

---

133 FYI this is 100% true. Try it.

Trudy Smith (mother-in-law)

Mom. Thank you for all your help with the kids these past six years. They love you so much and you are always there for them, and for me. I won the mother-in-law lottery with you. Thanks for adopting my whole family and feeding us all mountains of food whenever we come over. Thank you for sewing Hazel ten million adorable dresses. You are the best.

Elena and Amaya

I'm acknowledging you both here because if I didn't you would never forgive me. But that isn't the only reason. Elena, thanks for being my mama icon and helping me with my two littles. Hazel calls you "my Mexican auntie." My dearest Amaya, you are truly my third child and I can't believe you are almost an adult. I love you so much. Please be nice to your mom and don't do anything too crazy for a few years. Her heart can't take it.

Mom Friends (Ciara, Lauren, Sara, Erica, Sharon, Jen, Robyn, Kathleen and anyone I start hanging out with after I finish this book but before it was published)

Thank you for having adult conversations with me while our kids played. Thanks for kevetching, and listening to my kevetching. This book is filled with your insights and stories. Thank you for giving me permission to share some of what you told me. You all make me a better mom. Thank you for inspiring me to be funny...so I can make you laugh.

Ariana Kosmides, Drew Goldsman, Seth Wessler, Yasmine Farhang, Rae Garringer

This group text exchange has really kept me going. You guys are all incredibly accomplished people and half of you are low-key famous. Who would have ever thought that Hampshire College would have produced such high functioning adults? We really showed them.

Lastly,

My kids…I couldn't have written this without you. I almost couldn't do it because of you and your all-consuming needs. There would have been nothing to write about if you didn't exist. And because you exist… it took me almost six years to finish this thing.

Fredrik (Fritz) Bernard Kaye Smith

Never has a human being brought me more joy. You are the most Zen person I have ever met. You don't care that much about the past, and you don't think that much about the future. You exist in the here and now and you take us all with you to the present moment. You are joyous and energetic and hilarious and so sweet and loving. You have a heart of gold. You cry when you see a dead mouse. I can't wait to watch you play sports. I really love my Saturdays and I know I am about to give them up, but it's okay because that is how much I love you.

Hazel Kaye Smith

Thank you for making me a mom. I have never felt closer to anyone than I do to you. From the moment you were born, you have been an inquisitive, relentless spark of joy and creativity. Your intelligence shocks us. Nothing escapes your notice. Your brain is always thinking, worrying, wondering, questioning, working. You have challenged me in ways I never thought possible. It isn't easy to be your mom. It is a blissful, rewarding challenge. You delight me. You surprise me. You blow me away. I love you.

CPSIA information can be obtained
at www.ICGtesting.com
Printed in the USA
BVHW042029150421
605035BV00009B/984